REAL ESTATE

A HOUSEHOLD WEALTH PERSPECTIVE

BARRETT A. SLADE, PhD

PLAIN SIGHT PUBLISHING
AN IMPRINT OF CEDAR FORT, INC.
SPRINGVILLE, UTAH

ISBN 13: 978-1-4621-4173-9

Published by Plain Sight Publishing, an imprint of Cedar Fort, Inc.
2373 W. 700 S., Springville, UT 84663
Distributed by Cedar Fort, Inc., www.cedarfort.com

Library of Congress Control Number: 2022935439

Cover design by Shawnda T. Craig

Printed in the United States of America

10 9 8 7 6 5 4 3 2 1

Printed on acid-free paper

Contents

Preface

To understand the objectives and layout of this book, I must first tell you about my experience as a professor teaching real estate courses in the Department of Finance at the Marriott School of Business at Brigham Young University.

The business school does not provide a real estate major or degree. Therefore, real estate courses are considered electives and are taken by students pursuing a career in other business disciplines. When I began teaching a real estate elective course, I found that most of the students had two primary learning objectives for taking the class. First, they wanted to learn how to buy a home successfully, and second, they wanted to learn how to invest in real estate to create household wealth.

Because most real estate textbooks tend to be either too broad (e.g., real estate principles) or too narrow (e.g., real estate finance, valuation, or investments), most are designed for students majoring in real estate. Therefore, to achieve my students' two primary learning objectives, I had to supplement the course with other materials. I looked for a popular press book that might be more comprehensive and be sufficient for the course. Unfortunately, most focused on quick get-rich schemes rather than teaching the reader sound principles to achieve the two primary objectives. So, I decided to write a book that gets at the heart of these two objectives—to learn how to buy a home successfully and invest in real estate to create household wealth.

With these objectives in mind, the book is laid out as follows: First, chapter 1 provides an introduction. Second, chapters 2–8 teach the reader how to successfully purchase a home (the first primary objective of the book). Third, chapters 9–15 teach the reader how to invest in real estate to create household wealth (the second primary objective of the book). The remaining chapters provide supplementary material supporting the two primary learning objectives. For instance, chapters 16–18 present nontraditional or alternative real estate investment options, and chapters 19–22 provide reference material that expands and enlarges concepts or principles introduced in previous chapters.

PART I

INTRODUCTION

CHAPTER 1

Using Real Estate to Create Household Wealth

INTRODUCTION

Real estate has been and will continue to be an effective means of creating household wealth. The first half of this chapter highlights why real estate is a significant component of both the world and US economies as well as a substantial contributor to household wealth. The second half of the chapter discusses five specific reasons that real estate can be more effective at building wealth than are other asset classes.

REAL ESTATE AND THE ECONOMY

Savills World Research provides some perspective on the contribution of real estate to the world's wealth. In 2017, Savills found that residential real estate had a total value of $168.5 trillion, more than two times the value of the world's equity markets ($70.1 trillion). Combined, all real estate totaled more than $228 trillion, exceeding the combined amount of all debt and equity ($170.3 trillion). On a percentage basis, more than half (56.3%) of the world's wealth is in residential, commercial, and agricultural real estate, whereas only 42.1% is in debt and equity. Exhibit 1.1 graphically illustrates these findings:

Exhibit 1.1: Value of World Economy

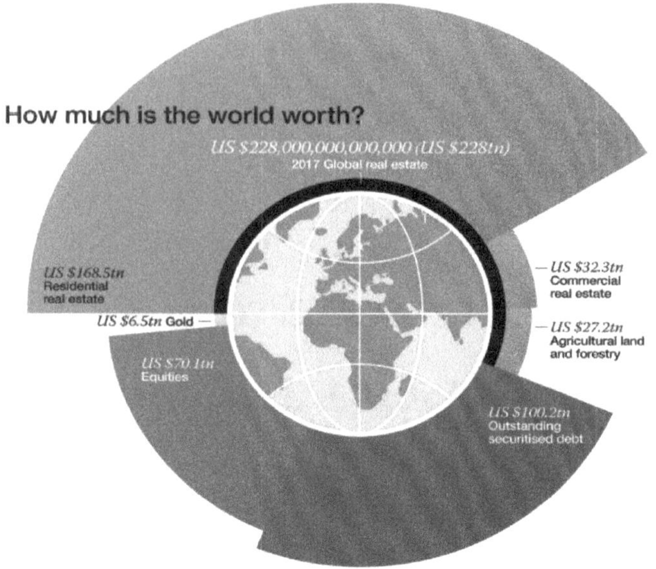

Source: Savills[1]

Not only do real estate assets make up a large proportion of the world's wealth, but the real estate industry is a significant contributor to many individual countries' economic output. For example, in the United States—the world's largest economy—spending on housing and residential investment accounts for more than 16% of the annual gross domestic product (GDP).[2] To put this percentage in perspective, in the United States in 2019, spending on housing, utilities, and residential investment exceeded nonresidential fixed investment spending, which includes all business spending on structures, equipment,

1. Paul Tostevin, "How Much Is the World Worth?" *The Savills Blog*, Savills, April 10, 2017, https://www.savills.com/blog/article/216300/residential-property/how-much-is-the-world-worth.aspx#:~:text=In%20early%202016%2C%20the%20Savills,shows%20that%20figure%20has%20risen.
2. "Gross Domestic Product, First Quarter 2020 (Third Estimate)' Corporate Profits, First Quarter 2020 (Revised Estimate)," Bureau of Economic Analysis, June 25, 2020, https://www.bea.gov/sites/default/files/2020-06/gdp1q20_3rd_1.pdf.

Exhibit 1.2: Real Estate Spending as Percentage of Nominal GDP (US, 2019)

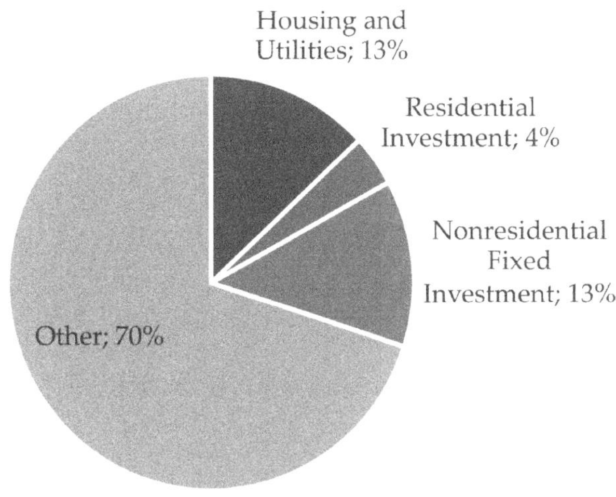

Source: Bureau of Economic Analysis, News Release: Gross Domestic Product, First Quarter 2020

transportation, technology, software, and research and development (see Exhibit 1.2).

In addition to its financial value and direct link to certain spending accounts, real estate has the ability to stimulate activity in seemingly unrelated sectors of the economy. Because real estate assets have tangible and relatively stable value, they are frequently offered as collateral for business and personal loans, including first and second mortgage loans, home equity lines of credit, and commercial loans. These loans provide cash flow that allows households and businesses to increase their consumption and invest in other assets. Loans collateralized by real estate have a particularly powerful impact at the household level, where home value typically accounts for more than 25% of net worth (see Exhibit 1.3 on following page).

EXHIBIT 1.3: HOME VALUE AS A PERCENTAGE OF NET WORTH

Source: Federal Reserve, Financial Accounts of the United States, Table B.101.H Balance Sheet of Households.

Notes: Total household net worth measures assets minus liabilities. Home value is measured as the market value of owner-occupied real estate, including vacant land and mobile homes.

Because real estate is such an important part of the world economy, real estate agents, brokers, and developers are not the only professionals who need to thoroughly understand real estate to work effectively. In fact, countless other less-obvious professionals can benefit from obtaining a solid understanding of real estate, including the following:

- Local, state, and national **politicians** considering the impact of proposed zoning or legislative changes
- **Attorneys** negotiating commercial real estate purchase contracts or corporate mergers involving considerable real estate assets
- **Estate planners** and **private wealth advisers** whose clients own real estate
- **Tax professionals** (including accountants and attorneys) advising clients on the tax implications of holding real estate
- **Institutional investors** considering investing in real estate investment trusts, mortgage-backed securities, or collateralized debt obligations
- **Bankers** and **loan officers** analyzing prospective mortgage loans

- Federal and state **regulators** (e.g., from the FDIC, OCC, or Federal Reserve) examining financial institutions that hold real estate assets or accept real estate as loan collateral
- **Appraisers** and other valuation experts tasked with valuing land and buildings
- **Economists** studying the effects of asset values on consumer spending and business cycles
- **Management consultants** advising companies with substantial real estate holdings

Though by no means exhaustive, this list illustrates both the importance of understanding real estate for many professionals and the extent of real estate's influence on the economy.

WHY REAL ESTATE BUILDS WEALTH

Many professionals benefit from learning about real estate's unique characteristics because they encounter real estate in their day-to-day work. However, individuals who never deal with real estate in their professional lives can still benefit from learning about it because real estate investing can be an exceptionally effective way to build household wealth. The following sections outline five reasons real estate is a more attractive vehicle for building wealth than other asset classes.

Reason #1: Leverage

Financial leverage is perhaps the primary reason real estate tends to build more wealth than other financial assets. Nowadays, home buyers can put down as little as 3% and borrow 97% of the value of a property at very favorable interest rates with payment terms as long as thirty years. The ability to control substantial value with a relatively small investment provides a unique opportunity to reap significant financial gains. For instance, assume that a buyer purchases a home worth $100,000 with a down payment of $3,000 and obtains a mortgage loan for $97,000. If the property value were to appreciate 5% over the following year, the owner could sell the property for $105,000 and net $8,000 after paying off the lender. This comes out to a $5,000 return on the initial $3,000 investment, or a net return of 166%.

Though this example clearly ignores transaction costs and mortgage interest, it nonetheless illustrates the power of leverage to increase investment returns. Since real estate investments are typically easier to leverage than other types of investments, they are an attractive vehicle for building wealth.

Reason #2: Appreciation

Over the long haul, real estate has shown to be an appreciating asset, meaning that the value tends to increase over time. Despite periodic fluctuations, housing prices have appreciated at an average rate of about 4% annually over the past twenty years (see Exhibit 1.4). The tendency of home values to increase over time makes real estate an attractive asset for household investment.

Exhibit 1.4: Case-Shiller Twenty-City Composite Housing Price Index

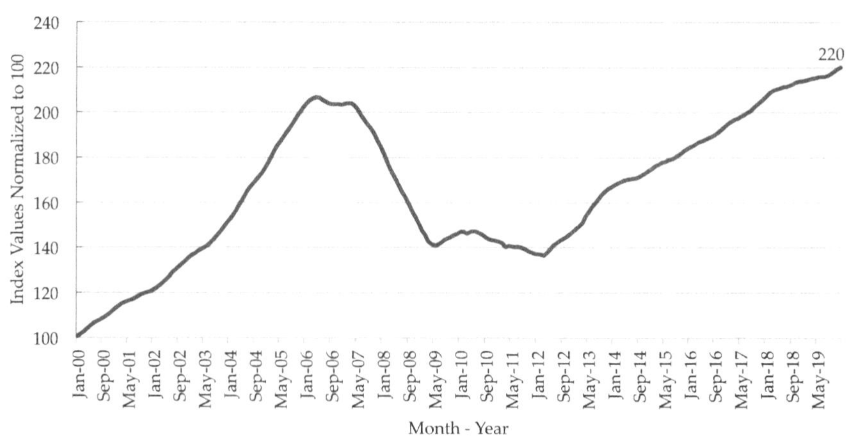

Source: FRED Economic Data, St. Louis FED

Reason #3: Physical Accommodation

Real estate is a unique asset class because it provides tangible, functional benefits in addition to monetary returns. Because people need places to rest, eat, work, worship, and play, real estate properties are in near-constant demand. Additionally, real estate investors can enjoy the nonpecuniary benefits of their properties while simultaneously profiting from their properties' financial investment value. For instance, a restaurant owner can obtain both a suitable business location and a stream of rental income by investing in a small strip mall. Similarly, individuals who purchase homes benefit from their homes' value as both a source of shelter and an investment. Thus, real estate presents an attractive investment opportunity for those who want to take advantage of its functional benefits while building their wealth.

Reason #4: Forced Equity (Savings)

The overwhelming majority of real estate purchases are completed with mortgage debt, which is typically amortized over a long period of time (e.g., thirty years). Since mortgage payments include both principal and interest, the outstanding debt balance declines over time, while the equity balance increases. This process is effectively the same as a forced savings plan, building up equity that can be profitably employed in the future. For example, *U.S. News and World Report*[3] found that about 20% of retirees plan to use home equity to help fund their retirement. Real estate is therefore an appealing investment alternative because it facilitates regular saving, leading to increased wealth.

Reason #5: Tax Benefits

Real estate is currently one of the best tax shelters for households and investors. As long as they have lived in a home for at least two of the last five years, homeowners are allowed to shelter up to $500,000 in capital gains if they are married filing jointly, and $250,000 if they are filing alone. Homeowners are also allowed to deduct mortgage interest from their taxable income.[4] Real estate investors are also

---

3. Emily Brandon, "The 10 Biggest Sources of Retirement Income," *U.S. News and World Report*, May 10, 2010, https://money.usnews.com/money/retirement/articles/2010/05/10/the-10-biggest-sources-of-retirement-income.
4. In 2020, taxpayers were allowed to deduct interest on up to $750,000 of mortgage debt (or $375,000 if married filing separately). For more information, visit https://www.irs.gov/pub/irs-pdf/p936.pdf.

allowed to take depreciation deductions in addition to their mortgage interest deductions.

DISADVANTAGES OF REAL ESTATE

Of course, the advantages of real estate do not come without costs, including both pecuniary and nonpecuniary costs. For instance, real estate properties require intensive management and maintenance that cannot be ignored. Additionally, finding properties and negotiating acquisitions requires high search costs due to market inefficiencies. Real estate properties are also less liquid than other types of investments, such as stocks and bonds, meaning that they can be both difficult and costly to sell, especially in an economic downturn.

CONCLUSION

Real estate is a tremendously important asset because it plays a large role in both the world economy and household finances. Furthermore, real estate investments provide an attractive way to build household wealth because of their many unique characteristics, including access to leverage, functional use, tax benefits, forced savings, and tendency to increase in value.

RELATED RESOURCES

Is Real Estate an Efficient Market?
http://betterinvestingre.blogspot.com/2011/06/is-real-estate-efficient-market.html

The Housing Market in the US Economy:
https://fas.org/sgp/crs/misc/IF11327.pdf

Why Real Estate Builds Wealth:
https://www.forbes.com/sites/davidgreene/2018/11/27/why-real-estate-builds-wealth-more-consistently-than-other-asset-classes/#60b732875405

Millionaire Investors Name Real Estate as Most Popular Alternative Asset Class:

https://www.morganstanley.com/pub/content/msdotcom/en/press-releases/millionaire-investors-name-real-estate-as-most-popular-alternative-asset-class-by-wide-margin_404f321a-29ad-438c-afab-ff18ceb302ac.html

Primer on Investment Income:

https://www.investopedia.com/terms/i/investmentincome.asp

Research on Real Estate Wealth Effects:

https://www.nar.realtor/ncrer.nsf/pages/rewealtheffect?opendocument

PART II

BUYING A HOUSE

CHAPTER 2

Getting Started

INTRODUCTION

When university students are asked if they would like to purchase a home someday, their response is almost always unanimous in the affirmative. Home ownership is still a vibrant part of the American dream. This chapter addresses essential considerations before purchasing a home, including choosing between renting and buying, understanding the risks of homeownership, preparing financially, determining affordability, and understanding the ongoing costs of homeownership.

RENT-OR-BUY DECISION

Although the American dream is homeownership, there are times when renting is more advantageous. Therefore, we should consider the advantages and disadvantages of each.

Advantages of Renting

Perhaps one of the greatest advantages renters have is the ability to move quickly with a minimal financial loss. Generally, short-term housing lease contracts require that each tenant make an upfront payment that includes first and last month's rent and a security deposit. If a tenant needs to move quickly, such as for a job relocation, the tenant's landlord will immediately place the property back on the rental market. Since most jurisdictions do not allow landlords to collect double rent, if the landlord successfully relets the property, the tenant is absolved of any future liability.

If the landlord is unable to relet the property, the tenant may be liable for any lease payments due over the remaining term of the lease. In most situations, the landlord would simply keep the deposit and last month's rent that were collected at the beginning of the lease term and release the tenant from any future obligation. Even with the possibility of losing a security deposit, however, the overall liability of renting is minuscule in comparison to the long-term liability of owning a home with a thirty-year mortgage.

Another advantage of renting is its relatively low upfront costs. As mentioned previously, tenants are typically required to pay first and last month's rent and a security deposit at the beginning of a residential lease, yet this is only a fraction of the ordinary upfront costs of buying a home.

Renting can also be advantageous because landlords are typically responsible for all repairs and maintenance on their properties. This arrangement makes it much easier for renters to budget their expenses than for homeowners, who have to plan for unexpected but necessary repairs.

Disadvantages of Renting

Although renting has many attractive advantages, it also carries several prominent disadvantages. First, when a tenant's lease term ends, the landlord has the power to increase rent for subsequent terms. This forces the tenant to either pay increased rent or incur substantial moving costs. Second, landlords can add living restrictions to their lease contracts. For instance, some landlords restrict their tenants' ability to own pets, repaint their living area, or use candles. Third, unlike home ownership, renting does not produce tax benefits. Fourth, tenants do not participate in the financial returns that are available when property values increase; these returns flow exclusively to property owners.

Advantages of Buying

While they do not strictly disadvantage renting, some advantages of buying are worth reviewing at this stage:

1. **Fixed Payments.** Since monthly payments are fixed for long-term, fixed-rate mortgages, mortgage payments that may financially stretch a household at first become less burdensome as the household's income increases over time.
2. **Pride of Ownership.** Many households find great enjoyment and flexibility in owning their own home. For instance, some families enjoy the freedom of being able to have a pet or choosing what color to paint a room. These nonpecuniary benefits are a genuine advantage to homeownership.
3. **Forced Savings.** Paying off a mortgage over time results in accumulating home equity, which can be used to supplement retirement income or stave off a family financial emergency.
4. **Tax Benefits.** Homeowners can deduct mortgage interest as an itemized deduction on their tax returns if their mortgage amount is less than $750,000. Additionally, households may qualify for a capital gain exclusion if they have lived in a property for two of the last five years. The maximum capital gain exclusion is $250,000 for single filers and $500,000 for joint filers.

Overall, these advantages of owning a home tend to tip the scales toward homeownership, making it an important goal for most American households.[5]

UNDERSTANDING THE RISKS AND RESPONSIBILITIES OF OWNING

Owning a home with a mortgage is a significant financial responsibility. Therefore, households must consider the primary risks and responsibilities of homeownership before committing to an acquisition. First, families should recognize that real estate tends to cycle (i.e., experience ups and downs) like most financial markets. A surprising number of people think that real estate prices always go up,

5. Now that we have discussed the qualitative aspects of renting versus owning, a quantitative analysis is in order. See chapter 24 for a case study that shows this analysis.

yet the empirical evidence tells a different story. Exhibit 2.1 illustrates the intertemporal nature of housing prices since January 2000. Notice that between January 2000 and June 2006, housing prices essentially doubled. However, also notice that from June 2006 through March 2012, housing values fell 33%.

Exhibit 2.1: Case-Shiller Twenty-City Composite Housing Price Index

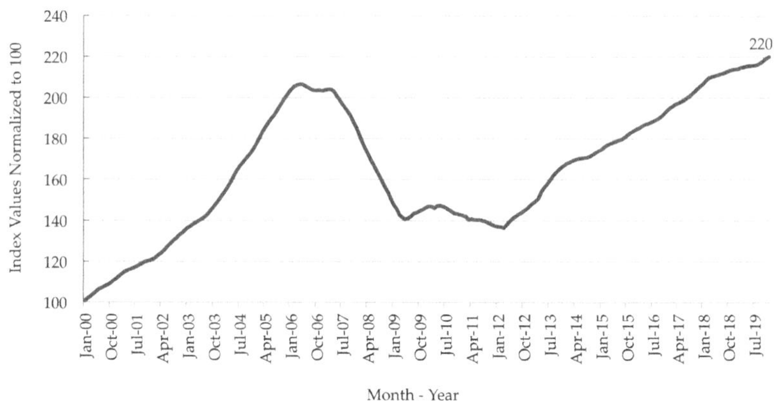

Source: FRED Economic Data, St. Louis FED

Housing markets have recovered nicely since that trough, but the data clearly shows that real estate housing markets can go down as well as up. During the downturn that lasted from 2006 to 2012, many families found themselves in a financial bind because they owed more on their house than it was worth. With negative home equity and reduced employment opportunities, many households lost their homes through foreclosure. Bad times are temporary, so this should not dissuade able households from buying homes. Even so, individuals and families should account for downside risk when deciding to purchase a home.

Households should also recognize that regional housing markets are unique and may experience price volatility that is counter to other areas. For instance, Exhibit 2.2 shows that San Jose, the top housing market by median home price, experienced a slight decline in prices during 2019. However, Salt Lake City, which has a much lower median home price, experienced a robust 12.2% increase in home prices during this same period.

EXHIBIT 2.2: TOP TWENTY METRO HOUSING MARKET BY MEDIAN HOME PRICE

Metro Area	Median Home Price	% Change 1 Year	% Change Since Peak	% Change Since Bottom	Affordable Index
San Jose, Calif.	$1,086,000	-0.9%	46.9%	134.4%	10
San Francisco, Calif.	$875,000	1.0%	24.4%	133.4%	10
Los Angeles, Calif.	$650,000	4.4%	11.4%	99.1%	10
Oxnard, Calif.	$598,000	1.3%	-3.1%	75.3%	10
Honolulu, Hi.	$580,000	1.3%	44.6%	59.7%	10
San Diego, Calif.	$568,000	4.2%	8.2%	92.4%	10
Seattle, Wash.	$460,000	4.8%	56.8%	119.1%	9
Boston, Mass.	$421,000	3.7%	20.8%	69.8%	8
New York, N.Y.-N.J.	$418,000	5.3%	3.5%	47.4%	10
Denver, Colo.	$400,000	4.1%	70.5%	111.8%	8
Sacramento, Calif.	$399,000	6.0%	0.0%	127.3%	8
Washington, D.C.-No. Va.	$397,000	5.8%	-8.2%	47.7%	9
Portland, Ore.	$385,000	3.9%	49.0%	94.5%	9
Bridgeport, Conn.	$374,000	-1.3%	-19.0%	28.7%	6
Riverside-San Bernadino, Calif.	$355,000	5.0%	-9.9%	110.2%	10
Stockton, Calif.	$355,000	4.4%	-14.5%	155.1%	10
Provo, Utah	$340,000	5.9%	77.6%	105.2%	10
Modesto, Calif.	$315,000	5.5%	-16.3%	149.7%	9
Salt Lake City, Utah	$310,000	12.2%	95.8%	133.3%	9
Colorado Springs, Colo.	$304,000	9.9%	49.8%	80.2%	8

Source: Kiplinger.com[6]

Exhibit 2.3 on the following page provides additional insight into the characteristics of the US housing market by showing the relative proportions of various residential units. Notice that over 60% of housing units are detached homes, with multifamily (i.e., condos) being the next most common unit type.

6. "Home Prices in the 100 Largest Metro Areas," Kiplinger, January 23, 2020, https://www.kiplinger.com/article/real-estate/T010-C000-S002-home-price-changes-in-the-100-largest-metro-areas.html.

Exhibit 2.3: US Housing Unit Breakdown

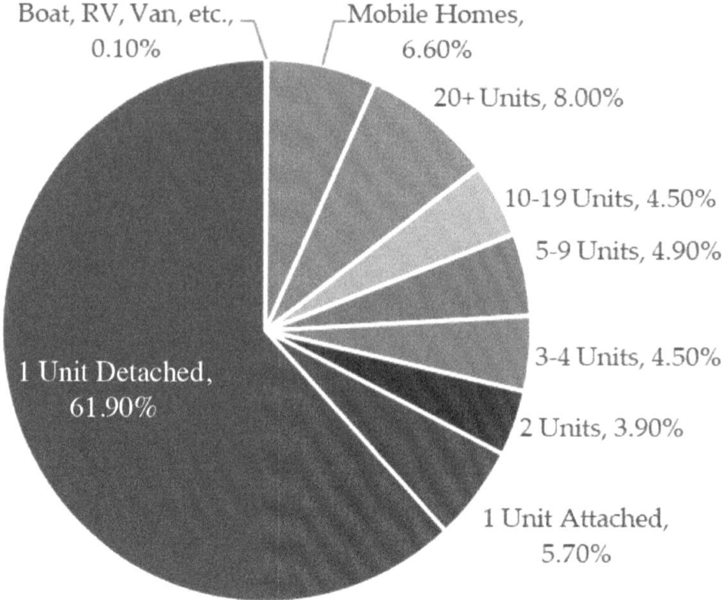

Source: US Census Bureau 2008

PREPARING FINANCIALLY

Simply considering the pros and cons of renting and owning is insufficient preparation for homeownership. Households must also consider the following essential steps of financial preparation.

Preparing a Budget

First, a household must assess its ability to make a mortgage payment. Typically, a mortgage payment consists of amortized mortgage principal and interest as well as a pro rata share of yearly property taxes and property insurance (i.e., homeowner's insurance). Industry professionals refer to these components as PITI (P = mortgage principal, I = mortgage interest, T = property taxes, I = property insurance).

Households can use their monthly housing expenditure while renting as a starting point for estimating a housing budget. Typically, a renter's current housing expenditure includes a monthly rent payment and a portion of the annual renter's insurance premium. Utility payments, if included in the rent figure, should be deducted to provide a clearer indication of how much money the household can apply toward a mortgage payment (PITI).

Next, a household should assess its other financial commitments and identify any surplus funds that could go toward a mortgage payment. This step is especially crucial because individuals and families often plan to acquire a home to upgrade their housing situation. Adding budget surplus to the current monthly housing expenditure produces a good estimate of the maximum amount a household could afford in housing expenses (PITI).[7]

After estimating a budget for PITI, a prospective homeowner should consider other pecuniary and nonpecuniary costs associated with homeownership. These include pecuniary costs such as monthly utility expenses and property maintenance and nonpecuniary costs, such as overseeing or performing property maintenance.[8] These costs can be substantial and are irrelevant to renters, so it is imperative that prospective homebuyers budget for them appropriately.

Estimating the Mortgage Amount

Once a household has a good handle on how much of its monthly budget can apply to PITI, it can then deduct estimated property taxes and insurance to arrive at an estimated mortgage payment. This figure can then be used to calculate the maximum loan amount the household can afford. Exhibit 2.4 contains an example of how to perform this calculation.

---

7. Of course, there are some other items that households should consider in financial preparation, such as current employment stability, expected income growth, and future career plans. Self-employed individuals should also realize that, for them, the mortgage approval and underwriting process is more rigorous and time-consuming.
8. Please note that maintenance costs are highly correlated with the age of a property; older homes require substantially more maintenance on average than newer homes.

EXHIBIT 2.4: ESTIMATING THE MORTGAGE AMOUNT—EXAMPLE

Jen wants to buy a home. She can afford to pay $1,500 per month (principal and interest) toward a mortgage. The current interest rate on thirty-year fixed-rate mortgages is 4%.

What is the maximum loan amount Jen can afford?

Solution:

Discount all 360 (30 years x 12 months) monthly payments at 0.33% (4% divided by 12 months).

$$\frac{\$1,500}{1+.0033} + \frac{\$1,500}{(1+.0033)^2} + \frac{\$1,500}{(1+.0033)^3} + \dots + \frac{\$1,500}{(1+.0033)^{360}} = \$314,191.86$$

Jen can afford to borrow about $315,000 to buy a home.

Down Payment and Closing Costs

After a household has estimated its potential mortgage loan total, its next step should be to estimate a down payment. How much a family is able and willing to allocate for a down payment is a function of their income, savings, and financial goals. Additionally, different mortgage structures have different down payment requirements. For example, a typical home buyer might be required to put at least 3% down for a conforming conventional loan, while a veteran who qualifies for a VA loan might not even be required to pay a down payment. Therefore, each household should consider its financial situation and available mortgage options before deciding which mortgage product to select and how much money to put down.

Once a household has determined how much it is willing to pay as a down payment, it can add that number to its estimated mortgage loan amount to estimate the price it could pay for a home. For example, if a household has $15,000 saved for a down payment and can afford a loan of $315,000, it could purchase a property worth up to $330,000.

In addition to estimating a down payment and mortgage loan amount, it is imperative that prospective homebuyers also account for closing costs. Closing costs vary by geographic area but are generally a function of the purchase price and loan type. Zillow provides a list of possible closing costs (see Exhibit 2.5).

Exhibit 2.5: Possible Closing Costs

Application Fee: The application fee covers the cost for the lender to process your application. Before submitting an application, ask your lender what this fee covers. It can often include things like a credit check for your credit score or appraisal as well. Not all lenders charge an application fee, and it can often be negotiated.

Appraisal: The appraisal cost is paid to the appraisal company to confirm the fair market value of the home.

Attorney Fee: The attorney fee pays for an attorney to review the closing documents on behalf of the buyer or the lender. This is not required in all states.

Closing Fee or Escrow Fee: The closing or escrow fee is paid to the title company, escrow company, or attorney for conducting the closing. The title company or escrow oversees the closing as an independent party in your home purchase. Some states require a real estate attorney be present at every closing.

Courier Fee: The courier fee covers the cost of transporting documents to complete the loan transaction as quickly as possible.

Credit Report: A tri-merge credit report is pulled to get your credit history and score. Your credit score plays a big role in determining the interest rate you'll get on your loan.

Escrow Deposit for Property Taxes and Mortgage Insurance: Often you are asked to put down two months of property tax and mortgage insurance payments at closing.

FHA Up-Front Mortgage Insurance Premium (UPMIP): If you have an FHA loan, you'll be required to pay the UPMIP of 1.75% of the base loan amount. You are also able to roll this into the cost of the loan if you prefer.

Flood Determination or Life of Loan Coverage: Flood determination or life of loan coverage is paid to a third party to determine if the property is located in a flood zone. If the property is found to be located within a flood zone, you will need to buy flood insurance. The insurance, of course, is paid separately.

Home Inspection: You will likely get your own home inspection to verify the condition of a property and check for home repairs that may be needed before closing.

Homeowners' Association Transfer Fees: The seller pays for this transfer fee, which covers the cost of preparing the documents that show what the dues are and confirm that they are paid current. The documents also include a copy of the association financial statements, minutes, and notices. The buyer should review these documents to determine whether the homeowners' association has enough reserves in place to avert future special assessments. The buyer should also check to see if there are special assessments, legal action, or any other items that might be of concern. Also included will be association by-laws, rules and regulations, and CC&Rs.

Homeowners' Insurance: Homeowners' insurance covers possible damages to your home. Your first year's insurance is often paid at closing.

Lead-Based Paint Inspection: This inspection fee covers the cost of evaluating lead-based paint risk.

Lender's Policy Title Insurance: Lender's policy title insurance assures the lender that you own the home and that the lender's mortgage is a valid lien, and it protects the lender if there is a problem with the title. Lender's policy title insurance is similar to the title search but is always a separate line item.

Loan Discount Points: Points are prepaid interest. One point is 1% of your loan amount. This is a lump-sum payment that lowers your monthly payment for the life of your loan.

Origination Fee: The origination fee covers the lender's administrative costs. It's usually about 1% of the total loan, but you can sometimes find mortgages with no origination fee.

Owner's Policy Title Insurance: Owner's policy title insurance protects you in the event someone challenges your ownership of the home. It is usually optional.

Pest Inspection: The pest inspection fee covers the cost to inspect for termites or dry rot, which is required in some states and is also required for government loans. Repairs can get expensive if evidence of termites, dry rot, or other wood damage is found.

Prepaid Interest: Most lenders will ask you to prepay any interest that will accrue between closing and the date of your first mortgage payment.

Private Mortgage Insurance (PMI): If you're making a down payment that's less than 20% of the home's purchase price, chances are you'll be required to pay PMI. If so, you may need to pay the first month's PMI payment at closing.

Property Tax: Typically, lenders will want any taxes due within sixty days of purchase by the loan servicer to be paid at closing.

Recording Fees: Recording fees are charged by your local recording office, usually city or county, for the recording of public land records.

Survey Fee: The survey fee goes to a survey company to verify all property lines and things like shared fences on the property. This is not required in all states.

Title Company Title Search or Exam Fee: The title search or exam fee is paid to the title company for doing a thorough search of the property's records. The title company researches the deed to your new home, ensuring that no one else has a claim to the property.

Transfer Taxes. Transfer tax is the tax paid when the title passes from seller to buyer.

Underwriting Fee: The underwriting fee also goes to your lender, covering the cost of researching whether or not to approve you for the loan.

VA Funding Fee: If you have a VA loan, you may be required to pay a VA funding fee at closing (or you can roll this fee into the cost of the loan if you prefer). This is a percentage of the loan amount that the VA assesses to fund the VA home loan program; however, some borrowers are exempt from this fee. The percentage depends on your type of service and the amount of your down payment.

Source: Zillow.com[9]

9. "What Are Closing Costs and How Much Are They"? Zillow, https://www.zillow.com/mortgage-learning/closing-costs/.

Zillow reports that closing costs typically range between 2% and 5% of the purchase price, or between $6,600 and $16,500 for a $330,000 home. These costs are not trivial, so homebuyers must plan appropriately for them. Lenders typically provide closing cost estimates after borrowers apply for a loan. However, borrowers are responsible for confirming that all closing costs have been accounted for and are accurate. In some cases, homebuyers are surprised by unanticipated expenses at loan closing and must scramble to come up with the additional funds. Contemporary mortgage regulations have reduced the prevalence of surprise closing fees, yet borrowers should still be careful and attentive to prevent unpleasant surprises.

RELATED RESOURCES

What Are Closing Costs, and How Much Are They?
https://www.zillow.com/mortgage-learning/closing-costs/

Why Should You Buy a Home?
https://www.thebalance.com/eight-reasons-to-buy-a-home-1798233#:~:text=Homeownership%20is%20a%20superb%20tax,deductible%20on%20your%20tax%20return.

Pros and Cons of Homeownership
https://www.incharge.org/housing/homebuyer-education/homeownership-guide/advantages-and-disadvantages-of-owning-a-home/

Rent versus Buy Considerations
https://www.fidelity.com/viewpoints/personal-finance/rent-vs-buy#:~:text=Rather%20than%20simply%20focusing%20on,the%20end%20of%20your%20stay.&text=On%20the%20other%20hand%2C%20if,20%2C%20renting%20might%20be%20better.

Rent versus Buy Calculator
https://smartasset.com/mortgage/rent-vs-buy#BLculKpVg9

CHAPTER 3

Mortgage Finance I—Working with a Lender

INTRODUCTION

A mortgage loan is the primary means of financing the purchase of a home, so understanding mortgage financing with its unique terms and calculations is essential to minimizing financing costs. The root of the word mortgage comes from the Latin *mortuum vadium*, which means "dead pledge."[10] Indeed, some people worry that taking on a mortgage is a sort of death pledge, but the reality is not so frightening.

First, this chapter identifies the characteristics of different types of lenders and things to consider when selecting a lender. Second, it explains the inputs that lenders use to determine the terms of a loan, such as credit score and income verification. Third, it discusses how houses are financed and the importance of understanding mortgage structures, annual percentage rate (APR), points and effective interest rates, alternative mortgage products, government-sponsored enterprises, and the secondary mortgage market. Fourth, it reviews the mortgage application process and the differences between prequalification and preapproval. Fifth, the chapter explains typical closing

10. "What Is Mortuum Vadium"? The Law Dictionary, https://thelawdictionary.org/mortuum-vadium/.

costs and the regulation about good faith estimates, and sixth, it examines how to determine when to refinance an existing mortgage.

SELECTING A LENDER

As prospective homebuyers search for a mortgage lender, they need to understand the different types of lenders and the subfields that the lenders work in. For the most part, residential mortgage lenders are classified as either mortgage bankers, mortgage brokers, retail lenders, or online lenders.

Mortgage Bankers

Mortgage bankers are individuals, companies, or institutions that originate mortgages. Mortgage loans originated by a mortgage banker can either be personally funded or borrowed from warehouse lenders. Mortgage bankers usually sell the loans they originate to mortgage investors and only sometimes retain loans for their portfolios. After originating loans, mortgage bankers can also choose to retain mortgage servicing rights, including payment collection rights, or sell them to another financial institution.[11] Mortgage bankers primarily make money through mortgage origination fees and generally offer a mix of both conventional and nonconventional loans (i.e., jumbo loans).[12]

Mortgage Brokers

Mortgage brokers are intermediaries in the mortgage market. They bring together borrowers and lenders but do not use their funds to originate loans. The primary responsibility of a mortgage broker is to match borrowers with lenders who offer products appropriate for the borrowers' financial situations and needs. Mortgage brokers also

---

11. Julia Kagan, "Mortgage Banker," Investopedia, January 29, 2020, https://www.investopedia.com/terms/m/mortgagebanker.asp
12. "Mortgage Banker Definition." Bankrate, 2020, https://www.bankrate.com/mortgages/mortgage-banker/.

facilitate transactions by handling paperwork and transferring information between borrowers and lenders.[13]

RETAIL LENDERS (BANKS AND CREDIT UNIONS)

Retail lenders generally include banks and credit unions. These lenders are highly regulated and are generally required to be state or federally chartered. These institutions usually provide a wide range of financial products (e.g., checking and savings accounts, home equity lines of credit, personal loans, and business loans) in addition to mortgage loans. Most potential homebuyers already have a bank account with a retail lender, which makes their retail lender an obvious candidate for a mortgage loan.

Online Lenders

Online lenders operate online to provide loans, including residential mortgages. Because online lenders have low overhead costs, their rates and fees tend to be very competitive. These convenience-focused lenders also enable borrowers to apply online and be approved quickly.

Peer-to-peer lending services were the earliest online lenders and allow anyone to lend money to loan applicants. Currently, however, banks and larger financial institutions, rather than individuals, are the primary funding source for online lenders.[14]

START WITH MULTIPLE LENDERS

Which type of lender is best for obtaining a residential home loan? It is wise to shop all of them. Mortgage bankers, mortgage brokers, and online lenders are virtually indistinguishable to most people. Whether they use their funds or someone else's, these institutions all focus on originating as many loans as possible to earn origination fees.

---

13. Julia Kagan, "Mortgage Broker," Investopedia, January 29, 2020, https://www.investopedia.com/terms/m/mortgagebroker.asp.
14. Justin Pritchard, "Online Lenders Make Borrowing Easy (and Cheap)," The Balance, June 25, 2019, https://www.thebalance.com/online-loans-315614.

These lenders' relationships with a borrower are typically limited to one transaction.

The primary difference between mortgage bankers/brokers and online lenders is that online lenders do not host face-to-face meetings. Most mortgage bankers and brokers, on the other hand, have offices to host physical meetings with potential borrowers. Face-to-face meetings with lenders are preferable to some individuals who are unnerved by a lack of personal interaction when conducting a significant financial transaction.

Retail lenders are significantly different from the other three types of lenders. Most borrowers already have a relationship with a retail lender (usually a bank or credit union). Additionally, retail lenders have a greater interest in building positive relationships with borrowers so they can sell them other financial services in the future.

Since these different types of lenders all have different characteristics and incentives, prospective borrowers should shop between two or three of them before deciding from whom to borrow.

BORROWER ANALYSIS

In addition to understanding the players in the mortgage industry, borrowers need to learn how to manage their finances to qualify for favorable loan terms. This includes learning how to build a strong credit score and prepare for income verification.

Managing Your Credit Score

At least six months before starting to look at houses, homebuyers should examine their credit history and take steps to improve their credit score. Two numbers from a borrower's financial information dominate today's semi-automated mortgage financing: (1) gross income and (2) Fair Isaac Co. (FICO) credit score. Borrowers should take reasonable steps to increase their gross income. However, most find it easier and more beneficial to focus on increasing their FICO score.

Credit Reporting Agencies

Three leading credit reporting agencies operate within the United States: Experian (www.experian.com), Equifax (www.equifax.com), and TransUnion (www.transunion.com). Lenders look at reports from at least one, if not all, of these agencies to learn about borrowers' credit history. Data in these reports come from public records and creditors.

Each of the credit reporting agencies is required by law to provide everyone with one free credit report per year. Additional copies can be obtained relatively cheaply ($10 or less). Borrowers should regularly examine their credit reports from each of the three agencies because although studies show that a high percentage of credit reports are accurate, some have errors that may impact a credit score.[15] Correcting inaccuracies can be as simple as writing a letter to the rating agency but may take some time to resolve, so it's smart to get on this early.

If a lender denies a prospective borrower credit based on his or her credit history, the lender is required to provide the borrower with a copy of the credit report that formed the basis for the credit denial.

FICO Score

Since credit information remains on an individual's record for seven years (bankruptcy lasts for ten years), preparing to apply for credit often feels discouraging to people with past credit mistakes. Fortunately, however, recent credit history (particularly the last six months) is given greater weight in computing the most important number in credit analysis today, the FICO score.

A FICO score can range from 300 to 850, with a higher number signaling higher creditworthiness. The average FICO score is 703.[16] The following factors make up a FICO score:

---

15. How Accurate Are Your Credit Reports, https://www.cardrates.com/advice/how-accurate-are-your-credit-reports/
16. Alexandria White, "Average FICO Score Hits Record High," CNBC Select, January 6, 2021, https://www.cnbc.com/select/average-fico-score-hits-record-high-703/. Accessed February 10, 2020.

- Payment history (35%): Track record of paying creditors
- Amounts owed (30%): Number of creditors and amount of outstanding debt
- Length of credit history (15%): Length of track record with past creditors
- New credit (10%): Number of new accounts and credit requests
- Types of credit in use (10%): Mix of different types of debt

Individuals usually have to pay to learn their FICO score, despite advertisements that suggest otherwise. Obtaining a regular score report can be a good idea for those who are unsure of their credit score or who want to track their score progress. Reputable sites such as www.myfico.com offer score information for a nominal monthly fee.

The best way for an individual to improve his or her FICO score is to simply contract a reasonable amount of debt and pay it off promptly over several years. Several quicker fixes can also help someone maximize his or her score in the short term. For instance, an individual preparing to apply for a mortgage could do the following:

1. Take special care to pay all of his or her bills on time.
2. Ask for a credit limit increase on his or her credit card (part of a person's FICO score is based on the total percentage of his or her available balance that he or she has drawn).
3. Pay down current debt commitments as much as possible.
4. Refrain from opening new credit or retail discount accounts.

Higher FICO scores often translate directly into lower available mortgage rates, so prospective homebuyers greatly benefit from maximizing their FICO score. Even so, potential buyers should not unilaterally focus on increasing their FICO score at the expense of other aspects of home-buying preparation.

INCOME VERIFICATION AND ANALYSIS

Mortgage loan officers are required to verify applicants' income and provide supporting documentation. Also, loan officers need to verify the source of monies used for down payments and closing costs.

For W-2 employees who have diligently saved for a down payment and closing costs, the verification process is straightforward. It is more complicated, however, for those who are self-employed (1099) or have received funds from a nontraditional source, such as a gift.

If an applicant is self-employed, the loan officer will generally ask to see the applicant's tax returns for the last two years. The loan officer will then average adjusted gross income from the two returns and divide by twelve to estimate average monthly income. The loan officer may also review the applicant's bank statements to verify the flow of funds over time.

Self-employed people also face unique challenges when applying for a mortgage because their interests as a borrower clash with their tax incentives. Self-employed people are incentivized to reduce their taxable income to decrease their tax liability, but doing so reduces the income they can claim on a mortgage application. Self-employed individuals should, therefore, start working with a lender as soon as possible to work through all the complexities that may arise.

For an individual to be able to use a gift to pay part of a down payment or closing costs, the gift generally needs to be from a family member, and the funds need to be trackable (documentable). Usually, lenders want to see the family member's bank statements that include the donated funds as evidence that the funds came from the family member, not a loan shark down the street. Also, a gift recipient and his or her donating family member must sign a gift letter verifying that the transferred funds are a gift and not a loan. Rather than go through this process, some borrowers elect to "season" gift funds by receiving the gift funds into their bank account months before applying for a loan. This method generally prevents any verification issues.

HOW HOUSES ARE FINANCED

When shopping for a mortgage loan, it is essential to understand that there are two primary mortgage structures. The first is a fixed-rate mortgage, and the second is an adjustable-rate mortgage.

Fixed-Rate Mortgage Loan

As the name suggests, fixed-rate mortgages have a fixed interest rate over the entire term. Even within fixed-rate mortgages, however, amortization structures[17] vary considerably. For instance, fixed-rate loans may be fully amortizing (level payment mortgage), partially amortizing, or negatively amortizing and may include accelerated payments. Each of these structures is discussed in the following paragraphs.

Level Payment Mortgage (LPM)

The most popular type of mortgage is the level payment mortgage (LPM), or fully amortizing mortgage. LPMs use a constant payment over the term of the loan that reduces the principal balance to zero at the maturity date of the loan. Calculating the monthly payment required to pay off an LPM is a relatively simple exercise in Excel. For reference, the formula is provided here:

= *Pmt (rate, nper, pv, [fv], [type])*

This formula contains three required arguments—interest rate (rate), term (nper), and principal amount (pv)[18]—and two optional arguments, which are omitted for LPMs. Borrowers love LPMs because of their predictability. Additionally, since incomes tend to rise over time, borrowers often find that their LPM payments become easier to manage from year to year.

---

17. Amortization-schedule loans on real property often require principal payments throughout the course of the loan. In such a loan, the principal is said to be amortized. The rate at which this amortization takes place varies widely, but the most common rates for home mortgages are fifteen years (180 payments) and thirty years (360 payments). A loan with no amortization is called an interest only (IO) loan. A loan that requires payments (for a time) lower than the interest payments has "negative" amortization, as the size of the loan increases, rather than decreases, over time.
18. In this formula, negative numbers indicate cash outflows for the borrower, while positive numbers indicate cash inflows. Under this convention, the = PMT() formula output should be negative.

EXHIBIT 3.1: AMORTIZATION TABLE—LEVEL PAYMENTS

Amortization Table					
Inputs					
Loan Amount				$100,000	
Annual Interest Rate				4.50%	
Term of Loan (Yrs.)				30	
Number of Payments per Yr.				12	
Outputs					
Monthly Payment				$506.69	
Month	Beginning Loan Balance	Payment	Interest	Principal	End Loan Balance
1	$100,000	$506.69	$375.00	$131.69	$99,868.31
2	$99,868.31	$506.69	$374.51	$132.18	$99,736.14
3	$99,736.14	$506.69	$374.01	$132.67	$99,603.46
4	$99,603.46	$506.69	$373.51	$133.17	$99,470.29
5	$99,470.29	$506.69	$373.01	$133.67	$99,336.62
6	$99,336.62	$506.69	$372.51	$134.17	$99,202.44
7	$99,202.44	$506.69	$372.01	$134.68	$99,067.77
8	$99,067.77	$506.69	$371.50	$135.18	$98,932.59
9	$98,932.59	$506.69	$371.00	$135.69	$98,796.90
10	$98,796.90	$506.69	$370.49	$136.20	$98,660.70
11	$98,660.70	$506.69	$369.98	$136.71	$98,523.99
12	$98,523.99	$506.69	$369.46	$137.22	$98,386.77

In this formula, negative numbers indicate cash *outflows* for the borrower, while positive numbers indicate cash *inflows*. Under this convention, the = PMT() formula output should be negative.

Exhibit 3.1 shows the first twelve months of an amortization table for a level payment mortgage. Notice how the payment stays fixed over the term of the mortgage, while the portion allocated to interest decreases, and the portion allocated to principal increases.

ACCELERATED-PAYMENTS MORTGAGE

If a mortgage is the first mortgage for a borrower's primary residence, then the borrower is typically allowed to prepay principal,

EXHIBIT 3.2: AMORTIZATION TABLE—ACCELERATED PAYMENTS

Amortization Table

Inputs

Loan Amount	$100,000
Annual Interest Rate	4.50%
Term of Loan (Yrs.)	30
Number of Payments per Yr.	12

Outputs

Monthly Payment	$506.69
Double Payment	$1,013.37

Month	Beginning Loan Balance	Payment	Interest	Principal	End Loan Balance (Double Payments)
1	$100,000.00	$1,013.37	$375.00	$638.37	$99,361.63
2	$99,361.63	$1,013.37	$372.61	$640.76	$98,720.86
3	$98,720.86	$1,013.37	$370.20	$643.17	$98,077.70
4	$98,077.70	$1,013.37	$367.79	$645.58	$97,432.12
5	$97,432.12	$1,013.37	$365.37	$648.00	$96,784.12
6	$96,784.12	$1,013.37	$362.94	$650.43	$96,133.69
7	$96,133.69	$1,013.37	$360.50	$652.87	$95,480.82
8	$95,480.82	$1,013.37	$358.05	$655.32	$94,825.50
9	$94,825.50	$1,013.37	$355.60	$657.77	$94,167.73
10	$94,167.73	$1,013.37	$353.13	$660.24	$93,507.48
11	$93,507.48	$1,013.37	$350.65	$662.72	$92,844.77
12	$92,844.77	$1,013.37	$348.17	$665.20	$92,179.56

accelerating the paydown of the debt. Exhibit 3.2 displays the amortization table for a borrower who pays twice the minimum monthly payment each month.

Notice how quickly the principal owed declines compared to the previous example. In this case, the remaining principal after twelve months is $92,179, while in the prior case, it was $98,386. If the borrower continued to make double payments, the loan would be paid off in 123 months, or about ten years, compared with thirty years in the previous example.

Partially Amortizing Mortgage

A partially amortizing mortgage, often referred to as a balloon mortgage or a bullet loan, stipulates a balance to be due at the end of the loan term. The advantage of this type of loan is that it reduces monthly payments. On the other hand, a bullet loan leaves a balance remaining at the end of the loan term for the borrower to either repay or refinance. In reality, these types of mortgages are quite rare in residential lending.

To calculate the payment for a partially amortizing loan, include the future balloon payment amount as the future value (fv) in Excel's payment function. For example, consider a level payment mortgage with the following inputs:

$$= PMT(\frac{0.045}{12}, 30 * 12, 100000)$$

This would provide a level payment of $506.69. To convert this loan to a partially amortizing loan with a remaining balance of $30,000 at the end of the loan term, modify the payment function as follows:

$$= PMT(\frac{0.045}{12}, 30 * 12, 100000, -30000)$$

This provides a reduced monthly payment of $467.18, or savings of $39.51 per month over the level payment structure.

Negatively Amortizing Mortgage

A negatively amortizing loan actually allows the loan balance to grow over time. In a negatively amortizing loan, the monthly payment does not cover the accrued interest, and the deficit is added to the loan balance. Generally, these loans are provided to individuals who expect to have a much higher income in the future than they do in the present. For example, a young surgeon just starting his or her career might consider this type of loan. Rather than wait for his or her income to increase, the young surgeon might choose to purchase an expensive home immediately, financing the purchase with a negatively amortizing mortgage. A lender would likely grant the surgeon a negative amortizing loan out of confidence that his or her income would increase dramatically in the future, allowing the surgeon to refinance or pay off the loan. Exhibit 3.3 shows the amortization table for a negatively amortizing loan.

Notice that the payment is less than the accrued interest in each period, which leads to an increasing loan balance.

EXHIBIT 3.3: AMORTIZATION TABLE—NEGATIVE AMORTIZATION

Amortization Table

Inputs	
Loan Amount	$100,000
Annual Interest Rate	4.50%
Term of Loan (Yrs.)	30
Number of Payments per Yr.	12
Remaining Balance at End	$130,000

Outputs	
Monthly Payment	$335.49
Monthly Payment without Neg Amort	$506.69

Month	Beginning Loan Balance	Payment	Interest	Principal	End Loan Balance
1	$100,000	$335.49	$375.00	($39.51)	$100,039.51
2	$100,039.51	$335.49	$375.15	($39.65)	$100,079.16
3	$100,079.16	$335.49	$375.30	($39.80)	$100,118.96
4	$100,118.96	$335.49	$375.45	($39.95)	$100,158.91
5	$100,158.91	$335.49	$375.60	($40.10)	$100,199.01
6	$100,199.01	$335.49	$375.75	($40.25)	$100,239.27
7	$100,239.27	$335.49	$375.90	($40.40)	$100,279.67
8	$100,279.67	$335.49	$376.05	($40.55)	$100,320.22
9	$100,320.22	$335.49	$376.20	($40.71)	$100,360.93
10	$100,360.93	$335.49	$376.35	($40.86)	$100,401.79

Adjustable-Rate Mortgage Loan (ARM)

Another option a buyer may choose when shopping for a mortgage is the adjustable-rate mortgage (ARM). An ARM has periodic dates during which its interest rate "resets," usually based on an index such as a US Treasury rate. ARMs are attractive to lenders (especially banks) because they mitigate much of the interest-rate risk characteristic of long-term LPMs. Due to their attractiveness to lenders, ARMs are often offered with very low initial interest rates.

Calculating the payments on an ARM over its life is more complicated than calculating the payments on an LPM because a change in interest rates causes a change in the required payment. In addition, a number of contract terms can affect how an ARM's interest rate resets. Exhibit 3.4 defines important terms related to ARMs.

Exhibit 3.4: ARM Key Terms

Index: The index is the reference point on which the interest rate is based. The prime rate and US Treasury rates are frequently used indices.

Margin: An ARM's margin is its interest rate's spread above the index rate. The margin is based on the loan's risk. For example, a "T + 4%" spread is equal to the current Treasury rate plus 4%.

Rate Adjustment Period: A rate adjustment period states how often an ARM's interest rate resets. One year is the most common rate adjustment period. An ARM's monthly payment is recalculated based on the new interest rate after each rate adjustment period.

Rate Adjustment Cap: Most adjustable-rate loans have an interest rate cap, or "collar." This limits the rate's up-and-down movements, usually with a small limit (e.g., 1%–2%) each period and a larger limit (e.g., 5%–6%) over the life of the loan. This helps mitigate the effects of large interest-rate swings and provides both parties with some predictability.

Teaser: A teaser rate is a temporarily low interest rate used to encourage a buyer to sign an ARM. Teaser rates likely played a part in causing the Great Recession because buyers often "qualified" for loans based solely on their low initial teaser rate. When real estate values dropped, and credit markets suddenly dried up during the downturn, these buyers were unable to refinance their loans when their teaser rates expired, leaving them with payments they could not afford.

ARMs, despite their abuse in the real estate bubble of the mid-2000s, enable borrowers and lenders to share in interest-rate risk and are likely here to stay. However, buyers should not pay too much attention to the stated rate on an ARM, which is almost always a teaser rate. If a loan's interest rate can contractually increase to an interest rate the buyer is unable to pay, he or she should probably not sign the loan.

Prime versus Alt-A versus Subprime

Mortgages are also classified into three broad subcategories based upon their perceived risk. The most creditworthy buyers are classified as prime, while those with poor credit are known as subprime. In between these two general classifications are alt-A buyers, who may not have documentation for all income or investment properties and may have other complicating factors, making them riskier or more difficult to assess than prime buyers. Subprime (and to a lesser extent alt-A) buyers often receive less-favorable terms on mortgages, such as higher interest rates and prepayment penalties. Subprime lending practices were criticized during the Great Recession, and lending to that segment has decreased significantly since that time.

ANNUAL PERCENTAGE RATE (APR)

Renting money is never free; lenders make their money by charging interest and fees on loans. Mortgage lenders are required to disclose the annualized total costs per year of a loan as a percentage of the loan's total principal amount. This figure is called the annual percentage rate, or APR. Though APR is not a precise yield calculation, it allows for easy comparison across lenders. Note that a mortgage's APR is often higher than its quoted interest rate because an APR includes any fees paid upfront or amortized into the mortgage. For a valid comparison across lenders, compare the APR on a "no-cost" or "no-fee" loan.

The APR was first introduced in 1968 through the Truth in Lending Act. The United States government passed the Truth in Lending Act to help its citizens better understand the true cost of their mortgage and to provide a standardized method of reporting mortgage rates to help consumers quickly compare rates from different lenders. Since 1968, there have been multiple revisions to the Truth in Lending Act to eliminate loopholes discovered by lenders. The most recent legislation passed was the Mortgage Disclosure Improvement Act of 2008. The act states that a loan's final APR cannot be more than 0.125% off from the APR initially disclosed by the lender.

A loan's APR is what the lender charges to borrow money on a yearly basis. APR is calculated by taking the sum of the interest and fees paid and dividing by the loan amount. This number is divided by the number of days in the loan term and then multiplied by 365. This yields the APR in decimal form, which can be converted to a percentage by multiplying by 100:

$$APR = \left[\left(\frac{\frac{Fees+Interest\ Paid}{Loan\ Amount}}{Number\ of\ Days\ in\ Loan\ Term}\right) * 365\right] * 100$$

APR can also be calculated in Excel or on a financial calculator.

Lenders are typically willing to lower the APR on a loan by introducing fees and points. This is known as buying the rate down. However, a lower APR does not always translate into a lower effective rate. Buyers should, therefore, compare rates from lenders under the same conditions, preferably with no points or fees.

POINTS AND EFFECTIVE RATES

Advertisements frequently champion extremely low interest rates on loans. These types of advertisements are often misleading because they include points and fees in the fine print that is often overlooked and misunderstood. Picking out the right mortgage loan typically involves wading through several confusing mortgage quotes with different points and fees.

LOAN POINTS

When buyers begin shopping for a mortgage, they quickly notice that some mortgage rates are quoted with points. For instance, an internet search of mortgage rates might produce the following screen (see Exhibit 3.5):

Exhibit 3.5: Internet Search Results—Mortgage Rates

Featured CFBANK NMLS #409132 ★★★★★ 141 Reviews	4.000% 30 year fixed	4.044%	$1,146	$1,257 Points: 0.524 5 year cost: $47,079
CFBANK NMLS #409132 ★★★★★ 141 Reviews	4.124% 30 year fixed	4.124%	$1,163	$0 Points: 0 5 year cost: $47,287
Featured BLUE SPOT HOME LOANS NMLS #3001 ★★★★★ 73 Reviews	4.124% 30 year fixed	4.200%	$1,163	$2,179 Points: 0.908 5 year cost: $49,466

Notice that the top quote from CFBank provides a rate quote of 4.000% with 0.524 points, while right below is another quote from the same bank of 4.124% with no points. This evokes the natural question, Which is best? To answer that question, it is necessary to understand some important concepts relating to mortgage points.

TERMS AND CONCEPTS

Mortgage points are sometimes referred to as origination points and sometimes as discount points. Origination points are essentially fees paid to the lender to take out a loan, while discount points are paid to lower the nominal interest rate on the loan. Regardless of what a lender calls them, points are always a cost to the borrower.

One-point equals 1% of the loan amount. When a lender distributes loan proceeds, the lender retains the amount of the loan attributed to its points, but the loan's monthly payment is based on the entire contract loan amount.

Now that we understand some of the fundamental concepts associated with mortgage points, let's work through a few examples of how to calculate the effective interest rate of a mortgage with points to learn how to properly evaluate loan options.

EFFECTIVE RATE (FULL TERM)

Assume that a bank has agreed to loan a borrower $275,000 at 4.25% interest for thirty years but will charge two points to make the loan. Given these terms, what is the effective interest rate on the loan? To answer this question, first calculate the loan's monthly payment. This is done using the Excel PMT function:

$$= PMT(\frac{0.0425}{12},\ 30 * 12,\ \ -275000)$$

The previous calculation results in a monthly payment of $1,352.83. Next, calculate the amount dispersed. In this case, the points amount to $5,500 ($275,000 * 0.02), which results in an amount dispersed of $269,500. Third, calculate the effective rate of the mortgage using the following Excel function and inputs:

$$= rate(30 * 12, -\ 1352.83,\ 269500)$$

This calculation provides an effective interest rate of 4.421%. Notice that this is higher than the stated rate of 4.25%. The effective interest rate is really the rate the borrower pays for funds he or she receives and is higher because the borrower does not receive the full or contract loan amount of $275,000.

This type of analysis provides important insights when comparing mortgage alternatives, so let's work through the analysis with two alternative loan arrangements.

EFFECTIVE RATE WITH EARLY PAYOFF

Assume a borrower is working with two different lenders, Lender A and Lender B. Lender A agrees to loan the borrower $300,000 over thirty years at a 4.5% interest rate and will charge no points. Lender B, on the other hand, will also lend $300,000 over thirty years but at a rate of 4.25%. Lender B will charge 1.75 points for this lower rate. Assume that the borrower wants to live in the property only for five years, so he or she plans to sell the property and pay the loan off at that time. Given these terms, which loan provides the lowest effective interest rate?

To answer this question, follow this four-step process for each loan alternative:

1. Calculate the payment of each loan given the nominal interest rate quoted by the respective lenders.
2. Calculate the amount dispersed given the points charged.
3. Calculate the remaining balance of each loan after five years.
4. Calculate the effective interest rate.

First, let's calculate the effective interest rate for Lender A.

Exhibit 3.6a: Effective Interest Rate—Lender A

Lender A agrees to loan $300,000 over thirty years at a 4.5% interest rate and will charge no points.

Step 1: Calculate the payment (Excel).

$$= PMT\left(\frac{0.045}{12}, 30 * 12, 300000\right)$$

Monthly Payment: $1,520.06

Step 2: Calculate the amount dispersed.

$$\$300,000 * 0.00 = \$0$$
$$\$300,000 - \$0 = \$300,000$$

Amount Dispersed: $300,000

Step 3: Calculate the remaining balance (Excel).

$$= PV(\frac{0.045}{12}, 25 * 12, 1502.06)$$

Remaining Balance: $273,473.75

Step 4: Calculate the effective interest rate (Excel).

$$= rate(5 * 12, - 1502.06, 300000, - 273473.75)$$

Effective Interest Rate: 4.5%

Note: The effective rate of a loan with no points is the nominal interest rate. Now, let's calculate the effective interest on the proposed loan by Lender B.

EXHIBIT 3.6B: EFFECTIVE INTEREST RATE—LENDER B

Lender B agrees to loan \$300,000 over thirty years at a 4.25% interest rate and will charge 1.75 points.

Step 1: Calculate the payment (Excel).

$$= PMT(\frac{0.0425}{12}, 30 * 12, 300000)$$

Monthly Payment: \$1,475.82

Step 2: Calculate the amount dispersed.

$$\$300,000 * 0.0175\ (points) = \$5,250$$
$$\$300,000 - \$5,250 = \$294,750$$

Amount Dispersed: \$294,750

Step 3: Calculate the remaining balance (Excel).

$$= PV(\frac{0.0425}{12}, 25 * 12, 1475.82)$$

Remaining Balance: \$272,423.09

Step 4: Calculate the effective interest rate.

$$= rate(5 * 12, -1475.82, 294750, -272423.09)$$

Effective Interest Rate: 4.66%

The effective interest rate for loan A is 4.5% and for loan B is 4.66%, despite the fact that loan B has a lower stated start. From this analysis, it is clear that loan A is less costly than loan B.

Which Lender Is Offering the Best Deal?

The previous analysis shows two ways to determine which lender is offering the best loan terms. First, we can ask the lenders to quote a rate with no points or fees. The lender quoting the lowest rate is preferred. Second, we can calculate the effective interest rate with points and fees. The lender with the lowest effective interest rate is preferred.

A third approach, not previously shown, requires that the borrower first decide on what rate he or she prefers and then ask the lender if there are any points or fees associated with that rate. The lender with the lowest points or fees is the preferred lender.

Getting Cash Back for Closing Costs

As borrowers, we need to understand that lenders use a rate sheet when quoting loan terms. A rate sheet includes the points associated with alternative interest rates and alternative lock periods. For instance, the sample rate sheet in Exhibit 3.7 shows the relationship between interest rates, lock period, and points.

Exhibit 3.7: Sample Lender Rate Sheet

30 Year Fixed Conventional				
	15 Day	30 Day	45 Day	60 Day
3.000	96.369	96.369	96.381	96.268
3.125	97.151	97.151	97.100	97.050
3.250	99.681	99.619	99.579	99.459
3.375	100.286	100.204	100.164	100.044
3.500	100.791	100.697	100.657	100.537
3.625	101.211	101.191	101.151	101.031
3.750	101.548	101.528	101.488	101.368
3.875	101.950	101.930	101.890	101.770
4.000	102.380	102.360	102.320	102.200
4.125	102.760	102.740	102.700	102.580
4.250	102.774	102.754	102.714	102.594
4.375	102.882	102.862	102.822	102.702
4.500	103.269	103.249	103.209	103.089
4.625	103.620	103.600	103.560	103.440
4.750	103.560	103.540	103.500	103.380
4.875	103.890	103.870	103.830	103.710

The left column is the interest rate, the top row is the lock period, and the intersection is the points at par (100). For all rates below par, the borrower would pay the lender points, and at all rates above par, the lender would pay the borrower points that can be used by the borrower to pay for closing costs. For instance, at a 3% interest rate, assuming a thirty-day lock, the borrower would pay the lender 3.631 points (100 – 96.369). At a 4% rate, assuming a thirty-day lock, the lender would pay the borrower 2.36 points. In the latter case, the borrower would be committing to a higher interest rate with a higher monthly payment but would have 2.38% of the loan amount to pay for closing costs.

If a borrower plans to occupy the property for a relatively short period of time, say three years, then it is probably advantageous to pay a higher interest rate and receive cash back to pay for closing costs.

OTHER IMPORTANT POINTS ABOUT POINTS

Here are a few important takeaways from our conversation about mortgage points:

1. Mortgage points, either origination or discount points, increase the effective interest rate of a loan.
2. Early prepayment of a loan with points increases its effective rate. Lenders do not refund the points on loans that are paid off early.
3. As a rule of thumb, borrowers should pay points only if they are going to keep a loan for a long time.
4. Borrowers should shop mortgages by always having lenders quote loans with no points because the effective interest rate of a loan with no points is the quoted nominal rate. This simplifies comparisons across lenders.
5. Borrowers who plan to be in a property for a relatively short period should consider paying a higher rate and use the cash back to pay for closing costs.

OTHER LOAN FEES

Lenders also charge for other services or expenses they incur. Other fees may include application fees, processing fees, appraisal fees, and credit fees. These can add up quickly; borrowers should pay close attention to loan details and try to get the lender to waive as many fees as possible. In other words, borrowers should negotiate with their lender. Most mortgage lenders will charge similar fees across all of their products, but when comparing different mortgage lenders, borrowers need to include different lenders' fees as part of their calculations. Buyers can adjust for fees just like point charges to compare loans on an apples-to-apples basis. Once again, for borrowers who are planning to keep a loan for a long time, a lender with higher fees and a lower interest rate may be most attractive. For short-term shoppers, a low- or no-cost lender is generally preferable.

RELATED RESOURCES

How My FICO Score Is Calculated
http://www.myfico.com/crediteducation/whatsinyourscore.aspx

What Is APR?
Video: https://www.youtube.com/watch?v=gwNWEZJOCQw

What Does APR Mean?
http://banking.about.com/od/APR/fl/What-does-APR-Mean.htm

How to Calculate APR with Excel
http://banking.about.com/od/loans/a/calculateapr.htm

APR Pitfalls—Why the Lowest APR Isn't Necessarily Best
http://banking.about.com/od/mortgages/ss/compare_apr.htm

CHAPTER 4

Mortgage Finance II—Residential Mortgage Products and Markets

INTRODUCTION

To effectively compare different mortgage loan products, borrowers need to understand a few key terms. This chapter lists and defines some of the most important terms related to mortgage lending.

TERMS AND DEFINITIONS

Loan-to-Value (LTV) Ratio

When mortgage lenders sell a foreclosed property, they are entitled to collect only an amount equal to the remaining balance on the mortgage loan plus contract interest and fees. However, if a foreclosed property sale yields less than the principal amount left on the mortgage, lenders must often record a loss on the property. Because of the limited upside and substantial downside potential of foreclosure, lenders are usually willing to lend out only a percentage of a property's value. This percentage is called a loan-to-value, or LTV, ratio. The numerator of this ratio is simply the principal amount of the loan, while the denominator is the appraised value or cost of the property.

$$LTV = \frac{Principal\ Loan\ Amount}{Appraised\ Property\ Value}$$

Lenders typically use the lesser of the appraised value or purchase price for the denominator of their LTV ratios. Thus, in situations where the estimated value of the property is less than the purchase price, the buyer may receive a smaller loan than he or she anticipated. Similarly, if an appraisal comes in higher than the property's purchase price, mortgage lenders usually base their loan amount on the purchase price.

Private Mortgage Insurance (PMI)

Though mortgage lenders are reluctant to lend the entire purchase price of a property, most homebuyers lack the means to make a significant (20%+) down payment on a home purchase. For this reason, mortgage lenders almost always require borrowers to purchase private mortgage insurance (PMI) when their down payment is less than 20% of the value of the home. When borrowers purchase PMI, an insurance premium is included in their monthly loan payments. In return, the mortgage insurer promises to compensate the lender if the borrower defaults on the loan. In a conventional mortgage market, lenders are required to terminate the PMI premium once the LTV ratio reaches 78% or lower.

Maturity Date

A loan's maturity date is the date on which the loan's final payment comes due. If the loan is not fully amortized (i.e., a large principal amount, called a balloon payment, is required on the last payment date), this date is often called the loan's balloon date. On the street, partially amortized loans are sometimes referred to as bullet loans.

Prepayment

Prepayment terms deal with the rights of a buyer to pay extra principal on his or her mortgage loan balance before the maturity date of the loan. Borrowers like to have the ability to prepay the loan, especially when they want to sell the property or refinance the loan.

The value of the prepayment option on a level payment mortgage depends primarily on how interest rates change from the date the interest rate locks to the date the buyer contemplates prepayment. When interest rates decline substantially, a buyer's prepayment option becomes very valuable to the buyer and very expensive to the lender. Because buyers get to choose when to refinance their loan, most loans are refinanced under these exact circumstances. The embedded option of prepayment is thus valuable to the buyer. However, the high potential cost to lenders has led them to charge more in interest to compensate for the added risk. Note that in the less-regulated commercial mortgage industry, prepayment is usually not included as an option on loans unless buyers pay a "yield maintenance" premium to compensate their lender for lost income.

Debt-to-Income (DTI) Ratio

A critical ratio analyzed by lenders in awarding mortgage loans is the debt-to-income (DTI) ratio. The DTI is calculated by taking the borrower's total monthly debt obligations (e.g., car payments, credit card debt, student loans), including estimated PITI on the mortgage, and dividing by the applicant's monthly gross (pretax) income:

$$\frac{\textit{All Debt Obligations}}{\textit{Gross Monthly Income}} \leq 45\%$$

The result expresses the percentage of a buyer's total income committed to all of his or her debt obligations. Currently, the industry's recommended benchmark for this ratio is less than or equal to 45%, meaning all debt obligations (including PITI) should not exceed 45% of a borrower's gross monthly income.

Acceleration Clause

Today, most mortgage documents have an acceleration clause that allows the lender to accelerate all future loan payments if the borrower defaults on one payment. In other words, if the borrower defaults on one payment, the lender can call the remaining mortgage balance due immediately. This option allows for a timely foreclosure. Otherwise, a borrower could claim that he or she was in default on only one payment, not all future payments.

Due-on-Sale Clause

Similar to an acceleration clause, a due-on-sale clause allows a lender to call all future payments due immediately if a borrower sells the property. This clause effectively prohibits a new buyer from assuming an existing loan, which may have favorable terms. Instead, this clause allows a lender to demand immediate payment of the loan balance after a property sells. A due-on-sale clause protects lenders who are unwilling to extend credit to a new buyer with a different financial condition and creditworthiness.

Insurance and Property Tax Clause

Insurance and property tax clauses protect lenders from two scenarios in which a loan's collateral value might be destroyed. First, if borrowers do not pay their property insurance and their property is destroyed (i.e., in a fire), they can default on their mortgage and force their lender to bear the loss from the property damage. Second, if borrowers do not pay their property taxes, the county treasurer can foreclose on the property, wiping out all other liens on the property. To mitigate these risks, most lenders require that the borrower pay a pro rata share of property insurance and property taxes into an escrow, or impound, account to ensure that they are paid on time.

MORTGAGE OFFERINGS

Now that we have a general understanding of mortgage terms and classifications, let's analyze the most common mortgage offerings on the market today.

Government-Sponsored Enterprises

A government-sponsored enterprise (GSE) is a quasigovernmental entity. In the case of the mortgage market, GSEs, including Fannie Mae, Freddie Mac, and Ginnie Mae, were set up to provide liquidity to the residential mortgage market by purchasing conforming conventional loans in the secondary market. After buying the loans, GSEs issue short- and long-term bonds known as mortgage-backed securities. During the Great Recession, the federal government took over mortgage market GSEs, eliminating their status as quasigovernmental entities. There has been recent discussion, however, about returning them to quasigovernmental status.

Conforming Conventional Loans

The conventional mortgage is the most common form of mortgage financing today, making up more than 80% of the mortgage market. There is a fair amount of variance in the mortgage market. Still, most conventional loans are "conforming" conventional loans, which means they meet the requirements needed for purchase by Fannie Mae and Freddie Mac in the secondary market. These essential characteristics include the following:

- A 5% down payment (LTV < 95%) (3% for first-time buyers) is required.
- The maximum loan amount is $510,400 (for single-family residences).
- Private mortgage insurance must be purchased (if LTV > 80%).
- The debt to income (DTI) ratio must be less than 45% of gross monthly income.
- The buyer must have a "prime" classification (credit and documentation standards).

Note that the loan limit of $510,400 for conventional loans is the general rule for the continental US but can be as high as $765,600 in "high-cost" areas. A higher loan limit makes sense for areas such as Honolulu, where housing costs are quite high but are typically offset by higher wages.

Nonconforming Conventional loans

Standard mortgage loans that do not fulfill one or more of the requirements needed for purchase by Fannie Mae and Freddie Mac are known as nonconforming conventional loans. The most common type of nonconforming loan is the jumbo loan, which meets each of the requirements for secondary market purchases by GSEs except the loan amount limit. Jumbo loans are often purchased and securitized by private conduits but are somewhat more expensive than conforming conventional loans because they are ineligible for purchase by Fannie or Freddie.

Alt-A loans are also a type of nonconforming conventional loan. Like jumbo loans, alt-A loans have a secondary market that is more limited than that for conforming loans.

GOVERNMENT HOUSING AGENCIES

Within the US, three government agencies play a prominent role in providing government-insured home loans: the Federal Housing Administration (FHA), the Veterans Benefits Administration (VA), and the US Department of Agriculture (USDA).

Federal Housing Administration (FHA)

To help more Americans qualify for mortgage loans, the Federal Housing Administration insures loans (through Ginnie Mae) made to customers who have difficulty qualifying for a conventional mortgage. The relaxed qualification requirements are a boon to some homebuyers but come at a cost. For instance, FHA loan borrowers are required to pay a 0.85% upfront mortgage insurance premium (UFMIP) to the FHA in return for insuring their loan (FHA guarantees the full amount to the lender). This premium is usually rolled into the total loan amount and paid over the course of the mortgage. Following are other important qualification requirements and characteristics of FHA-insured loans.

- A 3.5% down payment is required (max 96.5% LTV).
- Borrowers need to have a credit score of 580 or higher.

- The maximum loan amount varies geographically but is typically $275,665 for low-cost areas.[19]
- Sellers, builders, and lenders may pay some of the borrower's closing costs.
- Two-part mortgage insurance is required: (1) an upfront premium (1.75% of the loan amount; can be financed as part of the loan), and (2) an annual premium (paid monthly).[20]
- The mortgage insurance premium (MIP) remains for the life of the loan.
- The buyer is not limited to the "prime" classification (the credit standards are more relaxed compared to conventional loans).

The FHA also has a particular product for borrowers who plan to make repairs to their homes. This is known as a 201(k) loan.

Veterans Benefits Administration (VA)

The Veterans Benefits Administration (VA) loan program helps veterans finance the purchase of a home with loan terms favorable in comparison to other types of mortgage loans. The VA guarantees loans made to American military veterans and their surviving spouses (who do not remarry). In return for obtaining a loan guarantee, veterans must pay the VA a funding fee, which may be included in the loan. Other important requirements and characteristics of VA loans are as follows:

- No down payment is required.
- The interest rate is negotiable and competitive.
- The buyer can finance the VA funding fee (plus reduced funding fees with a down payment of at least 5% and the exemption for veterans receiving VA compensation).
- VA rules limit the amount charged for closing costs.
- Closing costs are comparable to other financing types (and may be lower).

---

19. Check http://www.fha.com/lending_limits to find out the FHA lending limits for each county.
20. The annual premiums vary depending on the down payment and term of the loan. For a thirty-year loan with less than a 5% down payment, the annual premium is 0.85% of the loan amount.

- Closing costs may be paid by the seller.
- No private mortgage insurance premiums are required.
- The loan may be assumable.
- The buyer has the right to prepay the mortgage without penalty.
- For homes inspected by the VA during construction, a warranty from builder and assistance from the VA to obtain cooperation of builder.
- The VA provides assistance to veteran borrowers in default due to temporary financial difficulty.[21]

US Department of Agriculture (USDA)

The USDA provides a guaranteed loan program that allows lenders to underwrite home loans for low- and moderate-income households who reside in eligible rural areas. Applicants must meet income requirements, agree to occupy the property as their primary residence, and be US citizens. These loans generally require no down payment and have below-market interest rates.[22]

Second Mortgage

Homeowners who need cash, and have equity in a home, often seek out a second mortgage. Second mortgages usually charge higher rates of interest to compensate for their lower priority upon default.

Home Equity Line of Credit (HELOC)

A home equity loan or home equity line of credit (HELOC) allows a homeowner to borrow against the equity in their home on an as-needed basis. In other words, a borrower who has equity in a home may qualify for a line of credit to use at his or her discretion. Interest-only accrues on a HELOC as the borrower accesses the funds, making them an excellent option for personal financial planning. For example, a household may

---

21. https://www.zillow.com/mortgage-learning/va-home-loans/
22. More information about USDA loans can be found at https://www.rd.usda.gov/programs-services/single-family-housing-guaranteed-loan-program.

obtain a HELOC with the intent of using the funds only in a financial emergency. The benefits of a home equity loan include relatively low financing fees and tax deductibility on interest for balances up to $100,000. The tax benefits of home equity loans often make them more attractive than consumer loans, which are generally not tax-deductible.

Reverse Mortgage

Many Americans, particularly retired Americans with limited pension and Social Security income, find reverse mortgages to be an attractive option. Reverse mortgages allow homeowners to receive regular cash payments (usually monthly) in exchange for equity in their house. They are like a home equity line of credit that automatically increases each month until the equity in the home is exhausted. As with a standard mortgage, homeowners must carefully compare the rates and terms offered by reverse mortgage lenders to obtain a favorable reverse mortgage product. The FHA provides reverse mortgage insurance, so refinancing through an FHA-approved lender is often a homebuyer's best option.

SECONDARY MORTGAGE MARKET

Shortly after origination, most loans are sold into the secondary mortgage market. The following chart (Exhibit 4.1) illustrates the various players and components of both the primary and secondary mortgage markets.

Exhibit 4.1: Secondary Mortgage Market

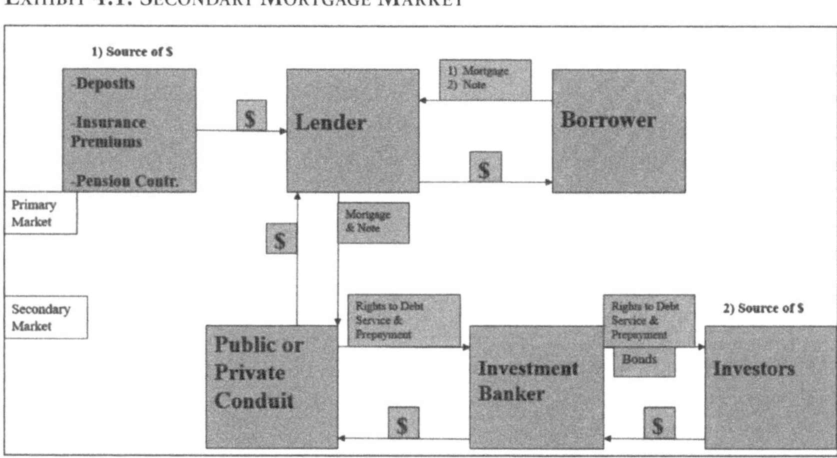

Notice that in the primary market that the lender has funds, such as deposits, that he or she needs to put to work to earn a rate of return. At the same time, the borrower would like to purchase a home but does not have enough cash to do so. So, he or she seeks to borrow funds from the lender. After completing the loan approval process, the lender transfers funds to the borrower, who buys the home. In exchange for the funds, the borrower conveys a signed mortgage and promissory note to the lender, giving him or her a financial security interest in the property. Afterward, the borrower makes a monthly payment to the lender.

This simple illustration captures the essentials of the primary mortgage market, and most people think that this is where the story ends. However, the mortgage market is much more complex. To replenish funds to make more loans and earn more in loan origination fees, the lender would ordinarily sell the loan into the secondary mortgage market. The buyers of these loans are typically referred to as mortgage conduits or mortgage aggregators (public or private). The two largest public aggregators are Fannie Mae (Federal National Mortgage Association) and Freddie Mac (Federal Home Loan Mortgage Corporation). After acquiring a pool of loans, aggregators typically work with investment bankers to securitize and sell mortgage-backed bonds or securities. The rate of return on these mortgage securities is slightly lower than the mortgage interest rates paid by the original mortgagors (borrowers), allowing the servicers and conduits to earn a slight return for assisting with the process.

APPLYING FOR A MORTGAGE LOAN

The first step in applying for a mortgage loan is to gather and organize the data and documents required by the loan application. This typically includes the following items:

- Full name, birth date, Social Security number, and phone number.
- Marital status and number of children and ages.
- Residence history for at least two years. If you're a renter, your rent payment is needed. If you're an owner, all mortgage,

insurance, and tax figures are needed for your primary residence and all other properties owned.

- Employment history for at least two years, including company name(s), address(es), phone number(s), and your title(s).
- Income history for at least two years. If you receive commissions or bonuses or are self-employed, you must provide two years of bonus, commission, or self-employed income received. Most lenders average variable and self-employed income over two years.
- Asset account balances, including all checking, savings, investment, and retirement accounts.
- Debt payments and balances for credit cards, mortgages, student loans, car loans, alimony, child support, or any other fixed-debt obligations.
- Confirmation whether or not you've had bankruptcies or foreclosures within the past seven years, are party to any lawsuits, or have co-signed on any loans.
- Confirmation whether or not any part of your down payment will be borrowed.[23]

The second step is completing the lender's loan application. Most lenders use the federally required mortgage application (Form 1003, Uniform Residential Loan Application), especially if a borrower is applying for a conforming conventional loan that will be purchased by Fannie Mae or Freddie Mac. Most borrowers complete this application online.

GETTING PREQUALIFIED OR PREAPPROVED

Once a homebuyer has selected a lender and completed the loan application, the lender will likely offer to "prequalify" the buyer free of charge. Prequalification has limited value, as it places no obligations on the lender. Instead, homebuyers should ask their originator to "preapprove" them for a loan. The preapproval process is more involved and can cost a few hundred dollars (though some lenders will

23. https://www.zillow.com/mortgage-learning/mortgage-application-documents/

preapprove borrowers free of charge). A preapproval is not an ironclad loan commitment but generally speeds up the underwriting process. Sellers also see a preapproval as a positive signal that a buyer is serious and can afford to purchase the home. Reportedly, less than 10% of homebuyers obtain a loan preapproval, suggesting that requesting a preapproval can be a relatively simple way for a buyer to set him- or herself apart from other buyers.

OBTAINING CLOSING COST ESTIMATES

After a borrower completes a loan application, the lender is required to provide him or her with a Loan Estimate Form[24] that discloses loan terms, projected payments, closing costs, loan costs, other costs, and cash to close. Borrowers are required to sign and date this form, but doing so does not obligate them to accept the loan. The Loan Estimate Form is sometimes referred to as a good faith estimate, but in reality, it is much more than that.

Before the Great Recession, many lenders abused the way they used good faith estimates. In some cases, loan officers deliberately underestimated loan closing costs to lure borrowers into a deal and then hit them with additional costs right before closing. This required borrowers to scramble at the last minute to obtain additional funds to close their loan. Because of these abuses, Congress implemented several regulations that prohibit this type of conduct. Now, once a loan officer has provided a completed Loan Estimate Form, he or she must adhere to strict rules and regulations to deviate from these estimates. Violations of these rules and regulations come with punitive fines levied by the Consumer Financial Protection Bureau, so most lenders today adhere to the estimates provided in their initial Loan Estimate Form.

---

24. A Loan Estimate Form can be obtained at https://files.consumerfinance.gov/f/201311_cfpb_kbyo_loan-estimate.pdf

THE REFINANCE DECISION

In an environment in which interest rates have declined since loan origination, refinancing a mortgage loan can often save a borrower thousands of dollars in interest costs. Deciding whether to refinance depends on several factors, including:

- The outstanding loan interest rate
- The current proposed mortgage interest rate
- The remaining term of the existing mortgage
- Prepayment penalties
- The costs of refinancing

The optimal way to calculate a refinance is through NPV or IRR analysis using a discounted cash flow (DCF) model. DCF models will be reviewed in detail in later chapters. For now, we'll present a simplified analysis utilizing time value of money (TVM) calculations.

A common refinance situation lends itself well to this simplified analysis. Many homeowners who have held a mortgage loan for several years and built equity in their home consider switching from a thirty-year mortgage loan to one with a fifteen-year term (and often a lower interest rate). Exhibit 4.2 (on the following pages) presents the analysis required to make this decision.

In this example, refinancing yields a very attractive rate, which is essentially a risk-free rate of return given that the borrower keeps the loan to maturity.

EXHIBIT 4.2: SIMPLIFIED REFINANCING ANALYSIS

Suppose that fifteen years ago, Jackie bought a home and took out a mortgage loan of $370,000 (including all points) with a 5% interest rate and a thirty-year fully amortizing term.

Now, a fifteen-year loan with an interest rate of 3.5% and $5,000 in loan points and fees is available on the market. Assuming that a new loan would be for exactly the current balance on her mortgage, what rate of return could Jackie earn by refinancing?

Solution:

1. **Calculate the monthly payment on the original loan (Excel).**

$$= PMT(\frac{0.05}{12}, 30 * 12, 370000)$$

Monthly Payment: –$1,986.24

2. **Calculate the remaining principal balance on the loan after fifteen years (Excel).**

$$= PV(\frac{0.05}{12}, 15 * 12, -1986.24)$$

Remaining Balance: $251,170.46

3. **Calculate the new monthly payment with the refinanced loan (Excel).**

$$= PMT(\frac{0.035}{12}, 15 * 12, 251179.46)$$

New Monthly Payment: –$1,795.57

4. **Calculate the difference in monthly payments to calculate the monthly savings.**

$$= \$1,986.24 - \$1,795.27$$

Monthly Savings: $190.67

5. **Calculate the rate of return on the refinance with the $5,000 upfront cost included.**

$$= rate(15 * 12, 190.67, -5000)$$

Annual Rate of Return: 3.81% x 12 = 45.71%

RELATED RESOURCES

Uniform Residential Loan Application

https://singlefamily.fanniemae.com/delivering/uniform-mortgage-data-program/uniform-residential-loan-application

Loan Estimate Form

https://www.consumerfinance.gov/policy-compliance/guidance/mortgage-resources/tila-respa-integrated-disclosures/forms-samples/

How It Works: The Secondary Mortgage Market

http://www.freddiemac.com/blog/homeownership/20160125_secondary_mortgage.page?

Mortgage Prequalification versus Preapproval
https://www.bankofamerica.com/mortgage/learn/mortgage-prequalification/

What Is the Consumer Financial Protection Bureau (CFPB)?
https://www.creditkarma.com/advice/i/what-is-the-cfpb

CHAPTER 5

Housing Search and Negotiation

INTRODUCTION

With a solid understanding of their budget and a plan for financing their home, homebuyers are ready to begin searching for a home. Looking for a home can be fun, especially at first, but finding the right property at the right price is usually challenging. People in the midst of searching for a home are often colloquially referred to as house hunters, and some buyers start to feel like a hunter in search of elusive prey. To increase their chances of having a successful search, homebuyers should, if possible, employ the following strategies before starting to scour the internet for their next residence.

REDUCE TIME PRESSURES

Depending on market conditions, real estate can be illiquid. Most real estate purchases are made at about the current market value of the property in what is known as an arm's-length transaction. However, parties under time pressure often pay more or receive less than they would in a typical market value transaction. Examples of parties with time pressure include buyers that need to move in quickly (e.g., because they are living in a hotel) and sellers that need cash quickly (e.g., because they have already moved and are unable to pay both mortgages). Homebuyers (and sellers) should eliminate time pressures, if at all possible. When moving to a new area, buyers are often wise to rent an apartment for three to six months to avoid a time crunch. On the other hand, if a seller has time stress, a buyer may be able to use that to his or her advantage at the negotiating table.

DETERMINE NEEDS

Before starting to look at homes, homebuyers should establish a sound plan by detailing and ranking their individual needs and wants. Doing so prevents buyers from wasting time chasing houses that don't suit them. As a general rule, if a home has several characteristics that are misaligned with his or her desires, a buyer should not entertain the thought of purchasing it, even if it seems like a great deal. Buyers should consider the following characteristics:

- **Location**, including access (e.g., streets, freeways, subway, train), visibility (e.g., the attractiveness of the area and neighborhood), amenities (e.g., retail shopping, parks, and school reputation), and infrastructure (e.g., utilities and parks)
- **Home characteristics**, including style, house size, yard size, and house price
- **Future plans**, including how long they will likely stay and their family size

Often, the best way for a buyer to search is to first filter by location by selecting attractive neighborhoods that have several houses in his or her price range. Then, the buyer should filter further using home characteristics that he or she deems most important. When determining their needs, homebuyers should keep in mind that, on average, the typical American family moves every seven years.

SET REALISTIC EXPECTATIONS

When asked about the type of home they want to purchase, buyers often have a laundry list of amenities difficult to find in the nicest of luxury homes but a price range that justifies only a starter home. In some exceptional cases, buyers manage to acquire properties for less than their market value. However, as a rule, homebuyers should plan to pay market value for the home they purchase. Therefore, buyers should let their most important characteristics guide a search within their price range. Furthermore, buyers should not allow themselves to get overly attached to any property unless they are willing to pay a premium for it. Instead, they should be patient and modify their plans if they prove to be unrealistic.

BEGINNING THE HUNT

A generation ago, people hunted for houses by driving around residential neighborhoods looking for "for sale" signs, scouring local periodicals, or employing a buyer's agent with limited knowledge of houses in a given area. Thankfully, this is no longer the case. The internet, with its wealth of information, has overturned the real estate search industry. Buyers can now explore dozens, if not hundreds, of options online. A multitude of tools can be used for this purpose, and only a few of them are discussed in this chapter. Prospective buyers should take a few minutes to explore each of these websites in addition to reading the summary of the tools each provides.

USING TECHNOLOGY

MLS (Multiple Listing Service)

In real estate, like most industries, knowledge is power. In any given area, the local MLS (Multiple Listing Service) is likely the greatest repository of information available to those searching for a home. The MLS allows users to view extensive details and photos for most listed properties. It also provides engines for running reports and mapping that would enable a macro analysis of neighborhoods and markets. The MLS's data and capabilities are so extensive that it could probably be a one-stop internet resource for someone buying a home.

Unfortunately, the MLS suffers from the glaring issue of limited access. Access to the hundreds of MLSs across the country is generally limited to licensed, dues-paying members in the area. For obvious reasons, not all information (such as the key code to gain access to the interior of listed properties) is shared online. Still, MLS boards across the country restrict access to their information largely to keep local members (licensed agents and brokers) employed. Since the boards incur the cost of acquiring and presenting the information, paid subscription access is quite sensible. Buyers shouldn't plan on getting access to the full power of the MLS system unless they enlist the aid of a real estate agent in the area.

For buyers who choose not to work with a real estate agent, limited access to the MLS is often provided from a web portal. MLS login sites often allow nonsubscribing users to search for listings, albeit with limited access to listing information. Their information is likely more updated and valid than that found on other web pages.

Realtor.com

While access to the MLS is limited, many sites provide similar information that is updated periodically from actual MLS listings. One primary site that does this is Realtor.com (www.realtor.com). Realtor.com pulls information from the MLS on properties listed by real estate agents and presents it in a reasonably user-friendly format. Realtor.com also has a mobile app that enables homebuyers to search on the go. This site has the agenda of promoting the use of REALTORS®, but its information can be useful to buyers who never plan to use one.

Housing Search Engines

Some independent companies provide housing search capabilities and other tools to prospective home buyers and renters across the United States. The two largest of these companies are Zillow, Inc. (Nasdaq: Z, www.zillow.com) and Trulia, Inc. (NYSE: TRLA, www.trulia.com). Both of these sites allow for a variety of search techniques. They contain listings submitted by property owners in addition to those listed with Realtors®. They also have extra features that can assist in real estate purchases. For example, Zillow provides limited data on sold properties, a "Zestimate" of many home values, and access to the interior and exterior design ideas and aides. The biggest downfall of sites such as Zillow and Trulia is that their information is not always updated and accurate. Still, they provide valuable services to customers as a first step in the home search.

Classifieds

Classified advertisements are a good source for home listings, particularly for homes that are being sold without the involvement of a licensed agent. Large classified engines such as www.craigslist.com or smaller local classified ads (such as www.ksl.com) may contain information on properties that some buyers find attractive. Regulation of these classified advertisements is minimal, so the same properties may be listed over and over again. Still, they contain useful information about properties not available on any other website.

Finding FSBOs (For Sale by Owners)

If a buyer is interested in a specific area and does not want to risk missing the few listings that are not posted online, he or she may want to drive through the area periodically to look for sale signs or any other signs of turnover. Alternatively, he or she might ask someone living in the area to watch out for similar signals.

WORKING WITH A LICENSED AGENT

Purchasing real estate is a time- and effort-intensive process. Various resources exist to aid buyers in this process, including real estate agents, who assist buyers throughout the entire buying process. These professionals provide buyers with benefits, but their assistance comes at a cost. Following are some of the advantages and disadvantages of using an agent when buying real estate.

Advantages

Training and Knowledge

Agents have experience and training to aid in the buying process. They organize contract documentation and other necessary paperwork. Agents also answer buyers' questions, including clarifying and explaining the provisions of documents signed by the buyer. They can also help buyers avoid delays and costly missteps and gain necessary disclosures from the seller.

Access to the MLS and Critical Information

Agents help buyers cut down the time and energy required to search for a home that meets their needs. Agents are familiar with the MLS and may be privy to information on properties that have not yet hit the market. They have experience finding what clients are looking for and doing due diligence on properties. Agents also have valuable information about local markets and neighborhoods, including information about home pricing, zoning codes, and school districts.

Agents can also aid buyers in the pre-inspection process. Their experience can give buyers insight into the standing of different properties and help them know what to look out for during an inspection. Agents may also have access to the CLUE (Comprehensive Loss Underwriting Exchange) report, giving buyers information on the dates of claims, cause of losses, and amounts paid. They can even help in negotiating repairs or concessions with the seller.

Negotiation Skills

Because of their experience, agents can help with negotiations. They are familiar with the purchase process, especially how to work with sellers and sellers' agents. Without the help of an agent, an inexperienced buyer may not be equipped to take charge of pre-purchase negotiations. Preparing for these negotiations is crucial, and agents can conduct much of the necessary market and pricing analysis.

Costs

Licensed agents are typically compensated on commission (a percentage of the sales price), meaning that if their buyer, who they are helping, purchases a property that is listed for sale with another agent, then that agent splits the commission with them. This commission structure then allows a buyer to work with a licensed agent to acquire a property without directly paying for the agent's services.

Disadvantages

As previously noted, one of the advantages of working with a licensed agent to buy a home is that the buyer typically does not pay the agent directly because the agent shares in the commission paid by the seller to the listing agent. This compensation agreement leads to an obvious conflict of interest. On the one hand, the buyer's agent is helping the buyer find and negotiate the acquisition of a property. On the other hand, their compensation is tied to the purchase price—the higher the purchase price, the higher the commission.

To mitigate this problem, some buyers will enter into an exclusive right-to-represent contract with an agent. This contract generally sets forth the commission to be paid to the agent/broker, even if the buyer finds the home him- or herself. Usually, these are long-term contracts that tie the hands of buyers and are therefore not advisable.

Given these two potential concerns, most experienced real estate buyers use a buyer's agent but do not enter into an exclusive right-to-represent contract. These same buyers also realize that when it comes time to make an offer, they are on their own because their agent is biased and wants to get the highest price he or she can for the home. Therefore, it is recommended that prospective buyers use a buyer's agent to obtain market data and to search for a property but not be unduly influenced by the buyer's agent when determining the offer price.

Requires a Middleman

A buyer's agent usually handles most of the communication with sellers and sellers' agents. This sometimes forces the buyer to wait to receive information. Other times, an agent might not accurately communicate a buyer's interest. Depending on the agent and their experience, these issues may not surface. Regardless, without an agent, buyers can take charge of their communication. This is an important consideration since it is essential for buyers to be aware of all conversations with sellers.

Some Buyers Already Have Direct Connections

Some buyers are interested in purchasing a home from someone they already know or a property with which they are already familiar. In these cases, an agent may not be as helpful in terms of providing the buyer with listing information.

Being One of Many Clients

If an agent is working with a large number of buyers, each buyer's home-buying process may not get the attention it requires. This can force buyers to conduct their due diligence at each stage of the buying process. It may also increase communication barriers and time lag between the buyers and their agent.

Depending on Agent's Timeline/Schedule

Buyers have to account for their agent's schedule when scheduling showings and negotiations with sellers. The agent's schedule will likely hold more weight in deciding timing due to the agent's access to properties and expertise in negotiations. This can be especially frustrating for buyers who are actively engaged in the purchase process.

Takeaways

Agents can be helpful in the process of buying property. If a buyer chooses not to hire an agent, he or she will spend much more time and energy on research and negotiation. Buyers should also be aware that not all agents have the training and expertise that is required to offer a professional service. When deciding who to hire, they should ask some of the following questions:

- Can you provide some references?
- How extensive is your professional network?
- Do you have errors and omissions insurance?
- How many clients have you assisted in buying?
- What are your policies regarding canceled agreements?
- How familiar are you with the local community where I am searching?

PERFORMING INSPECTIONS

During their search online, buyers should identify a few properties that seem appealing and contact their owner or agent to schedule a walk-through. Nothing allows a prospective buyer to get a feel for a home better than visiting the neighborhood and property in person.

Buyers should walk through several homes before making a purchase. If a buyer is happy with a property after a physical visit, he or she is probably ready to make an offer.

REPEATING THE CYCLE

While it would be ideal for every buyer to know exactly what he or she wants before looking at a single property, most buyers learn things during the search process that adjust their criteria somewhat. Homebuyers should continually refine their search based on what they learn to maximize their chance of finding the right house.

SETTLING ON AN OFFER PRICE

Knowing the market value of a property is fundamental to achieving financial success in real estate. Chapter 7, "Obtaining a Residential Appraisal," outlines the processes that appraisers use to estimate the market value of residential real estate. Some buyers actually hire an appraiser prior to making an offer on a property, but this is the exception rather than the rule. Instead, most buyers estimate the value themselves by reviewing comparable sales in the neighborhood, studying value estimates from online services such as Zillow, and researching the property characteristics and asking prices of similar properties.

When using online services, buyers should be aware that value estimates, such as Zillow's "Zestimate," may not be very reliable. The accuracy of these prediction models depends entirely on the inputs used, and the inputs available for use depend on state law. Predictions on home values are usually somewhat accurate when recent sales volume is sufficient and transaction prices are disclosed. However, in about a half-dozen states, sale prices are not disclosed to the public, so valuation models have to estimate the values based on another method and are generally less accurate.

NEGOTIATING THE ACQUISITION

Now that you have a good feel for the value of the property, it is time to begin the negotiation. Let's review some of the fundamental principles of negotiation.

Negotiation is the process whereby two or more parties decide what each will give and take in a relationship. In negotiation, experience is a great teacher. Great negotiators take risks. The two main types of negotiations are distributive and integrative. Distributive negotiations involve a single issue and typically result in zero-sum bargaining because of the parties' conflicting goals. Integrative negotiations include multiple issues. They present the opportunity for joint gain but require mutual trust and collaborative problem-solving to achieve optimal outcomes.[25]

Negotiations have five main phases:

- **Investigating** or information gathering. In this phase, buyers determine what their goals are for the negotiation. They also decide what they will and will not concede. This preparation is key to a successful negotiation. By recalling their ultimate goals and desires, buyers can maintain clarity throughout the entire process. Buyers should also prepare by determining their maximum, or "reservation," price. A buyer's reservation price is the price above which the buyer would leave the negotiation. Buyers should not reveal their reservation price to sellers. Finally, buyers should complete their investigation by assessing the seller's perspective. They should estimate the seller's goals, target price, and reservation price. Properly understanding the seller's perspective increases a buyer's power in negotiation.
- **Determining the BATNA**, or "Best Alternative to a Negotiated Agreement." Knowing their BATNA helps buyers pick their reservation price. Additionally, considering alternatives beforehand helps buyers analyze deals more critically. In negotiations, the party with the best BATNA

25. Lisa Jones Christensen, chapter 10 of *Class 25: Conflict and Negotiation*, November 2019.

ultimately holds the most influential negotiating position, so buyers should explore alternatives to strengthen their BATNA. They should also remember that a seller's perception of the buyer's BATNA is often more important than the buyer's actual alternatives. As with reservation price, buyers should never reveal their BATNA. After determining their own BATNA, buyers should take some time to understand what the seller's alternatives might be.

- **Presenting**. The presentation phase is the beginning of the actual negotiation. In this phase, both parties present the information they have gathered in previous phases in a way that supports their position. Buyers should focus on making a clear and direct presentation.
- **Bargaining**. In the bargaining phase, the parties discuss goals and desires and seek to come to a satisfactory agreement. Concessions (i.e., giving up one thing in return for something else) are a natural and important part of this process. Concessions allow the negotiation to progress toward a conclusion, and they demonstrate open-minded cooperativeness. The key to successful bargaining is asking questions. The better a buyer understands the seller's position, the better the outcomes he or she will achieve. Buyers should also keep in mind the idea of the bargaining zone, or zone of possible agreement, during this phase. The bargaining zone lies between the buyer's reservation price (Br) and the seller's reservation price (Sr). When Br < Sr, no zone of possible agreement exists. When Br > Sr, the zone of agreement lies between Sr and Br.
- **Closing**. At the end of negotiating, both parties must reach an acceptable agreement or agree to walk away from the transaction. Buyers should not see walking away from a deal as a failure but rather as an opportunity to learn. Great negotiators reflect on their experiences and ask questions to find out what it would have taken to reach an agreement.

Buyers can improve their negotiation results by avoiding certain tendencies of ineffective negotiation. These include letting ego get in the way, maintaining unrealistic expectations, accepting the first offer (satisficing), getting overly emotional, letting past negative outcomes affect present ones (self-reinforcement), and not having relevant and diagnostic feedback. Practicing to overcome these obstacles leads to improved results in negotiations.[26]

RELATED RESOURCES

Should You Hire a Real Estate Agent or Lawyer to Buy a House?
http://www.nolo.com/legal-encyclopedia/hire-real-estate-agent-or-lawyer-29527.html

Why Use a Realtor®? Six Important Reasons
http://www.realtor.com/advice/why-use-a-realtor-6-important-reasons/

Hiring Buyer's Agents: Should Buyers Sign Exclusive Broker Agreements with a Buyer's Agent?
http://homebuying.about.com/od/buyingahome/qt/071907-buy-agt.htm

The Three Types of Buyer-Broker Agreements
https://www.realtor.com/advice/buy/3-types-buyer-broker-contracts/

Real Estate Broker
http://en.wikipedia.org/wiki/Real_estate_broker

How to Find the Right Home: Making Decisions Before You Buy
http://homebuying.about.com/od/buyingahome/a/buyerinfo.htm

The Data-Driven Home Search
http://www.nytimes.com/2014/07/20/realestate/using-data-to-find-a-new-york-suburb-that-fits.html?_r=1

---

26. "Chapter 10: Conflict and Negotiations," *Organizational Behavior* (University of Minnesota Libraries Publishing Edition, 2017). This edition was adapted from a work originally produced in 2010 by a publisher who has requested that it not receive attribution. https://open.lib.umn.edu/organizationalbehavior/part/chapter-10-conflict-and-negotiations/.

Home Inspection Checklist
http://www.totalhomeinspection.comTotalHomeInspection-Checklist.pdf

Home Inspection Training Video #1 with Ben Gromicko
https://www.youtube.com/watch?v=HlXtrW8DKAM

Broad Search Engines (Good Place to Start)
www.realtor.com
www.zillow.com
www.trulia.com

Crime Levels
www.crimereports.com
www.familywatchdog.us
www.mylocalcrime.com

School Reputation and Crime Levels
www.neighborhoodscout.com

CHAPTER 6

Executing a Real Estate Purchase Contract (REPC)

INTRODUCTION

Real estate purchase contracts are formal documents that specify the terms of a transaction and the responsibilities of both parties (buyer and seller). To avoid conflict and subsequent litigation, buyers and sellers must understand the critical components of a contract before signing. Therefore, the purpose of this section is to review some of those components. This review is from a practitioner's perspective and does not circumvent the need to seek competent legal counsel before executing the contract.[27]

STANDARD STATE-APPROVED CONTRACTS

Many states have a standard Real Estate Purchase Contract (REPC) that has been well vetted, and almost all real estate brokers use it. Most real estate agents and brokers will provide buyers with a free copy. Standard REPCs are also frequently available online. Buyers should be careful to get the standard REPC applicable to the state in which the property is located.

---

27. The author is not an attorney and is not offering legal advice. You should always seek competent legal counsel before signing a contract.

Although all parts of the contract are important, several areas warrant more consideration, including the purchase price, earnest money deposit, contract dates, contingencies, and remedies for breach of contract. After discussing each of these items, we will review the process for submitting offers and opening escrow.

IMPORTANT CONTRACT TERMS AND CONCEPTS

Before signing a contract, the parties must first decide on a price and how the buyer will pay for the property. Once the buyer has completed his or her analysis of the property value, determining an offer price is pretty straightforward. Deciding how to pay for the property and how to disperse funds is much more difficult. Exhibit 6.1 provides a snapshot of the contract details associated with the purchase price.

Exhibit 6.1

2. PURCHASE PRICE.

2.1 Payment of Purchase Price. The Purchase Price for the Property is $ ________________. Except as provided in this Section, the Purchase Price shall be paid as provided in Sections 2.1(a) through 2.1(e) below. Any amounts shown in Sections 2.1(c) and 2.1(e) may be adjusted as deemed necessary by Buyer and the Lender (the "Lender").

$______________	(a) **Earnest Money Deposit.** Under certain conditions described in the REPC, this deposit may become totally non-refundable.
$______________	(b) **Additional Earnest Money Deposit** (see Section 8.4 if applicable)
$______________	(c) **New Loan.** Buyer may apply for mortgage loan financing (the "Loan") on terms acceptable to Buyer. If an FHA/VA loan applies, see attached FHA/VA Loan Addendum.
$______________	(d) **Seller Financing** (see attached Seller Financing Addendum)
$______________	(e) **Balance of Purchase Price in Cash at Settlement**
$______________	PURCHASE PRICE. **Total of lines (a) through (e)**

Source: https://realestate.utah.gov/forms/New_REPC_2017.pdf

Item 2.1 (a) pertains to the earnest money deposit. Earnest money is like a deposit and generally goes toward the down payment if a purchase goes through. Buyers should always offer the lowest possible amount of earnest money because the earnest money may not be refundable if they back out of the contract. Buyers also want the earnest money to be refundable for as long as possible, so they should be attentive to both the amount of earnest money and the associated dates when making an offer to buy a property.

Item 2.1 (c) pertains to the funds that will come from the mortgage lender. At this stage, buyers who have been working with a lender should have a clear idea of how much of the total purchase price will come from their savings in the form of a down payment and how much will come from the mortgage lender.

Item 2.1 (e) is the remaining down-payment amount the buyer will owe, assuming that the earnest money is applied to the down payment.

The next section of the contract that warrants careful consideration is the contract deadlines. Exhibit 6.2 provides a snapshot of this section of the contract.

Exhibit 6.2

24. CONTRACT DEADLINES. Buyer and Seller agree that the following deadlines shall apply to the REPC:

(a) Seller Disclosure Deadline ______________________ (Date)

(b) Due Diligence Deadline ______________________ (Date)

(c) Financing & Appraisal Deadline ______________________ (Date)

(d) Settlement Deadline ______________________ (Date)

Source: https://realestate.utah.gov/forms/New_REPC_2017.pdf

Item 24 (a) is the deadline for the seller to provide seller disclosures. An example of these is provided in Exhibit 6.3.

Exhibit 6.3

7. SELLER DISCLOSURES. No later than the Seller Disclosure Deadline referenced in Section 24(a), Seller shall provide to Buyer the following documents in hard copy or electronic format which are collectively referred to as the "Seller Disclosures":

(a) a written Seller property condition disclosure for the Property, completed, signed and dated by Seller as provided in Section10.3;
(b) a *Lead-Based Paint Disclosure & Acknowledgement* for the Property, completed, signed and dated by Seller (only if the Property was built prior to 1978);
(c) a Commitment for Title Insurance as referenced in Section 6.1;
(d) a copy of any restrictive covenants (CC&R's), rules and regulations affecting the Property;
(e) a copy of the most recent minutes, budget and financial statement for the homeowners' association, if any;
(f) a copy of any long-term tenant lease or rental agreements affecting the Property not expiring prior to Closing;
(g) a copy of any short-term rental booking schedule (as of the Seller Disclosure Deadline) for guest use of the Property after Closing;
(h) a copy of any existing property management agreements affecting the Property;
(i) evidence of any water rights and/or water shares referenced in Section 1.4;
(j) written notice of any claims and/or conditions known to Seller relating to environmental problems and building or zoning code violations;
(k) In general, the sale or other disposition of a U.S. real property interest by a foreign person is subject to income tax withholding under the *Foreign Investment in Real Property Tax Act of 1980* (FIRPTA). A "foreign person" includes a non-resident alien individual, foreign corporation, partnership, trust or estate. If FIRPTA applies to Seller, Seller is advised that Buyer or other qualified substitute may be legally required to withhold this tax at Closing. In order to avoid closing delays, if Seller is a foreign person under FIRPTA, Seller shall advise Buyer in writing; and
(l) Other (specify) ______________________

Source: https://realestate.utah.gov/forms/New_REPC_2017.pdf

It is difficult for buyers to perform due diligence until they have received all the seller disclosures, so buyers must require that sellers provide these soon after they have signed the purchase contract.

The due diligence deadline is the next important contract date. Buyers must be careful to ensure that the seller disclosure deadline and the due diligence deadline are not too close together; otherwise, they will not have enough time to complete thorough due diligence of the property.

The financing and appraisal deadline is the next important contract date. Buyers should be sure to consult with their lender before committing to this date and add extra days to account for unexpected delays.

The last important contract date is the settlement deadline. This is the date that the deal closes, and the transaction is complete. As with the other dates, buyers should be careful to provide a buffer for unexpected delays. Buyers must also realize that these deadlines are attached to various consequences. They need to take the deadlines seriously and understand the consequences of not meeting them.

After understanding and identifying the critical deadlines in their contract, buyers next need to stipulate important contingencies. These are necessary conditions that must be met for the deal to close. On the street, contingencies are often referred to as weasel clauses because they allow the buyer or seller to weasel out of the contract with no negative ramifications if a condition is not met. REPCs generally contains four common contingencies:

1. **Inspection:** A third-party inspection must be completed and found satisfactory by the buyer.
2. **Appraisal:** The lender must obtain an appraisal of the property, and the appraised value must equal or exceed the offer price.
3. **Financing:** The buyer must apply for and seek to obtain mortgage financing. The terms offered by the mortgage company must be found satisfactory by the borrower/buyer.
4. **Title:** A title report must be obtained from a title company and found satisfactory by the buyer, and a clean title must be provided by the seller to the buyer at closing.

REMEDIES FOR BREACH OF CONTRACT

Sometimes, one of the parties to a contract either chooses not to or cannot fulfill one or more aspects of the contract. When either the buyer or seller breaches a contract, the other party may be entitled to certain remedies. Although the remedies may vary considerably depending on the type of breach and the jurisdictional law, two remedies tend to result more often than others. First, if the buyer decides not to fulfill his or her contract obligations, the remedy is generally for the seller to keep the earnest money and put the property back on the market to sell to someone else. Second, if the seller decides not to sell or breaches the contract, the buyer can file a suit for specific performance, forcing the seller to fulfill his or her obligation to sell and vacate the property.

SUBMITTING OFFERS AND COUNTEROFFERS

Typically, a buyer's first offer is below market value, so the seller must decide if he or she will accept, decline, or counter the offer. Often, the seller will respond with a counteroffer that is less than the listing price but higher than the buyer's initial offer price. The counteroffer is a formal document that stipulates the parts of the initial offer that are not acceptable and proposes alternatives. Counteroffers are generally addendums to the original offer and are valid contracts, so buyers must treat them as such. More often, the counteroffer process is completed online using DocuSign, so buyers should be sure to get good legal counsel when completing a counteroffer and make sure they understand everything in it before they sign. Sometimes the counteroffer process goes back and forth a number of times before a meeting of the minds occurs. When both parties have come to an agreement, and all signatures are in place, it is time to open escrow and prepare for the close.

OPENING ESCROW

Once a valid contract has been executed by both parties, the contract and any earnest monies are generally conveyed to an escrow officer who acts as an independent third party to assist the parties (buyer and seller) in completing the terms of the contract.

RELATED RESOURCES

How to Read the Fine Print on Real Estate Purchase Offers
https://www.homelight.com/blog/offer-to-purchase-real-estate/

New Utah Real Estate Purchase Contract
https://realestate.utah.gov/forms/New_REPC_2017.pdf

The Key Elements of a Real Estate Purchase Agreement
https://www.legalnature.com/guides/the-key-elements-of-a-real-estate-purchase-agreement

Breach of Real Estate Contract
https://www.themyerslg.com/blog/2019/04/breach-of-real-estate-contract-a-broken-promise/

CHAPTER 7

Obtaining a Residential Appraisal

INTRODUCTION

After someone enters into a contract to buy a property, the mortgage lender will usually require the buyer to pay for an appraisal of the property to assess its collateral value. A typical residential appraisal costs between $450 and $650. Lenders are required by federal regulation to order appraisals through an appraisal management company (AMC). AMCs are independent third parties who order appraisals from a licensed appraiser, preventing loan officers from being able to influence appraisal outcomes.

To begin the appraisal process, appraisers usually require their client, the AMC, to provide some important information:

First, appraisers need the address and legal description of the subject property. Second, appraisers need to know what property rights to value. These may include the fee simple absolute estate, the leased-fee estate, or the leasehold estate. For an owner-occupied residence, lenders want the appraiser to value the fee simple interest. Third, appraisers need to know the date of valuation because real estate appraisals are a snapshot in time. The date of valuation is typically the date of inspection, but there may be instances when an appraiser is asked to value a property as of another date, such as the date of death, in the case of estate planning. Fourth, appraisers need to understand which definition of value to use as the basis of the appraisal. Typically, appraisers are asked to estimate the market value of a property. However, market value is defined differently by different organizations. Fannie Mae uses the following definition of market value:

> Market value is the most probable price that a property should bring in a competitive and open market under all conditions requisite to a fair sale, the buyer and seller, each acting prudently, knowledgeably and assuming the price is not affected by undue stimulus. Implicit in this definition is the consummation of a sale as of a specified date and the passing of title from seller to buyer under conditions whereby:
>
> - buyer and seller are typically motivated;
> - both parties are well informed or well advised, and each acting in what he or she considers his/her own best interest;
> - a reasonable time is allowed for exposure in the open market;
> - payment is made in terms of cash in US dollars or in terms of financial arrangements comparable thereto; and
> - the price represents the normal consideration for the property sold unaffected by special or creative financing or sales concessions granted by anyone associated with the sale.[28]

Notice the phrase *most probable price* in the definition. This requirement has been the cause of many conflicts between borrowers and appraisers. Many people feel that market value should be whatever someone is willing to pay, but the definition does not allow for that way of thinking. Instead, the definition requires that appraisers estimate the value that represents the most probable price. If we were to survey market participants and ask them how much they would be willing to pay for a particular commodity, we would find a range of prices. The more people we surveyed, the more obvious the most probable price would become. In effect, market value, as defined in mortgage lending, is a distributional concept. Lenders do not want to know the highest possible sale price of a property; they want to know the most probable sale price. That way, if they have to foreclose and resell the property to recover their loan proceeds, lenders know what price to expect.

---

28. Fanniemae.com

Fifth, appraisers need to know the scope and use of the appraisal. The scope of an appraisal describes the level of detail and effort that must go into it and provides a general sense of its reliability. For instance, hiring an appraiser to conduct some cursory research and give a rough estimate of value for negotiation purposes is much different than hiring an appraiser to be an expert witness on a difficult legal case where the value must be precise and defensible. It is also vital that appraisers know how their appraisal will be used (e.g., for mortgage underwriting) so they can ensure that it covers the essential items required for that use.

Active real estate market participants have many occasions to interact with appraisers and review appraisal reports, so they need to understand the valuation process and the three approaches to valuation.

APPRAISAL PROCESS

Valuing a property typically involves the use of three approaches to valuation: (1) the sales comparison approach, (2) the cost approach, and (3) the income approach. The sales comparison approach compares a property's characteristics with those of similar properties that have recently sold and then makes adjustments for differences. The cost approach is based on the concept that a buyer will not pay more for a property than the cost to replicate it. It estimates the value of a property by recognizing the contributory value of both the land and building improvements. The income approach is useful when a rental market exists for the subject property. This approach is based on the income-producing potential of the property for investment purposes.

Sales Comparison Approach

Of the three approaches to valuation, the sales comparison approach is perhaps the most intuitive. In its simplest form, the sales comparison approach can be considered the "prudent shopper's" method. A prudent shopper carefully examines the item that he or she is interested in and then begins the comparison process by reviewing the prices of similar items. After considering differences (quantitative and qualitative) in the articles, the shopper adjusts the respective prices to evaluate which is the best deal. In effect, the prudent shopper exposes any arbitrage opportunities that result in an inefficient market.

Appraisers and investors using the sales comparison approach simulate a prudent shopper's experience to arrive at an estimate of value. Appraisers and investors first familiarize themselves with the characteristics of the subject property and then research the market for similar properties that have recently sold, are listed for sale, or are under contract. They then compare these properties and transactions to the subject property and adjust for material differences to arrive at an estimate of value for the subject property. The theoretical premise behind the sales comparison approach is the principle of substitution, the idea that it would be irrational for a buyer to pay more for a property than what he or she would pay for an equally desirable substitute.

The availability of substitute or comparable properties determines the applicability and reliability of the sales comparison approach. This approach is given considerable weight when there have been numerous recent transactions of similar properties. Inversely, this approach is given less weight when few properties have transacted or are offered for sale or when there are significant differences between the subject property and recently completed transactions. The latter case may result in large adjustments that could be difficult to support with market data.

To implement the sales comparison approach, appraisers and investors follow a seven-step process:

1. Become familiar with the characteristics of the subject property.
2. Research comparable sales, listings, and contracts.
3. Confirm these transactions with the related parties (buyer, seller, agent).
4. Organize the data and calculate units of comparison.
5. Identify value-influencing differences between the subject property and the comparable properties.
6. Adjust for these differences.
7. Reconcile the analysis to arrive at an estimate of market value.

THE SALES COMPARISON GRID

An adjustment grid (see Exhibit 7.1) is commonly used in residential appraisals. The grid helps organize data and shows the adjustments necessary to account for the differences between the subject and comparable properties.

When using a sales comparison grid, the analyst should be careful to make the adjustments the correct way. For example, if a comparable has a garage but the subject does not, then the comparable is superior to the subject in this characteristic, and the price should be adjusted downward to estimate the value of the subject property.

EXHIBIT 7.1: SAMPLE COMPLETED ADJUSTMENT GRID

SALES COMPARISON ANALYSIS

ITEM	SUBJECT	COMPARABLE NO. 1		COMPARABLE NO. 2		COMPARABLE NO. 3	
Address	1626 Montego Drive Bismarck, ND	1615 Contessa Drive Bismarck, ND		3023 Tyler Parkway Bismarck, ND		1756 Country West Drive Bismarck, ND	
Proximity to Subject		0.11 miles		0.31 miles		0.17 miles	
Sales Price	$ 255,000		$ 273,000		$ 226,000		$ 265,000
Price/Gross Living Area	$ 108.60	$ 106.14		$ 102.59		$ 109.87	
Data and/or Verification Source	Int/Ext. Inspe Contract	MLS, Ext. Inspection Assessor		MLS, Ext. Inspection Assessor		MLS, Ext. Inspection Assessor	
VALUE ADJUSTMENTS	DESCRIPTION	DESCRIPTION	+(−)$ Adjust.	DESCRIPTION	+(−)$ Adjust.	DESCRIPTION	+(−)$ Adjust.
Sales or Financing Concessions		Conventional None/SB$4425	+4,425	Cash None/SB$3347	+3,347	Conventional None/SB$195	+195
Date of Sale/Time		7/1/2004		4-19-2004		10/19/2004	
Location	Urban	Urban		Urban		Urban	
Leasehold/Fee Simple	Fee Simple	Fee Simple		Fee Simple		Fee Simple	
Site	13,136 SF	13202 SF		10400 SF		15501 SF	
View	City Street	City Street		City Street		City Street	
Design and Appeal	Split Level/Good	2 Story/Good		Split Level/Good		Split Level/Good	
Quality of Construction	Good	Good		Good		Good	
Age	1993/11/4-6E	1996/7A/2-3E	-2,000	1995/9A/4-6E		1988/16A/6-8E	+2,000
Condition	Good	Good		Good		Good	
Above Grade	Total Bdrms Baths	Total Bdrms Baths		Total Bdrms Baths		Total Bdrms Baths	
Room Count	7 3 2.5	9 4 2.5		8 4 3	-1,500	7 3 2.5	
Gross Living Area	2,348 Sq. Ft.	2,572 Sq. Ft.	-10,100	2,203 Sq. Ft.	+6,500	2,412 Sq. Ft.	-2,900
Basement & Finished	Full/1095 fin.	Full/1240 fin.	-2,200	Full/1249 fin.	-2,300	Full/1448 fin.	-5,300
Rooms Below Grade	FR 2BR Bath	FR 2BR Den Bath		FR 2BR Bath		FR 2BR Bath	
Functional Utility	Average	Average		Average		Average	
Heating/Cooling	FWA/CA	FWA/CA		FWA/CA		FWA/CA	
Energy Efficient Items	Furnace/Window	Furnace/Window		Furnace/Window		Furnace/Window	
Garage/Carport	3 Car Att/BI	3 Car Att		3 Car Att/BI		3 Car Att/BI	
Porch, Patio, Deck,	Deck, Patio	Deck	+1,000	Deck	+1,000	Deck, Patio	
Fireplace(s), etc.	2 Fireplaces	1 Fireplace	+2,000	1 Fireplace	+2,000	1 Fireplace	+2,000
Fence, Pool, etc.	UGS	Fence, UGS	-4,000	UGS		Wet Bar	
	Appliances	Appliances		Appliances		Appliances	
Net Adj. (total)		☐ + ☒ - $	10,875	☒ + ☐ - $	9,047	☐ + ☒ - $	4,005
Adjusted Sales Price of Comparable		$	262,125	$	235,047	$	260,995

Source[29]

29. https://www.voegeleappraisal.com/xsites/Appraisers/voegeleappraisal/content/uploadedFiles/WebSample-1.pdf

Using a sales comparison grid can be beneficial in valuing a home because it can help identify the importance of value-influencing variables. Note that while usually correlated, the difference between the cost of an attribute and its value may be significant. Many upgrades to a property add less to the property's value than they cost to install. Swimming pools are a good example. Adding a swimming pool to a property will increase its value but usually by less than its cost to install. However, some upgrades add more to a property's value than their cost. Some examples include modernizing a floor plan (often by knocking out walls or adding closets) and improving the condition of the landscaping and yard. Buyers should note that each upgrade affects value differently. By performing comparative market analysis, buyers can gain a greater understanding of which improvements are worth doing and which are not.

REGRESSION ANALYSIS

While the sales comparison grid example is relatively easy to complete and denotes exact values for each of the variables considered, regression analysis is a more dynamic method for approximating the marginal values of separate property attributes. It can also help estimate the size of the expected deviation due to factors that cannot be realistically modeled. Finally, regression analysis enables buyers to analyze a larger sample of comparable properties. The steps to perform a regression analysis are detailed here.

Step 1: Get the Proper Tools

Use Microsoft Excel with the Analysis ToolPak installed. Most versions of Excel should at least have the add-in available for installation. If the Analysis ToolPak is not installed, the user can install it by selecting Excel Options > Add-Ins and then selecting Excel Add-ins > Go from the Manage box. This brings up a window that enables the user to add the Analysis ToolPak. Once the add-in is installed, its capabilities are accessible through the Data ribbon tab. Note that, while very functional, Excel's regression capabilities are fairly simplistic. For some buyers, obtaining and learning a more robust statistics software package (such as the open-source "R") is worth the effort.

Step 2: Identify the Most Important Variables

The next step in preparing for regression analysis is to identify the variables (property characteristics) that most affect property value, such as location and property size. For this simplified example, we will assume that location, property size (square footage), and availability of a garage affect the price the most. Still, regressions with ten or more variables are not uncommon. Performing regressions with too many variables can, however, lead to data overload and increased information acquisition costs, so it is usually best to pick out three to seven of the most important factors and use those to get a reasonably good picture of a property's value.

Step 3: Quantify Each Variable

Once the variables have been selected, the next step is to quantify each of the variables. For data that is already quantified, such as square footage, generally no modification is necessary. However, qualitative data, such as true/false (garage) or location data (Phoenix or Tempe), needs to be transformed. Statisticians frequently quantify true/false values by using "binary" variables. For example, properties with a garage might be assigned a binary variable of 1, while properties that do not would be assigned a value of 0. Since 0 multiplied by any number is 0, properties that do not have a garage will remain unaffected by this variable. For the location, the same concept applies. For instance, if the comparable properties were located across two cities, Phoenix and Tempe, the analyst could specify a value of 1 if the property was in Phoenix and 0 otherwise. The results of this analysis would identify the differential between Phoenix and Tempe.

Step 4: Gather the Data

Once an analyst has decided what data to obtain and how to categorize the data, he or she should be ready to gather the data, which is often the most time-consuming part of the process. The analyst should create a table with columns that describe the characteristics of the property that he or she believes influence its value.

Step 5: Perform a Regression

Once the data is organized in a tabular format in Excel, it is time to perform the regression analysis. Opening the Analysis ToolPak produces a user form that looks something like Exhibit 7.2

Exhibit 7.2: Excel Data Analysis ToolPak

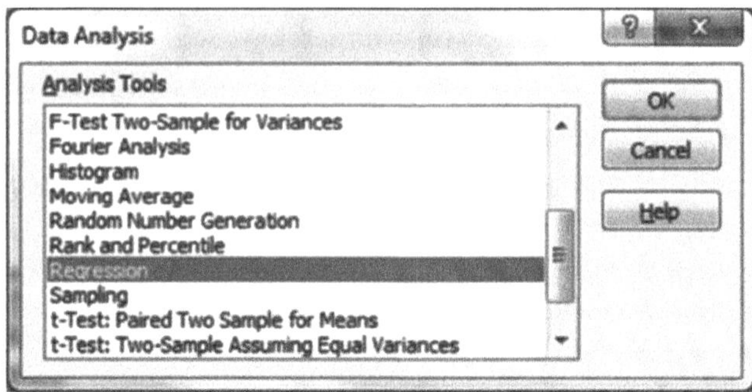

The analyst should click on the Regression option (highlighted in blue in Exhibit 7.2) and press OK. At that point, another form should load, as shown in Exhibit 7.3.

Exhibit 7.3: Regression Form

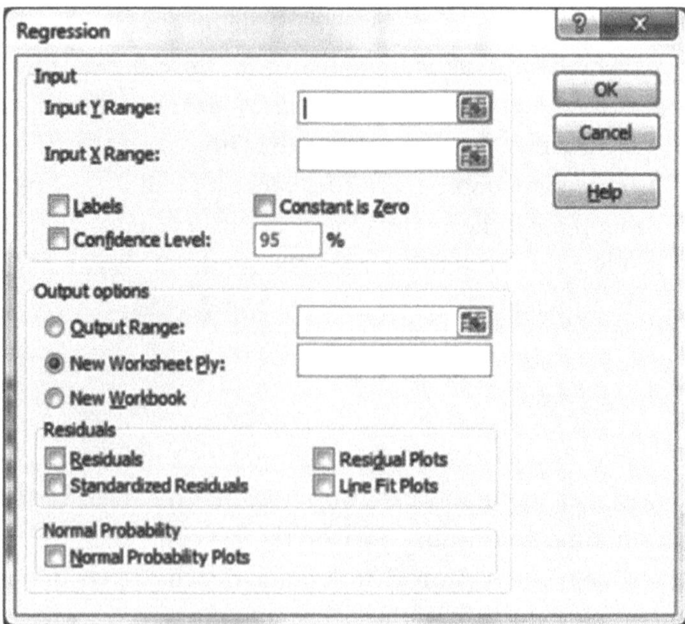

This window may look intimidating at first, but it is actually quite simple to use for those who understand the terminology. The first input box for "Y range" is where users put their control variable (usually "price" in this context). By clicking the red arrow to the right of the input box, the user can select the cells that contain prices. It is usually wise to include the column name and then click the Labels checkbox so that headings in the regression analysis are easier to understand.

The "X Range" comprises all of the variables whose effect the user is testing. These cells can be selected in the same manner as the "Y Range" cells. Note that it is easiest to list the control variable to the side of all the other variables.

Ninety-five percent is a good default confidence interval, though testing different confidence intervals can often be helpful. Users can also experiment with residual and probability plots. Clicking OK should produce a worksheet that looks like the example in Exhibit 7.4.

Exhibit 7.4: Regression Output in Excel

SUMMARY OUTPUT

Regression Statistics	
Multiple R	0.922421
R Square	0.85086
Adjusted R Squa	0.794933
Standard Error	19031.64
Observations	12

ANOVA

	df	*SS*	*MS*	*F*	*gnificance F*
Regression	3	1.65E+10	5.51E+09	15.21363	0.001142
Residual	8	2.9E+09	3.62E+08		
Total	11	1.94E+10			

	Coefficient	*andard Err*	*t Stat*	*P-value*	*Lower 95%*	*Upper 95%*	*ower 95.0%*	*pper 95.0%*
Intercept	51,545.65	19806.86	2.602413	0.031499	5870.939	97220.36	5870.939	97220.36
Size (sq. ft.)	2.31	0.475373	4.861829	0.001253	1.214971	3.407396	1.214971	3.407396
Excellent	48,365.05	17397.73	2.779964	0.023926	8245.819	88484.27	8245.819	88484.27
Average	10,796.52	14463.84	0.746449	0.476757	-22557.2	44150.19	-22557.2	44150.19

Step 6: Analyze the Regression Output

The summary output provides some regression statistics. Each of these is described in the following paragraphs.

Adjusted R Square: This number, the third number from the top (see Exhibit 7.4), represents the percent of the variation in the control variable (price) that is explained by the independent variables (in this case, size and condition). The number here, 0.794, or 79.4%, shows that the property size and condition explain 79.4% of the variation in the sales price in this example data set.

Coefficients: The coefficients column at the bottom left breaks out the relative importance of each data point in the regression. In this analysis, the "intercept" (baseline) price of a home in poor condition was $51,545.65. Each additional square foot added $2.31 to the price. A property in excellent condition netted an extra $48,365.05, and one in average condition netted an extra $10,796.52. These coefficients are very valuable in determining the relative importance of each attribute in contributing to the price.

P-value: The "P-value" column in the bottom middle shows the probability that the variable could have no effect on the dependent variable (price). For example, the chance that the size of a property has no effect (0.001253 or 0.1253%) is minuscule, suggesting that this variable is an important variable for explaining property value.

Lower X% and Upper X%: While the coefficients column seems to provide an exact number, this column reports the center of a probability distribution with a wide range of possible values. The lower and upper bounds (at the bottom right) show the confidence interval of the coefficient calculation. For example, given a 95% confidence interval here, the value of an additional square foot could be as low as $1.21 per square foot or as high as $3.41 per square foot, with an expected value based on the sample set of about $2.31 per square foot. Additional observations can help to decrease the size of confidence intervals.

Creating the equation for the price of a subject property is as simple as plugging the correct numbers into the formula suggested by the regression analysis. The equation, in this case, would read as follows:

Expected Price = $51,545.65 + $2.31 * (Square Feet)
+ $48,365.05 * (Excellent Variable) + $10,796.52 * (Average Variable)

So, the value of a home with 3,000 square feet in average condition would be estimated as follows:

Value = $51,545.65 + $2.31 * 3,000 + $48,365.05 * 0 + $10,796.52 * 1 = $131,642.17

COST APPROACH

The cost approach is an appraisal technique that assumes that a rational and prudent purchaser will pay no more for a property than the cost of reproducing, or replacing, a similar property with the same utility. Estimating a property's value via the cost approach has five steps:

Step 1: Estimate the reproduction cost new of all building improvements by identifying all direct and indirect costs, including entrepreneurial profit.

Step 2: Estimate all elements of accrued depreciation, including physical deterioration, functional obsolescence, and external obsolescence.

Step 3: Subtract the total accrued depreciation from the reproduction cost new of the building improvements. This result provides the depreciated cost new of the building improvements.

Step 4: Estimate the value of the subject property's site as though vacant and at the highest and best use.

Step 5: Add the estimated site value to the depreciated cost new of the improvements.

Each of these steps is examined in detail in the following paragraphs.

Step 1: Estimate Reproduction Costs New

The first step to conducting the cost approach is to estimate the reproduction cost new of the building improvements. Real estate development involves everything from finding a parcel of land to obtaining approvals to completing all improvements on that land. The breadth of real estate development is substantial and falls outside the scope of this book. But developers, when estimating the development costs of a newly constructed project, generally segregate the costs they will incur into three categories: (1) direct costs (hard costs), (2) indirect costs (soft costs), and (3) developer's (entrepreneurial) profit.

Direct Costs

Direct costs, sometimes known as hard costs, are costs that go mainly into site preparation and the vertical construction of buildings. For example, if a developer has plans and blueprints ready for a site but has not yet touched the site, the developer's cost to hire a general contractor to prepare the site and build the project would be equal to the total direct costs of the project. To estimate direct costs, analysts can use construction cost estimation software such as RSMeans or consult with a developer or contractor.

Indirect Costs

Indirect costs, sometimes known as soft costs, are costs that do not go directly to the contractor but are nonetheless necessary to complete a real estate development project. Many soft costs are professional fees, such as architecture, engineering, legal, financing, and advertising fees. These costs vary widely from region to region, so appraisers need to consult with a knowledgeable developer in their area to obtain valid estimates.

Developer's Profit

Real estate development is a time-consuming and risky field. Development is time-consuming because finding a worthwhile development site is difficult. Just gaining approvals from all of the necessary organizations (e.g., the local government) can take years. Finally, coordinating between designers, engineers, construction managers, attorneys, debt holders, equity holders, and the general public is a daunting task. Development is risky because of the large number of moving parts involved and the many types of risk incurred by developers, including, but not limited to, government risk, construction risk, financing risk, and market risk. Real estate developers need to be compensated for their time and the risks they take and thus usually charge a tidy sum known as developer's profit. Like soft costs, these can vary substantially from region to region and from developer to developer.

Calculating the sum of direct costs, indirect costs, and developer's profit is the first step of the cost approach.

Step 2: Estimate Accrued Depreciation

The next step is to determine the accrued depreciation on the building and other structures. While similar in concept to depreciation in an appraisal context, depreciation calculated for tax purposes is often vastly different from the number calculated by an appraiser. Accrued depreciation can be separated into three categories: (1) physical depreciation, (2) functional obsolescence, and (3) external obsolescence.

Physical Depreciation

The first type of accrued depreciation is the physical deterioration of the property. When they are not well maintained, buildings can show signs of age and wear quickly. Even when buildings are well maintained, exposure to the elements eventually necessitates remodeling and rebuilding. The number used in the cost approach for physical deterioration should represent the economic loss on the building due to wear and tear.

Functional Obsolescence

The second type of accrued depreciation does not result from wear and tear but rather from changes in consumer preferences that cause the value of existing buildings to decline. An example could include the lack of electrical service to accommodate electronic equipment in a modern household.

External Obsolescence

Though less common than the other two categories of depreciation, external obsolescence can lead to steep declines in property values. External obsolescence occurs when a situation outside the property's boundaries makes new construction on the property less financially plausible. One poignant example of external obsolescence occurred in Detroit, Michigan, with the construction of the $55.7 million Superdome in 1975. The building served for several years as the home for the Detroit Lions football team and other special events. In 2002, a new stadium was constructed in Detroit and attracted those events. At auction a few years later, the original stadium and the 127 acres of land on which the stadium and parking lot were located were auctioned to the highest bidder for $550,000. Not all of the 99%+ decline in value was due to external obsolescence (there was clearly some physical deterioration and functional obsolescence), but the "Lion's" share of the loss came from external obsolescence. External obsolescence is challenging to control and represents a significant risk in investing in real estate.

Understanding and measuring each of these types of accrued depreciation is crucial for a reliable value estimate. One relatively simple approach for estimating the impact of these effects is known as the Age-Life Method. In the Age-Life Method, the analyst first estimates the useful or economic life of buildings of the same type as the subject property. Then, the analyst determines the "effective" age of the subject building. Buildings that are well maintained and have little functional obsolescence may have an effective age that is much younger than their actual age. In contrast, the opposite may be true for poorly maintained or obsolete structures. Accrued depreciation can then be calculated with the following equation:

$$Accrued\ Depreciation\ Percent = \frac{Effective\ Age}{Economic\ Life}$$

Multiplying the accrued depreciation percent by the reproduction cost new results in the dollar amount of accrued depreciation from all sources.

Step 3: Deduct Accrued Depreciation from Reproduction Cost New

With steps 1 and 2 completed, determining the value of the structures on the subject site is as simple as subtracting the number calculated in step 2 from the number calculated in step 1.

Step 4: Estimate Land Value

Using the cost method to determine land value is inherently problematic because land is virtually impossible to create or destroy (though ground can undoubtedly be prepared for or hindered by real estate development). There is a set amount of land in the world, and the value of that land is simply a matter of supply and demand. Instead of using cost, analysts calculate the value of land using another approach. Two common techniques used by appraisers are (1) sales comparison and (2) extraction.

Sales Comparison

Valuing land by sales comparison requires an analysis of sales of land similar to the subject property. The objective of this approach is to value the site as though vacant. When vacant land sales near the subject property are available, sales comparison is usually the most effective method.

Extraction

In a market with little available vacant land, the land values for comparable properties can be estimated by taking a total sale price and then subtracting the value of the structures on that property (usually by using steps 1–3 of the cost approach as previously shown). For example, a new house that costs $200,000 to build (including developer's profit) but sells for $300,000 suggests a land value for the property of $100,000.

Step 5: Add Land Value to Step 3

Once an appraiser has estimated separate values for the building and the land, he or she can add the two values to estimate the total value of the subject property. One significant benefit of the cost approach relative to other techniques is its ability to distinguish the value of a building(s) from the value of the land. Knowing this information can aid managers in making decisions about the optimal use of a property.

RELATED RESOURCES

Appraisal Institute
www.appraisalinstitute.org

Understanding the Appraisal
https://www.appraisalinstitute.org/assets/1/7/understand_appraisal_1109_(1).pdf

Using Alternative Data for Property Valuation Models
https://therealdeal.com/national/2020/07/29/using-alternative-data-for-property-valuation-models-post-covid-19/

Rethinking Real Estate Valuations and Alternatives to Traditional Approaches
https://www.nar.realtor/newsroom/rethinking-real-estate-valuations-and-alternatives-to-traditional-appraisals

CHAPTER 8

Due Diligence, Title Insurance, & Completing the Transaction

INTRODUCTION

Once a buyer has a property under contract to purchase, he or she needs to perform due diligence and complete the transaction. During this critically important period, buyers need to pay attention to details; otherwise, they could end up with a disappointing outcome.

DUE DILIGENCE

Purchase contracts stipulate a due diligence period that allows buyers to thoroughly investigate the property to make sure they are buying what they think they are buying. Most people have purchased a boxed item only to bring it home and find that it is defective in some way that renders it unusable (e.g., missing a critical part or damaged). When that occurs for most commodities, the purchaser simply returns the item to the store for a full refund or replacement. However, this approach is impossible for real estate acquisitions. Instead, buyers are given a due diligence period before the purchase to investigate the property and make sure it meets their expectations. This due diligence usually includes hiring a professional home inspector.

Retaining a Professional Home Inspector

No one wants to buy another person's problems. Unfortunately, this happens far too often with home purchases. Structural deficiencies and wear and tear, often unobservable to the naked eye, can cost thousands to remedy. To avoid these problems, buyers can pay for a property inspection by a qualified inspector (even if they are buying a new home). The American Society of Home Inspectors (ASHI) is a good source for finding qualified and licensed home inspectors.

Single-family home inspections by ASHI-certified inspectors, like appraisals, usually cost between $300 and $600. The report they provide looks in many ways like an appraisal report, with pictures and detailed analysis. The analysis in these reports is focused on the physical condition of the property and details needed remedies with their expected costs. Handing a seller an official report with a list of required repairs and costs to a property can help buyers get a discount on the sale price or can force the seller to take care of the needed repairs before closing. Some deals fall apart when buyers and sellers cannot agree on who should pay for needed repairs, but being aware of any defects should be paramount for any prospective buyer.

A home inspection also usually provides useful information on expected future repairs and maintenance, such as the remaining useful life of a home's roof. Other services, such as testing for mold, radon, and hidden water damage, can be purchased for an additional fee if an initial inspection suggests more investigation is warranted. Like an appraisal, buyers should not pay for an inspection report until they have signed a purchase contract, but once they have one, buyers should almost always invest in a quality inspection.

Finalizing Your Financing and Reviewing the Final Numbers

After satisfying any concerns about the physical condition of the property, buyers need to work with their lender to ensure that the financing terms are consistent with their expectations. Buyers should not assume that the lender "has it covered." Instead, they should check on the status of their loan and review all written documentation so that they are not surprised at the time of close.

PREPARING TO CLOSE AND TITLE INSURANCE

As a buyer approaches the date of closing, the escrow officer should ask questions about how the buyer would like to take the title and provide a settlement statement and preliminary title report for the buyer to review.

Closing a deal and obtaining title to a property can be a complex and confusing process for first-time homebuyers. The closing process must be completed correctly to ensure peace of mind; otherwise, the outcome can be financially devastating. For instance, owners sometimes take advantage of buyers by fraudulently selling the same property to multiple people. To protect against this situation and other similar nightmares, most buyers work with a reputable escrow officer or attorney and purchase title insurance.

Historical Significance of Title

Throughout most of human history, private land ownership was rare and was usually reserved for the very wealthy. Even if someone owned land, his or her ownership was only valuable if he or she could ensure stability. For example, when areas were conquered by military force, ownership transferred to the conquering party, leaving the original owners landless. Worse still, disputes over land ownership were tough to settle in the past, allowing the most politically connected to take advantage of the less influential.

One of the first and most well-known attempts to solve problems associated with land ownership was undertaken by William I of England (a.k.a. William the Conqueror). William ordered that each parcel of land be recorded in a volume of books that became known as the Domesday (pronounced "Doomsday") Book. The book's ownership records were considered final, and though it was commissioned primarily to aid with tax collection, the book became the largest title repository to date. Over time, most of the land ownership has shifted from public to private ownership, and the concept of title (who really owns a piece of land) has become even more important.

To aid in tracking land ownership over time, each county in the United States has a recording office. At these offices, people can submit legal documents detailing property interests such as ownership, mortgage loans, and construction liens. State laws usually encourage people with property interests to record their interests early to have the best chance of maintaining their interest should an issue arise. However, the execution of these laws differs from state to state.

Documents recorded at the county recorder's office are public records. Anyone can perform their title search, but most buyers choose not to. Instead, sellers are usually required to purchase a title insurance policy indemnifying the buyer from potential losses due to title problems.

Title Insurance

The title insurance industry has grown significantly over the past century and is now involved in nearly every real estate transaction. Title insurance companies are valuable to real estate transactions for two primary reasons.

First, title insurance companies can easily search public records to determine ownership. Since most county recording offices index land transactions by ownership name, finding the ownership chain for a parcel of land is an incredibly time-consuming process. Title insurance companies, however, have spent a lot of money organizing recorded documents into "tract" indexes that can easily track transactions on a single parcel of land. Also, title insurance companies have digitized much of the older data available only in paper files at recorders' offices to make it easily searchable. In short, it would almost certainly cost a buyer more in time and trouble to conduct a title search than it costs to buy a title insurance policy.

The second reason title insurance is so important is that, unlike the Domesday Book, records from the county recorder's office are not the final say in property interests. In many jurisdictions, a person who finds and is entitled to a valid deed to a property, even if it is over a hundred years old, can claim and subsequently receive ownership of the property even if someone else occupies the property. Title insurance compensates buyers who encounter this unfortunate situation or a myriad of related title problems.

Types of Title Insurance

Before reviewing the types of title insurance, buyers should understand the "covenant of marketable title." The covenant of marketable title states that a purchaser is right to assume that a seller of land has a marketable title to the property unless disclosed otherwise. If a search turns up an issue with the title, regardless of what the contract says, the buyer can walk away from the deal and force the seller to return his or her earnest money. To assure buyers that they indeed have a marketable title to the property, shortly after a real estate purchase contract is signed, sellers are usually obliged to provide buyers with a preliminary title report proving that they own the property.

Assuming a title is marketable, title insurance companies generally issue two types of policies:

> **Owner's Policy:** Usually paid for by the seller, an owner's policy covers many potential title disputes up to a certain amount, often the purchase price or more of the property. The title insurance policy is limited to actions by prior owners of the land (if you cloud the title in some way due to your actions, you have no protection).

> **Lender's Policy:** Usually paid for by the buyer, this policy offers title protection to the lender. Lender's policies are effective even after a mortgage loan is sold on the secondary market.

Unlike most types of insurance, title insurance does not have regular premium payments. Instead, the full premium is paid upfront, and the policy remains in effect for as long as the buyer holds title to the property.

Escrow

Typically, escrow officers work for title insurance companies. However, in some areas, attorneys or specialized escrow officers handle these duties. Escrow officers are the referees in the real estate purchase process, but they are not attorneys and do not offer legal advice. They work as intermediaries between purchasing and selling parties to ensure that all contract requirements are completed.

A buyer's first contact with an escrow officer is usually when the buyer pays the earnest money deposit for a home. Earnest money goes toward the purchase of a property and signals that the buyer is serious about the transaction. It is also used to compensate the seller if the buyer fails to perform on the contract. Usually, an escrow officer holds the earnest money deposit until the deal closes, or the deposit is refunded in accordance with a provision in the REPC.

Escrow officers make sure everything occurs as specified in the contract. For example, an escrow officer would make sure that a seller does not receive any sale proceeds until he or she has signed over the deed. Likewise, an escrow officer would ensure that the buyer does not get keys until he or she has paid for the property. Also, if either the buying or selling party initiates a dispute during a transaction, the escrow officer puts everything on hold until the dispute is resolved.

Escrow is used in more aspects of real estate than just during closing. For example, most monthly mortgage payments require payment of PITI (principal, interest, property taxes, and property insurance). However, lenders generally forward the tax and insurance portions to the appropriate parties once per year. While tax and insurance payments wait to be forwarded, they usually sit in an escrow account held by the lender.

CLOSING PROCESS

Since 2013, the Consumer Financial Protection Bureau (CFPB) has been revamping the mortgage lending system. Mortgages can be complex and confusing to many people. Therefore, the new rules and initiatives primarily serve two purposes:

1. To simplify and consolidate some of the required loan disclosures
2. To alter the timing of some activities in the mortgage process

To achieve these objectives, the CFPB has developed two forms, the Loan Estimate form and Closing Disclosure form (see Exhibits

8.1 and 8.2, respectively, on pages 111 and 112). These forms replace the traditional good faith estimate, initial and final Truth-in-Lending Statements, and the HUD-1 Settlement Statement.

The new forms aim to provide a simplified way to understand all costs on a real estate transaction that includes a mortgage loan. However, even with these changes to improve clarity, buyers should still review everything carefully. If buyers notice things that look different from what they expected, they should ask why. The time to resolve problems is before a deal closes, so buyers should keep asking questions until they receive satisfactory answers.

Settlement, Recording, and Closing

Completing an acquisition takes place in a series of steps over a day or two. First, the buyer and seller complete their respective duties as stipulated in the contract. The escrow officer typically orchestrates this process. Second, all necessary documents are recorded at the county recorder's office. Third, the escrow is closed, funds are dispersed, and keys to the property are transferred to the buyer.

In the first step, buyers are required to sign all mortgage documents. They must be careful to read all the documents that they sign and should ask questions if they do not understand something. Buyers should also carefully review all of the numbers in the documents to ensure that the numbers match the numbers they previously agreed to with their lender. These include the total loan amount, interest rate, and any loan-related closing costs.

Once the other documents have been signed, the buyer must sign the deed and stipulate how he or she would like to take title to the property. Buyers may choose to take title as an individual, as joint tenants with right of survivorship, or as tenants in common. Buyers should investigate these options before the close by consulting with an attorney and an estate planner, especially if they have a complex estate.

After signing the deed, the buyer must deliver the funds he or she is responsible for, including the down payment and closing costs not covered by the lender. Most often, buyers fulfill this obligation by providing the escrow officer with "good funds." For many states, good funds can be cash, a cashier's check, or a wire transfer. Most escrow officers refuse to accept large cash amounts, so buyers should not plan on paying with cash. Cashier's checks are generally acceptable but can delay closing for a couple of days while the funds are verified. The best and most common payment approach is wire transfer because funds are immediately verifiable. Lenders also wire their portion of the sale proceeds to the escrow officer.

After both parties have signed the necessary documents and funds have been transferred to the escrow officer, some of the documents, such as the deed and mortgage, are recorded at the county recorder's office. Once the proper recording is verified, funds are dispersed, and the escrow is closed. At this point, the buyer is technically a new property owner and may obtain keys and access to the property.

Exhibit 8.1: Example of a Completed Loan Estimate Form from CFPB (pg. 1 of 3)

FICUS BANK
4321 Random Boulevard • Somecity, ST 12340

Save this Loan Estimate to compare with your Closing Disclosure.

Loan Estimate

DATE ISSUED	2/15/2013
APPLICANTS	Michael Jones and Mary Stone 123 Anywhere Street Anytown, ST 12345
PROPERTY	456 Somewhere Avenue Anytown, ST 12345
SALE PRICE	$180,000

LOAN TERM	30 years
PURPOSE	Purchase
PRODUCT	Fixed Rate
LOAN TYPE	☒ Conventional ☐ FHA ☐ VA ☐ ___________
LOAN ID #	123456789
RATE LOCK	☐ NO ☒ YES, until 4/16/2013 at 5:00 p.m. EDT *Before closing, your interest rate, points, and lender credits can change unless you lock the interest rate. All other estimated closing costs expire on **3/4/2013** at 5:00 p.m. EDT*

Loan Terms		Can this amount increase after closing?
Loan Amount	$162,000	NO
Interest Rate	3.875%	NO
Monthly Principal & Interest *See Projected Payments below for your Estimated Total Monthly Payment*	$761.78	NO
		Does the loan have these features?
Prepayment Penalty		YES • **As high as $3,240** if you pay off the loan during the first 2 years
Balloon Payment		NO

Projected Payments		
Payment Calculation	**Years 1-7**	**Years 8-30**
Principal & Interest	$761.78	$761.78
Mortgage Insurance	+ 82	+ —
Estimated Escrow *Amount can increase over time*	+ 206	+ 206
Estimated Total Monthly Payment	$1,050	$968

Estimated Taxes, Insurance & Assessments *Amount can increase over time*	$206 a month	**This estimate includes** ☒ Property Taxes ☒ Homeowner's Insurance ☐ Other: *See Section G on page 2 for escrowed property costs. You must pay for other property costs separately.*	**In escrow?** YES YES

Costs at Closing		
Estimated Closing Costs	$8,054	Includes $5,672 in Loan Costs + $2,382 in Other Costs – $0 in Lender Credits. *See page 2 for details.*
Estimated Cash to Close	$16,054	Includes Closing Costs. *See Calculating Cash to Close on page 2 for details.*

Visit **www.consumerfinance.gov/mortgage-estimate** for general information and tools.

LOAN ESTIMATE — PAGE 1 OF 3 • LOAN ID # 123456789

Source: https://www.consumerfinance.gov/owning-a-home/loan-estimate/

Example of a Completed Loan Estimate Form from CFPB (pg. 2 of 3)

Closing Cost Details

Loan Costs

A. Origination Charges	$1,802
.25 % of Loan Amount (Points)	$405
Application Fee	$300
Underwriting Fee	$1,097

B. Services You Cannot Shop For	$672
Appraisal Fee	$405
Credit Report Fee	$30
Flood Determination Fee	$20
Flood Monitoring Fee	$32
Tax Monitoring Fee	$75
Tax Status Research Fee	$110

C. Services You Can Shop For	$3,198
Pest Inspection Fee	$135
Survey Fee	$65
Title – Insurance Binder	$700
Title – Lender's Title Policy	$535
Title – Settlement Agent Fee	$502
Title – Title Search	$1,261

D. TOTAL LOAN COSTS (A + B + C)	$5,672

Other Costs

E. Taxes and Other Government Fees	$85
Recording Fees and Other Taxes	$85
Transfer Taxes	

F. Prepaids	$867
Homeowner's Insurance Premium (6 months)	$605
Mortgage Insurance Premium (months)	
Prepaid Interest ($17.44 per day for 15 days @ 3.875%)	$262
Property Taxes (months)	

G. Initial Escrow Payment at Closing	$413
Homeowner's Insurance $100.83 per month for 2 mo.	$202
Mortgage Insurance per month for mo.	
Property Taxes $105.30 per month for 2 mo.	$211

H. Other	$1,017
Title – Owner's Title Policy (optional)	$1,017

I. TOTAL OTHER COSTS (E + F + G + H)	$2,382

J. TOTAL CLOSING COSTS	$8,054
D + I	$8,054
Lender Credits	

Calculating Cash to Close

Total Closing Costs (J)	$8,054
Closing Costs Financed (Paid from your Loan Amount)	$0
Down Payment/Funds from Borrower	$18,000
Deposit	- $10,000
Funds for Borrower	$0
Seller Credits	$0
Adjustments and Other Credits	$0
Estimated Cash to Close	$16,054

LOAN ESTIMATE PAGE 2 OF 3 • LOAN ID # 123456789

Source: https://www.consumerfinance.gov/owning-a-home/loan-estimate/

Example of a Completed Loan Estimate Form from CFPB (pg. 3 of 3)

Additional Information About This Loan

LENDER	Ficus Bank	MORTGAGE BROKER	
NMLS/__ LICENSE ID		NMLS/__ LICENSE ID	
LOAN OFFICER	Joe Smith	LOAN OFFICER	
NMLS/__ LICENSE ID	12345	NMLS/__ LICENSE ID	
EMAIL	joesmith@ficusbank.com	EMAIL	
PHONE	123-456-7890	PHONE	

Comparisons	Use these measures to compare this loan with other loans.
In 5 Years	$56,582 Total you will have paid in principal, interest, mortgage insurance, and loan costs. $15,773 Principal you will have paid off.
Annual Percentage Rate (APR)	4.274% Your costs over the loan term expressed as a rate. This is not your interest rate.
Total Interest Percentage (TIP)	69.45% The total amount of interest that you will pay over the loan term as a percentage of your loan amount.

Other Considerations

Appraisal	We may order an appraisal to determine the property's value and charge you for this appraisal. We will promptly give you a copy of any appraisal, even if your loan does not close. You can pay for an additional appraisal for your own use at your own cost.
Assumption	If you sell or transfer this property to another person, we ☐ will allow, under certain conditions, this person to assume this loan on the original terms. ☒ will not allow assumption of this loan on the original terms.
Homeowner's Insurance	This loan requires homeowner's insurance on the property, which you may obtain from a company of your choice that we find acceptable.
Late Payment	If your payment is more than *15* days late, we will charge a late fee of *5% of the monthly principal and interest payment.*
Refinance	Refinancing this loan will depend on your future financial situation, the property value, and market conditions. You may not be able to refinance this loan.
Servicing	We intend ☐ to service your loan. If so, you will make your payments to us. ☒ to transfer servicing of your loan.

Confirm Receipt

By signing, you are only confirming that you have received this form. You do not have to accept this loan because you have signed or received this form.

Applicant Signature   Date   Co-Applicant Signature   Date

LOAN ESTIMATE   PAGE 3 OF 3 • LOAN ID #123456789

Source: https://www.consumerfinance.gov/owning-a-home/loan-estimate/

EXHIBIT 8.2: EXAMPLE OF A COMPLETED CLOSING DISCLOSURE FORM FROM CFPB (PG. 1 OF 5)

Closing Disclosure

This form is a statement of final loan terms and closing costs. Compare this document with your Loan Estimate.

Closing Information

Date Issued	4/15/2013
Closing Date	4/15/2013
Disbursement Date	4/15/2013
Settlement Agent	Epsilon Title Co.
File #	12-3456
Property	456 Somewhere Ave Anytown, ST 12345
Sale Price	$180,000

Transaction Information

Borrower	Michael Jones and Mary Stone 123 Anywhere Street Anytown, ST 12345
Seller	Steve Cole and Amy Doe 321 Somewhere Drive Anytown, ST 12345
Lender	Ficus Bank

Loan Information

Loan Term	30 years
Purpose	Purchase
Product	Fixed Rate
Loan Type	☒ Conventional ☐ FHA ☐ VA ☐ _______
Loan ID #	123456789
MIC #	000654321

Loan Terms		Can this amount increase after closing?
Loan Amount	$162,000	**NO**
Interest Rate	3.875%	**NO**
Monthly Principal & Interest *See Projected Payments below for your Estimated Total Monthly Payment*	$761.78	**NO**
		Does the loan have these features?
Prepayment Penalty		**YES** • **As high as $3,240** if you pay off the loan during the first 2 years
Balloon Payment		**NO**

Projected Payments		
Payment Calculation	**Years 1-7**	**Years 8-30**
Principal & Interest	$761.78	$761.78
Mortgage Insurance	+ 82.35	+ —
Estimated Escrow *Amount can increase over time*	+ 206.13	+ 206.13
Estimated Total Monthly Payment	$1,050.26	$967.91

Estimated Taxes, Insurance & Assessments *Amount can increase over time* *See page 4 for details*	$356.13 a month	**This estimate includes** ☒ Property Taxes ☒ Homeowner's Insurance ☒ Other: Homeowner's Association Dues *See Escrow Account on page 4 for details. You must pay for other property costs separately.*	**In escrow?** YES YES NO

Costs at Closing		
Closing Costs	$9,712.10	Includes $4,694.05 in Loan Costs + $5,018.05 in Other Costs – $0 in Lender Credits. *See page 2 for details.*
Cash to Close	$14,147.26	Includes Closing Costs. *See Calculating Cash to Close on page 3 for details.*

CLOSING DISCLOSURE PAGE 1 OF 5 • LOAN ID # 123456789

Source: https://files.consumerfinance.gov/f/201403_cfpb_closing-disclosure_cover-H25B.pdf

Example of a Completed Closing Disclosure Form from CFPB (pg. 2 of 5)

Closing Cost Details

Loan Costs	Borrower-Paid At Closing	Borrower-Paid Before Closing	Seller-Paid At Closing	Seller-Paid Before Closing	Paid by Others
A. Origination Charges	**$1,802.00**				
01 0.25 % of Loan Amount (Points)	$405.00				
02 Application Fee	$300.00				
03 Underwriting Fee	$1,097.00				
04					
05					
06					
07					
08					
B. Services Borrower Did Not Shop For	**$236.55**				
01 Appraisal Fee to John Smith Appraisers Inc.					$405.00
02 Credit Report Fee to Information Inc.		$29.80			
03 Flood Determination Fee to Info Co.	$20.00				
04 Flood Monitoring Fee to Info Co.	$31.75				
05 Tax Monitoring Fee to Info Co.	$75.00				
06 Tax Status Research Fee to Info Co.	$80.00				
07					
08					
09					
10					
C. Services Borrower Did Shop For	**$2,655.50**				
01 Pest Inspection Fee to Pests Co.	$120.50				
02 Survey Fee to Surveys Co.	$85.00				
03 Title – Insurance Binder to Epsilon Title Co.	$650.00				
04 Title – Lender's Title Insurance to Epsilon Title Co.	$500.00				
05 Title – Settlement Agent Fee to Epsilon Title Co.	$500.00				
06 Title – Title Search to Epsilon Title Co.	$800.00				
07					
08					
D. TOTAL LOAN COSTS (Borrower-Paid)	**$4,694.05**				
Loan Costs Subtotals (A + B + C)	$4,664.25	$29.80			
Other Costs					
E. Taxes and Other Government Fees	**$85.00**				
01 Recording Fees Deed: $40.00 Mortgage: $45.00	$85.00				
02 Transfer Tax to Any State			$950.00		
F. Prepaids	**$2,120.80**				
01 Homeowner's Insurance Premium (12 mo.) to Insurance Co.	$1,209.96				
02 Mortgage Insurance Premium (mo.)					
03 Prepaid Interest ($17.44 per day from 4/15/13 to 5/1/13)	$279.04				
04 Property Taxes (6 mo.) to Any County USA	$631.80				
05					
G. Initial Escrow Payment at Closing	**$412.25**				
01 Homeowner's Insurance $100.83 per month for 2 mo.	$201.66				
02 Mortgage Insurance per month for mo.					
03 Property Taxes $105.30 per month for 2 mo.	$210.60				
04					
05					
06					
07					
08 Aggregate Adjustment	– 0.01				
H. Other	**$2,400.00**				
01 HOA Capital Contribution to HOA Acre Inc.	$500.00				
02 HOA Processing Fee to HOA Acre Inc.	$150.00				
03 Home Inspection Fee to Engineers Inc.	$750.00			$750.00	
04 Home Warranty Fee to XYZ Warranty Inc.			$450.00		
05 Real Estate Commission to Alpha Real Estate Broker			$5,700.00		
06 Real Estate Commission to Omega Real Estate Broker			$5,700.00		
07 Title – Owner's Title Insurance (optional) to Epsilon Title Co.	$1,000.00				
08					
I. TOTAL OTHER COSTS (Borrower-Paid)	**$5,018.05**				
Other Costs Subtotals (E + F + G + H)	$5,018.05				
J. TOTAL CLOSING COSTS (Borrower-Paid)	**$9,712.10**				
Closing Costs Subtotals (D + I)	$9,682.30	$29.80	$12,800.00	$750.00	$405.00
Lender Credits					

CLOSING DISCLOSURE — PAGE 2 OF 5 • LOAN ID # 123456789

Source: https://files.consumerfinance.gov/f/201403_cfpb_closing-disclosure_cover-H25B.pdf

Example of a Completed Closing Disclosure Form from CFPB (pg. 3 of 5)

Calculating Cash to Close — **Use this table to see what has changed from your Loan Estimate.**

	Loan Estimate	Final	Did this change?
Total Closing Costs (J)	$8,054.00	$9,712.10	**YES** • See **Total Loan Costs (D)** and **Total Other Costs (I)**
Closing Costs Paid Before Closing	$0	- $29.80	**YES** • You paid these Closing Costs **before closing**
Closing Costs Financed (Paid from your Loan Amount)	$0	$0	**NO**
Down Payment/Funds from Borrower	$18,000.00	$18,000.00	**NO**
Deposit	- $10,000.00	- $10,000.00	**NO**
Funds for Borrower	$0	$0	**NO**
Seller Credits	$0	- $2,500.00	**YES** • See Seller Credits in **Section L**
Adjustments and Other Credits	$0	- $1,035.04	**YES** • See details in **Sections K and L**
Cash to Close	$16,054.00	$14,147.26	

Summaries of Transactions — **Use this table to see a summary of your transaction.**

BORROWER'S TRANSACTION

K. Due from Borrower at Closing	**$189,762.30**
01 Sale Price of Property	$180,000.00
02 Sale Price of Any Personal Property Included in Sale	
03 Closing Costs Paid at Closing (J)	$9,682.30
04	
Adjustments	
05	
06	
07	
Adjustments for Items Paid by Seller in Advance	
08 City/Town Taxes to	
09 County Taxes to	
10 Assessments to	
11 HOA Dues 4/15/13 to 4/30/13	$80.00
12	
13	
14	
15	
L. Paid Already by or on Behalf of Borrower at Closing	**$175,615.04**
01 Deposit	$10,000.00
02 Loan Amount	$162,000.00
03 Existing Loan(s) Assumed or Taken Subject to	
04	
05 Seller Credit	$2,500.00
Other Credits	
06 Rebate from Epsilon Title Co.	$750.00
07	
Adjustments	
08	
09	
10	
11	
Adjustments for Items Unpaid by Seller	
12 City/Town Taxes 1/1/13 to 4/14/13	$365.04
13 County Taxes to	
14 Assessments to	
15	
16	
17	
CALCULATION	
Total Due from Borrower at Closing (K)	$189,762.30
Total Paid Already by or on Behalf of Borrower at Closing (L)	- $175,615.04
Cash to Close ☒ From ☐ To Borrower	**$14,147.26**

SELLER'S TRANSACTION

M. Due to Seller at Closing	**$180,080.00**
01 Sale Price of Property	$180,000.00
02 Sale Price of Any Personal Property Included in Sale	
03	
04	
05	
06	
07	
08	
Adjustments for Items Paid by Seller in Advance	
09 City/Town Taxes to	
10 County Taxes to	
11 Assessments to	
12 HOA Dues 4/15/13 to 4/30/13	$80.00
13	
14	
15	
16	
N. Due from Seller at Closing	**$115,665.04**
01 Excess Deposit	
02 Closing Costs Paid at Closing (J)	$12,800.00
03 Existing Loan(s) Assumed or Taken Subject to	
04 Payoff of First Mortgage Loan	$100,000.00
05 Payoff of Second Mortgage Loan	
06	
07	
08 Seller Credit	$2,500.00
09	
10	
11	
12	
13	
Adjustments for Items Unpaid by Seller	
14 City/Town Taxes 1/1/13 to 4/14/13	$365.04
15 County Taxes to	
16 Assessments to	
17	
18	
19	
CALCULATION	
Total Due to Seller at Closing (M)	$180,080.00
Total Due from Seller at Closing (N)	- $115,665.04
Cash ☐ From ☒ To Seller	**$64,414.96**

CLOSING DISCLOSURE PAGE 3 OF 5 • LOAN ID # 123456789

Source: https://files.consumerfinance.gov/f/201403_cfpb_closing-disclosure_cover-H25B.pdf

Example of a Completed Closing Disclosure Form from CFPB (pg. 4 of 5)

Additional Information About This Loan

Loan Disclosures

Assumption
If you sell or transfer this property to another person, your lender
☐ will allow, under certain conditions, this person to assume this loan on the original terms.
☒ will not allow assumption of this loan on the original terms.

Demand Feature
Your loan
☐ has a demand feature, which permits your lender to require early repayment of the loan. You should review your note for details.
☒ does not have a demand feature.

Late Payment
If your payment is more than *15* days late, your lender will charge a late fee of *5% of the monthly principal and interest payment.*

Negative Amortization (Increase in Loan Amount)
Under your loan terms, you
☐ are scheduled to make monthly payments that do not pay all of the interest due that month. As a result, your loan amount will increase (negatively amortize), and your loan amount will likely become larger than your original loan amount. Increases in your loan amount lower the equity you have in this property.
☐ may have monthly payments that do not pay all of the interest due that month. If you do, your loan amount will increase (negatively amortize), and, as a result, your loan amount may become larger than your original loan amount. Increases in your loan amount lower the equity you have in this property.
☒ do not have a negative amortization feature.

Partial Payments
Your lender
☒ may accept payments that are less than the full amount due (partial payments) and apply them to your loan.
☐ may hold them in a separate account until you pay the rest of the payment, and then apply the full payment to your loan.
☐ does not accept any partial payments.
If this loan is sold, your new lender may have a different policy.

Security Interest
You are granting a security interest in
456 Somewhere Ave., Anytown, ST 12345

You may lose this property if you do not make your payments or satisfy other obligations for this loan.

Escrow Account
For now, your loan
☒ will have an escrow account (also called an "impound" or "trust" account) to pay the property costs listed below. Without an escrow account, you would pay them directly, possibly in one or two large payments a year. Your lender may be liable for penalties and interest for failing to make a payment.

Escrow		
Escrowed Property Costs over Year 1	$2,473.56	Estimated total amount over year 1 for your escrowed property costs: *Homeowner's Insurance* *Property Taxes*
Non-Escrowed Property Costs over Year 1	$1,800.00	Estimated total amount over year 1 for your non-escrowed property costs: *Homeowner's Association Dues* You may have other property costs.
Initial Escrow Payment	$412.25	A cushion for the escrow account you pay at closing. See Section G on page 2.
Monthly Escrow Payment	$206.13	The amount included in your total monthly payment.

☐ will not have an escrow account because ☐ you declined it ☐ your lender does not offer one. You must directly pay your property costs, such as taxes and homeowner's insurance. Contact your lender to ask if your loan can have an escrow account.

No Escrow		
Estimated Property Costs over Year 1		Estimated total amount over year 1. You must pay these costs directly, possibly in one or two large payments a year.
Escrow Waiver Fee		

In the future,
Your property costs may change and, as a result, your escrow payment may change. You may be able to cancel your escrow account, but if you do, you must pay your property costs directly. If you fail to pay your property taxes, your state or local government may (1) impose fines and penalties or (2) place a tax lien on this property. If you fail to pay any of your property costs, your lender may (1) add the amounts to your loan balance, (2) add an escrow account to your loan, or (3) require you to pay for property insurance that the lender buys on your behalf, which likely would cost more and provide fewer benefits than what you could buy on your own.

CLOSING DISCLOSURE — PAGE 4 OF 5 • LOAN ID # 123456789

Source: https://files.consumerfinance.gov/f/201403_cfpb_closing-disclosure_cover-H25B.pdf

EXAMPLE OF A COMPLETED CLOSING DISCLOSURE FORM FROM CFPB (PG. 5 OF 5)

Loan Calculations

Total of Payments. Total you will have paid after you make all payments of principal, interest, mortgage insurance, and loan costs, as scheduled.	$285,803.36
Finance Charge. The dollar amount the loan will cost you.	$118,830.27
Amount Financed. The loan amount available after paying your upfront finance charge.	$162,000.00
Annual Percentage Rate (APR). Your costs over the loan term expressed as a rate. This is not your interest rate.	4.174%
Total Interest Percentage (TIP). The total amount of interest that you will pay over the loan term as a percentage of your loan amount.	69.46%

Questions? If you have questions about the loan terms or costs on this form, use the contact information below. To get more information or make a complaint, contact the Consumer Financial Protection Bureau at **www.consumerfinance.gov/mortgage-closing**

Other Disclosures

Appraisal
If the property was appraised for your loan, your lender is required to give you a copy at no additional cost at least 3 days before closing. If you have not yet received it, please contact your lender at the information listed below.

Contract Details
See your note and security instrument for information about
- what happens if you fail to make your payments,
- what is a default on the loan,
- situations in which your lender can require early repayment of the loan, and
- the rules for making payments before they are due.

Liability after Foreclosure
If your lender forecloses on this property and the foreclosure does not cover the amount of unpaid balance on this loan,
- [x] state law may protect you from liability for the unpaid balance. If you refinance or take on any additional debt on this property, you may lose this protection and have to pay any debt remaining even after foreclosure. You may want to consult a lawyer for more information.
- [ ] state law does not protect you from liability for the unpaid balance.

Refinance
Refinancing this loan will depend on your future financial situation, the property value, and market conditions. You may not be able to refinance this loan.

Tax Deductions
If you borrow more than this property is worth, the interest on the loan amount above this property's fair market value is not deductible from your federal income taxes. You should consult a tax advisor for more information.

Contact Information

	Lender	Mortgage Broker	Real Estate Broker (B)	Real Estate Broker (S)	Settlement Agent
Name	Ficus Bank		Omega Real Estate Broker Inc.	Alpha Real Estate Broker Co.	Epsilon Title Co.
Address	4321 Random Blvd. Somecity, ST 12340		789 Local Lane Sometown, ST 12345	987 Suburb Ct. Someplace, ST 12340	123 Commerce Pl. Somecity, ST 12344
NMLS ID					
ST License ID			Z765416	Z61456	Z61616
Contact	Joe Smith		Samuel Green	Joseph Cain	Sarah Arnold
Contact NMLS ID	12345				
Contact ST License ID			P16415	P51461	PT1234
Email	joesmith@ficusbank.com		sam@omegare.biz	joe@alphare.biz	sarah@epsilontitle.com
Phone	123-456-7890		123-555-1717	321-555-7171	987-555-4321

Confirm Receipt

By signing, you are only confirming that you have received this form. You do not have to accept this loan because you have signed or received this form.

Applicant Signature   Date   Co-Applicant Signature   Date

CLOSING DISCLOSURE   PAGE 5 OF 5 • LOAN ID # 123456789

Source: https://files.consumerfinance.gov/f/201403_cfpb_closing-disclosure_cover-H25B.pdf

RELATED RESOURCES

Understanding the Loan Estimate and Closing Disclosure—Video Walkthrough
https://www.youtube.com/watch?v=hsx9Yk9zuh4

Official CFPB "Loan Estimate Form Explainer"
http://www.consumerfinance.gov/owning-a-home/loan-estimate/

Official CFPB "Closing Disclosure Form Explainer"
http://www.consumerfinance.gov/owning-a-home/closing-disclosure/

Understanding the Escrow Process
http://www.investopedia.com/articles/mortgages-real-estate/08/closing-escrow-process.asp

Understanding Title Insurance
https://en.wikipedia.org/wiki/Title_insurance

PART III

BUYING A SMALL INVESTMENT PROPERTY

CHAPTER 9

Preparing to Purchase Investment Real Estate

INTRODUCTION

When people think about investing in commercial properties, they tend to think about large properties such as high-rise office buildings, shopping centers, and multifamily apartments. Investing in large properties requires more financial capital than most people have available. Therefore, real estate investing for the typical household tends to be with smaller real estate properties. These tend to be rental properties such as homes; condominiums; two-to-four family (duplex, triplex, and fourplex) residential properties; small office, retail, and industrial buildings; and vacant land. Before diving into the investment characteristics of each of these property types, let's review some foundational items that investors should consider before purchasing an investment property.

LAYING THE FOUNDATION

Before buying an investment property, investors should identify their objective for doing so. For example, investors might want to supplement income, retire early, supplement future retirement income, or leave an estate to their posterity. In any regard, knowing why they want to invest in real estate will help investors understand which type of property to select to achieve their objectives. It will also help investors determine their expected holding period and the risk-return tradeoff inherent in investing in alternative property types.

Next, investors need to realize that personally investing in small properties can require a significant time commitment and some unpleasant hassles. For instance, small investment properties usually require substantial management and maintenance. Investors need to decide who is going to fix a broken water heater and who is going to collect rents, pay bills, and handle bookkeeping associated with the property. These are just a few of the things that investors must address if they want to invest in real estate.

Many investors choose to offload many of these duties to a property manager. Property managers offer numerous services, which include finding tenants, showing properties, negotiating leases, collecting rents, paying bills, and overseeing maintenance. To perform these duties, property managers typically charge 8%–10% of collected rent revenue. This management charge might seem high, but buyers need to recognize that if they perform these duties themselves, they must complete them competently or they risk violating local housing laws.

INVESTMENT CHARACTERISTICS OF ALTERNATIVE PROPERTY TYPES

Once the foundational questions have been answered, it is time to discuss different property types and the pros and cons of each. This section examines the investment characteristics of single-family detached homes; residential condominiums; two-to-four family residential properties; and small office, retail, and industrial properties.

Single-Family Detached Homes

Many real estate investors believe that investing in rental homes is a great way to start because most people are quite familiar with this property type and inherently understand what determines value. (Characteristics that drive value for single-family homes include physical characteristics as well as location characteristics, such as proximity to employment, shopping, and recreation.) Another advantage of this type of property is lease length. For the most part, renters of single-family detached homes are generally more stable than apartment dwellers, so their lease terms are typically longer. Longer lease terms translate to less hassle for landlords. Another benefit of rental homes is their favorable depreciation schedule. Residential properties qualify for a shorter depreciation schedule than commercial properties (27.5 years versus 39 years). This shorter depreciation schedule leads to superior tax benefits compared to commercial or nonresidential investment properties.

Last but not least, many investors believe that single-family homes are less risky than other property types because people always need shelter but may not need an office or retail space. In other words, during an economic downturn, people still need a place to live but can get by without commercial space. This is the situation that played out during the Great Recession.

Even though there are many benefits to investing in residential homes, there are some distinct disadvantages. The first pertains to yard maintenance. The quality and appearance of the yard have a material impact on a property's value. Tenants of residential homes tend to have little regard for quality maintenance and let their yard care deteriorate over time, making the property less valuable. Landlords can mitigate this challenge by hiring a landscaping maintenance firm to care for the yard and increasing monthly rent to cover the charge. Eviction is another challenge associated with investing in homes. Single-family tenants often have a family with young kids. When young families struggle to pay rent, many landlords struggle to force an eviction.

Residential Condominiums

Investing in residential condominiums has several benefits over investing in other property types. One obvious benefit is the amenities that come from a shared common area. Tenants generally like amenities such as swimming pools, but the maintenance and liability associated with a swimming pool make it an unwise investment in a single-family home. Condo owners, however, do not have to worry about either of these issues because condo HOAs oversee amenity maintenance and obtain insurance to mitigate liability risks. As with single-family residences, condominiums benefit from a favorable depreciation schedule of 27.5 years and mortgage financing that is similar to that of a detached home.

The cons of investing in this type of property revolve around HOA restrictions. For instance, investors who purchase residential condos cannot add value to their property's exterior because they give up the right to change the exterior of their building. In addition, many condo owners pressure their HOA to reduce monthly fees, which leads to inadequate maintenance and subsequent deterioration in property value.

Two-to-Four Family Residential Properties

Investing in a residential duplex, triplex, or fourplex multitenant property can be a sound approach for investors who prefer residential properties over commercial properties. One advantage of multitenant properties over single-tenant properties is their ability to generate some rental income and cash flow, even if one of the units is vacant. One of the downfalls of single-tenant investment properties is their lack of rental revenue when the unit is empty. In this case, the entire debt service (or mortgage payment) falls upon the property owner and can quickly become a significant financial burden.

Another benefit includes the potential for owners to increase their value through sweat equity. In other words, because the investor is in control of the entire property, he or she can make improvements to the property that increase rental income and value. Two-to-four family residential properties also qualify for favorable financing terms such as single-family homes and condos.

On the negative side, these properties have some of the same management challenges as larger multitenant properties. Those who choose to invest in two-to-four residential properties should plan to encounter some of the same landlord hassles as apartments, such as tenant complaints and a general lack of pride of ownership.

Commercial and Industrial (C&I)

After considering the pros and cons of investing in residential properties, some investors develop an interest in commercial or industrial properties, namely office, retail, or industrial properties. These property types have some favorable investment characteristics, including longer-term leases, well-established tenants, and less-intensive management. Generally, commercial and industrial properties are designed as shells that require specialized construction for each tenant. Interior construction is referred to as tenant improvements (TIs) and can be very costly. Therefore, tenants tend to lease commercial properties for a longer term, typically a minimum of three years. In addition, property owners may structure leases so that tenants are responsible for all of the operating expenses on the property, making property management a breeze.

These advantages are countered by significant disadvantages. Perhaps the most significant problem is the lack of demand for commercial rentals during economic downturns. People need shelter during good times and bad times, but during bad times, they can live without commercial space. Therefore, investors in commercial and industrial property need to realize that during an economic recession, their property could become vacant quickly and remain that way for quite some time. Additionally, financing for these types of properties is more onerous—meaning that the loan-to-value ratio is lower, the required down payment is higher, the interest rate is higher, and the loan term is shorter than for residential properties. These properties also provide fewer tax benefits because their depreciation schedule is 39 rather than 27.5 years.

Overall, while C&I properties have some clear advantages over residential investment properties, their benefits are offset by some significant disadvantages.

Market Research and Property Search

New investors in real estate tend to increase their probability of success if they specialize in a property type and a geographical location. The idea is for investors to become "the expert" in a particular market (property type and geographic area) so that they can quickly exploit information asymmetries. The area that an investor selects should be near his or her home or work so he or she can easily see properties and gather market data.

Investors should also identify reliable data sources associated with their chosen market. These data sources might include those generated by local real estate agents, government offices, or local universities. Investors should not underestimate the importance of this step. To become the "expert" in a particular market, investors should make sure they have access to the best data available in their market. These data might include information on transaction prices, market rents, vacancies, operating expenses, total inventory, and new inventory, as well as on general economic indicators of the local market.

Once an investor has identified and studied relevant market data, he or she should begin searching for a property. Generally, this search starts naturally as investors start to become knowledgeable about a particular market. They start networking with individuals, including real estate agents, who are active in the market and can assist them in finding properties. Investors should also study their local online property advertising resources and drive through their area to identify new properties that have come onto the market.

Initial Inspection and Offers

As investors begin searching, they will start to find possible candidate properties. Timing is important. The good deals do not remain on the market for very long, so investors need to be especially responsive to properties that have just come onto the market. If someone is one of the first to contact a seller or seller's agent, he or she should carefully inspect the property. Investors should not be timid in their initial inspection. Even though they are not trained property inspectors, investors should try to discover property anomalies and concerns that could prove problematic later. Investors can also use problems they identify in their negotiations for a reduced price. During an inspection, potential buyers should ask questions about the property's performance, including questions about rental rates, vacancies, and operating expenses. Investors should also obtain documents relating to these items if they are available. Once an investor has gathered subject property data, he or she can start the investment analysis to determine if the property is a good investment candidate.

RELATED RESOURCES

Why You Should Be Investing Your Money in Real Estate
http://www.entrepreneur.com/article/228506

Real Estate Investing
http://en.wikipedia.org/wiki/Real_estate_investing

Pros and Cons of Investing in Commercial Real Estate
http://www.nolo.com/legal-encyclopedia/pros-cons-investing-commercial-real-estate.html

CHAPTER 10

Income Property Valuation

INTRODUCTION

Most homes are owner-occupied. Therefore, the most applicable approaches to home valuation are the sales comparison approach and the cost approach. For investment properties, rental revenue and operating expense data are readily available, so the income approach tends to be the best valuation method. While the other approaches to valuation (sales comparison and cost) may also be informative, investors should pay particular attention to values estimated by the income approach.

THE INCOME APPROACH TO VALUATION

In corporate finance, there are three financial statements: the balance sheet, the income statement, and the statement of cash flows. Corporate managers and investors analyze these statements to gain insight into the financial health of a firm and to assess its value. Similarly, in real estate, there are two financial statements: the annual operating statement and the reversion statement, also referred to as the termination statement. Annual operating and reversion statements provide market participants with insights into the financial health of a property and the basis for its valuation. In practice, the annual operating statement takes the following form:

Potential Gross Income	(PGI)
– Vacancy & Collection Loss	(V&CL)
+ Other Income	(OI)
Effective Gross Income	(EGI)
– Operating Expenses	(OE)
Net Operating Income	(NOI)

One of the first steps in the income approach is to estimate the potential gross income (PGI) of the subject property. Potential gross income is the gross annual income that the property could realize assuming 100% occupancy at market rents. Because market conditions (demand and supply) vary intertemporally, investment properties encounter periods of vacancy. Also, some tenants may suffer financial setbacks, causing them to miss some lease payments or stop paying altogether. Therefore, to account for this, the operating statement includes a line item for vacancy and collection loss (V&CL). Next, other nonrental income (OI) is accounted for. Other income may include parking fees, vending machine revenue, etc.

The deduction of vacancy and collection loss and the addition of other income from potential gross income results in effective gross income (EGI), which is essentially an estimate of the cash flow that the owner expects to receive. Next, operating expenses (OE) are deducted from EGI. Operating expenses typically vary geographically and by property type. Frequently, a property's historical expenses provide a solid estimate of its future operating expenses. However, a careful examination of all relevant data leads to the best forecast of operating expenses for a subject property. Deducting operating expenses from effective gross income results in a figure called net operating income (NOI). A property's market value can be derived by applying a market capitalization rate to NOI.

INCOME VALUATION MODELS

Income valuation models can be divided into two basic categories: ratio models (direct capitalization and effective gross income multiplier) and discounted cash flow models. In the context of ratio models, the income estimate can be divided by an appropriate rate or multiplied by an appropriate factor to estimate value. The rate that is typically employed in this context is the overall capitalization rate. The factor typically employed is the effective gross income multiplier. Each of these methodologies is described in the following paragraphs.

Ratio Models

The first ratio model is direct capitalization that requires a three-step process:

Step 1: Estimate the net operating income (NOI_0) for the subject property and the comparables (be consistent in the calculation).

Step 2: Calculate the overall capitalization rate (R_0) for each comparable by dividing the net operating income (NOI_0) by the sales price.

Step 3: Select the appropriate capitalization rate (R_0), and capitalize the subject's net operating income (NOI_0) to provide an estimate of value.

Selecting an appropriate capitalization rate for the subject property from the comparable sales requires that the investor consider the comparability of the property's attributes, transaction characteristics, and risk characteristics. Investors must be careful not to use measures of central tendency that can be heavily influenced by outliers, such as the arithmetic mean.

For instance, assume an investor has researched the comparable sales summarized in Exhibit 10.1.

EXHIBIT 10.1: SUMMARY OF BUILDING COMPARABLES

Comparable No.	Subject	1	2	3	4	5
Sale Price		387,000	520,000	385,000	345,000	320,000
Price per Sq. Ft.		$122	$144	$117	$108	$110
Property Rights	Leased Fee	Leased Fee	Leased Fee	Leased Fee	Leased Fee	Leased Fee
Financing Terms	Market	Market	Market	Favorable	Market	Market
Conditions of Sale	Normal	Normal	Normal	Normal	Normal	Normal
Date of Sale	Current	2 mo. Ago	12 mo. Ago	6 mo. Ago	8 mo. Ago	13 mo. Ago
Location	Good	Similar	Similar	Superior	Similar	Inferior
Site Utility	Good	Similar	Similar	Similar	Inferior	Similar
Building Sq.Ft.	3,200	3,150	3,600	3,300	3,200	2,900
Age/Condition	5 yrs. Good	8 yrs. Good	1 yr. Good	3 yrs. Good	6 yrs. Good	4 yrs. Good
Cap Rate		6.10%	6.30%	6.50%	6.90%	6.70%
EGIM		7.30	7.67	7.55	6.80	7.20

In this instance, the capitalization rates range from 6.1% to 6.9%. It would be inappropriate to use an average because doing so would assume that each comparable is equally weighted, or equally comparable to the subject property. The most appropriate method would be to examine each of the transactions to determine an appropriate and market-supported capitalization rate for the subject property. This narrowing process includes considering the physical, locational, financial, and transactional characteristics of each property in comparison with the subject property.

After determining the proper capitalization rate, the following formula is used to find the value of the property:

$$Value = \frac{NOI_o}{R_o}$$

Using a 6.5% capitalization rate supported by the preceding data, we could estimate the value of a property with an NOI of $22,890 as follows:

$22,890/0.085 = $352,153 Which rounds to: $350,000

Mortgage-Equity Capitalization Rate

A capitalization rate may also be derived from the capital markets. Direct capitalization from mortgage-equity analysis recognizes that when debt is used, the lender and equity investors are due a return on and of their investment. The mortgage-equity technique, sometimes referred to as the band-of-investment technique, derives a capitalization rate by calculating the weighted average of the first-year cash returns to the lender and equity investor. The formula for mortgage-equity analysis is as follows:

$$R_o = M(R_m) + (1 - M)R_e$$

M = the loan-to-value ratio (1 – M) = the equity portion
R_m = the mortgage constant R_e = the equity dividend rate

This technique assumes that similar properties are being acquired with debt and equity—a mortgage loan from a financial institution (debt) and a down payment (equity) from the equity investor. The mortgage loan requires the owner to make a monthly payment. The annualized monthly payment is referred to as the annual debt service (DS). Deducting annual debt service from net operating income (NOI_0) results in before-tax cash flow (BTCF). We can think of NOI as being distributed to both debt and equity holders. This concept is illustrated as follows:

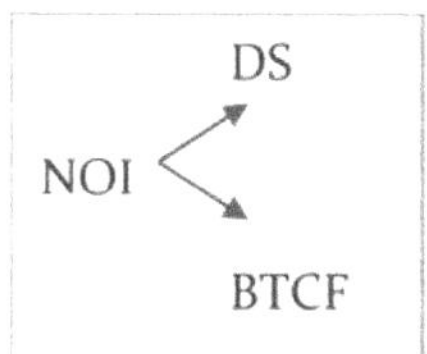

Because NOI can be partitioned between debt service and before tax cash flow, the debt service can be considered the net income to the debt, and the before-tax cash flow can be considered the net income to the equity. This produces the following equalities:

$$R_m = \frac{Debt\ Service}{Loan\ Amount} \quad R_e = \frac{BTCF}{Equity\ Amount}$$

$$R_o = \frac{NOI_o}{P}$$

R_m is the mortgage capitalization rate (or mortgage constant), and R_e is the equity capitalization rate (also referred to as the equity dividend rate or the before-tax cash-on-cash return). The purchase price (P) can be derived by combining the loan amount and the equity amount, so the capitalization rate (R_0) can be thought of as the weighted average of the mortgage capitalization rate (R_m) and the equity capitalization rate (R_e). Once R_0 is derived, the subject's value can be estimated by dividing the subject property's net operating income (NOI_0) by the capitalization rate (R_0).

The mortgage capitalization rate (R_m) can be derived in two ways: (1) annual debt service can be divided by the loan amount (as previously illustrated), or (2) the mortgage constant can be calculated if the terms of the mortgage (i.e., the interest rate, payment frequency, and loan term) are known. The derivation of the latter technique is shown here:

$$PVA = Ann\left[\frac{1-\frac{1}{\left(1+\frac{i}{m}\right)^{nm}}}{\frac{i}{m}}\right]$$

PVA = present value of an annuity
Ann = periodic annuity payment
i = annual mortgage interest rate
n = term of the mortgage in years
m = frequency of payments per year

The term in brackets is referred to as the present value annuity factor. Note that the loan amount and debt service can be substituted for PVA and Ann, respectively, as follows:

$$Loan\ Amount = DS\left[\frac{1-\frac{1}{\left(1+\frac{i}{m}\right)^{nm}}}{\frac{i}{m}}\right]$$

The reciprocal of the present value annuity factor is the mortgage constant (MC), as shown here:

$$\frac{Debt\ Service}{Loan\ Amount} = \frac{\frac{i}{m}}{1-\frac{1}{\left(1+\frac{i}{m}\right)^{nm}}} \times m = R_m = MC$$

Mortgage-Equity (Band-of-Investment) Example

After researching market data and talking with market participants, an analyst finds that cash-on-cash returns (equity dividend rates) cluster around 3%, that the NOI of the subject property is $22,890, and that typical loan terms are as follows:

LTV ratio	75%
Mortgage interest rate	5.50%
Loan amortization period	20 years
Periodic payments per year	12

Based on this information, we can calculate the overall capitalization rate using the band-of-investment technique and compute the value of the subject property:

$$R_o - M(R_m) + (1 - M)R_e$$

$$R_o = 0.75\left[\frac{\frac{0.0550}{12}}{1-\frac{1}{\left(1+\frac{0.0550}{12}\right)^{20(12)}}} \times 12\right] + 0.25(0.03)$$

$$R_o = 0.75(0.08254) + 0.25(0.030) = 0.06941$$

$$Value = \frac{NOI_o}{R_o}$$

$$\frac{\$22{,}890}{0.0694} = \$ \quad Value\ is\ rounded\ to: \$330{,}000$$

Effective Gross Income Multiplier

Applying the effective gross income multiplier (EGIM) is very straightforward. First, effective gross income multipliers are derived from the comparable sales. Second, an appropriate effective gross income multiplier is selected and applied to the subject property's effective gross income to arrive at an estimate of value, as shown in the following formula:

$$Value = EGIM \times EGI$$

The bracketing and narrowing process (finding the range of values and determining the correct value to use for a specific analysis) is very similar to the process described in the direct capitalization approach.

For example, assume that a property's first-year effective gross income was estimated at $45,300. Also assume the comparables are those shown in the sales comparison grid illustrated in Exhibit 10.1 and show a range in effective gross income multipliers from 6.8 to 7.67. Finally, assume that a multiplier of 7.5 is considered reasonable for the subject property. With this information, the value of the subject property would be determined as follows:

$$Value = 7.5 \times \$45{,}300 = \$340{,}000 \text{ rounded}$$

Discounted Cash Flow Analysis

The discounted cash flow analysis has three basic steps:

Step 1: Estimate cash flows before debt service over the projected holding period.

Step 2: Estimate the property reversion at the end of the holding period.

Step 3: Discount the cash flows before debt service and the property reversion to the present period at an appropriate discount rate.

The property reversion is synonymous with the forecasted value of the property at the end of the projection period less selling expenses. The forecast future value of the property is calculated by capitalizing the net operating income at time n + 1 (where n is the projection period) by a reversionary capitalization rate, sometimes referred to as a going-out cap rate or terminal cap rate or exit cap rate. A survey of market participants generally provides the best estimate of a reversionary cap rate. Together with the time n + 1 NOI, the reversionary cap rate can be used to estimate the future sales price with the following formula:

$$Future\ Sales\ Price = \frac{NOI_{n+1}}{Reversionary\ Cap\ Rate}$$

After estimating the future value of the property at the end of the holding period, the reversion is calculated by deducting selling expenses as follows:

$$Reversion = Future\ Sales\ Price - Selling\ Expenses$$

For example, if a property has a projected holding period of five years, a reversionary cap rate of 7.25%, an NOI of $28,658 in year 6, and selling expenses equal to 5% of the future sales price, its reversion would be calculated as follows:

Future Sales Price = $28,658/0.0725 = $395,282

Reversion = $395,282 x 0.95 = $375,514

Exhibit 10.2 shows a table of annual NOI cash flows with this reversion cash flow forecast.

Exhibit 10.2: Cash Flows Table

Year	1	2	3	4	5
NOI	$22,890	$24,035	$25,236	$26,498	$27,823
Reversion					$375,514
Total CF	$22,890	$24,035	$25,236	$26,498	$403,337

Selecting an Appropriate Discount Rate

Once total cash flows have been estimated over the projected holding period, the present value of those cash flows can be calculated by discounting them at an appropriate rate. In a real estate valuation context, the proper discount rate is the free-and-clear (i.e., without debt), before-tax rate of return required by a typical investor. Investors estimate the required rate of return for an investment by considering the risk involved and by comparing returns available on alternative and competing investment opportunities. Investors can build up a discount rate by considering proper compensation for four factors: (1) giving up control of money (compensation equals the risk-free rate), (2) giving up liquidity, (3) spending time in investment management, and (4) bearing unique investment risk. This "build-up" method of choosing a discount rate is illustrated here:

Risk-free rate	3%
Liquidity risk	1%
Management intensive	2%
Unique investment risk	3%
Total	9%

Even though individual investors may use this technique to formulate a discount rate when buying a property, investors should first focus on estimating market value—what the typical buyer would pay for the property.

A better method for estimating a discount rate involves carefully surveying market participants who are buying and selling similar properties in the area. Because of competitive market forces, discount rates tend to cluster for specific types of properties in specific locations. In the survey process, investors need to clearly communicate with market participants to ensure that they are comparing apples to apples. For instance, all discount rates should be the free-and-clear, before-tax rates of return and should be applied to cash flows before debt service.

After researching and surveying a primary market, investors often find it helpful to benchmark their results with third-party data providers.

Once an investor has selected an appropriate discount rate, he or she can discount future cash flows to the present by multiplying the cash flows by present value factors. Present value factors are calculated as follows:

$$PV = \frac{1}{(1+i)^n}$$

PV = present value　　i = discount rate
FV = future value　　n = term

Exhibit 10.3 shows the application of the present value factors to arrive at the present value of the property assuming a discount rate of 9%.

Summing the present values for each year results in a total present value of $341,628.

Exhibit 10.3: Example of Present Value Factors

Year	1	2	3	4	5
NOI	$22,890	$24,035	$25,236	$26,498	$27,823
Reversion					$375,514
Total CF	$22,890	$24,035	$25,236	$26,498	$403,337
PV Factors	0.91743	0.84167	0.77218	0.70842	0.64993
Present Value	$20,999.97	$20,229.12	$19,486.91	$18,771.74	$262,140.60

RELATED RESOURCES

What You Should Know about Real Estate Valuation
http://www.investopedia.com/articles/realestate/12/real-estate-valuation.asp

Real Estate Appraisal
http://thismatter.com/money/real-estate/real-estate-appraisal.htm

When to Use the Cost Approach
http://realestateandappraisal.blogspot.com/2008/02/cost-approach-appraisal-method.html

How to Calculate Capitalization Rate for Real Estate
https://www.thebalancesmb.com/how-to-calculate-capitalization-rate-for-real-estate-2866786

CHAPTER 11

Mortgage Financing for Investment Properties

INTRODUCTION

In an earlier chapter, we carefully reviewed the concepts and mathematics of mortgage financing for homeownership. This section builds on that foundation by discussing the nuances of mortgage financing for small investment properties.

COMMERCIAL MORTGAGE FINANCING

Although there is a market for commercial mortgage-backed securities, that market is reserved for large commercial properties that are out of reach for most households. Therefore, most financial institutions retain the mortgage loans they underwrite for small investment properties. This leads to greater customization in the mortgage underwriting process.

As an investor prepares to purchase a small investment property, he or she should begin working with a commercial loan officer at a local bank or credit union. When meeting with a potential lender, investors are typically required to bring pro forma operating statements for the property they are considering that show anticipated rental revenue and operating expenses. Commercial lenders have their unique underwriting standards, but investors may begin to notice considerable uniformity as they shop around in their area. Exhibit 11.1 provides an sample of standard loan characteristics for several smaller property types, including residential homes; condos; two-to-four family units; small office, retail, and industrial properties; and small tracts of land.

EXHIBIT 11.1: SAMPLE LOAN CHARACTERISTICS BY PROPERTY TYPE

	Loan-to-Value Ratios (LTVs)	Terms	Interest Rates	Debt Coverage Ratios (DCRs)	Points	Origination Fees
SFR Home Investment	< 70–80%	25- or 10-yr. fixed; 7-, 5-, 3-yr. adjustable	4–6% (adjustable is prime plus .2–.75%)	1.2:1	~1% due at origination	Admin., appraisal, inspection (for construction); case by case
Residential Condo Investment	< 70–80%	25- or 10-yr. fixed; 7-, 5-, 3-yr. adjustable	4–6% (adjustable is prime plus .2–.75%)	1.2:1	~1% due at origination	Admin., appraisal, inspection (for construction); case by case
2–4 Multifamily	< 70–80%	35- or 10-yr. fixed; 7-, 5-, 3-yr. adjustable	4–6% (adjustable is prime plus .2–.75%)	1.2:1	~1% due at origination	Admin., appraisal, inspection (for construction); case by case
Small Office, Retail, Industrial	< 60–70%	25- or 10-yr. fixed; 7-, 5-, 3-yr. adjustable	4–6% (adjustable is prime plus .2–.75%)	1.35:1	~1% due at origination	Admin., appraisal, inspection (for construction); case by case
Land	< 50–60%	25- or 10-yr. fixed; 7-, 5-, 3-yr. adjustable	5–6% (adjustable is prime plus .2–.75%)	1.35:1	~1% due at origination	Admin., appraisal, inspection (for construction); case by case

Source: *Data from Wells Fargo, Zions Bank, and Utah Community Credit Union (UCCU; May 2020)*

- The LTV ratios required by credit unions are usually lower than for commercial banks because they cannot bear the same level of risk.
- Loan terms are unique to each institution, but most offer fixed- and adjustable-rate loans. (For example, UCCU's ten-year fixed-rate mortgage uses the first ten years of payments for a twenty-year mortgage and balloons the remaining payments at year ten.)
- Interest rates depend on the borrower's credit rating and are often determined case by case. In general, interest rates for nonowner-occupied properties are higher than for standard mortgages. For adjustable-rate loans, interest rates are determined at signing as the prime rate plus a predetermined spread.
- Debt coverage ratios are consistent for residential properties but move higher for retail, office, and industrial properties

and for land due to their greater risk.

- Most lenders require at least 1% at signing. Some lenders refer to this as points, while others call it a loan origination fee.
- Some lenders charge administrative and appraisal fees for some property types. These fees are often determined on a case-by-case basis.
- Vacant land has many nuances due to its unique risks as an investment. Some lenders will not approve loans on vacant land, while others will but with stricter underwriting requirements. Raw or unimproved land poses the greatest risk to lenders. Therefore, the few lenders who offer loans on unimproved land charge high interest rates with low LTVs.

RELATED RESOURCES

Complete Guide to Investment Property Mortgages
https://mymortgageinsider.com/the-complete-guide-to-investment-property-mortgages-in-2018/

What to Know about Investment Property Mortgage Rates
https://www.lendingtree.com/home/mortgage/investment-property-mortgage-rates/

Six Types of Loans for Investment Properties
https://www.mashvisor.com/blog/6-types-loans-for-investment-properties/

CHAPTER 12

Real Estate Investment Analysis

INTRODUCTION

In the previous chapter, we examined some of the foundational qualitative decisions essential to successful real estate investment. In this chapter, we will work through the quantitative analysis necessary to make informed investment decisions. We'll do this by working step by step through an actual case study.

CASE STUDY

Let's start with our investor: Sally Haws. Sally is a single woman living in Dallas, Texas. She works for a consulting firm, and her adjusted gross income, after deductions, is $65,000. For the past year, Sally has been seriously considering purchasing a condo near the local university for investment purposes. She has saved $25,000 to invest in the condo, which she plans on keeping for about five years. Sally has looked at several properties and is interested in unit #102 at Courtside Condos. She wants the property to provide an after-tax rate of return of at least 9%. Sally is also interested in any tax benefits she would receive by investing in real estate. Exhibit 12.1 (on the following page) shows the federal marginal income tax rates for the 2020 tax year.

Given that Sally is a single woman and that her adjusted gross income is $65,000, her marginal tax rate is 22%. This means that each additional dollar Sally earns will be taxed at 22%, which is important to know as she analyzes an income-producing investment property.

EXHIBIT 12.1: MARGINAL INCOME TAX RATES (2020)

Tax rate	Single	Married, filing jointly	Married, filing separately	Head of household
10%	$0 to $9,875	$0 to $19,750	$0 to $9,875	$0 to $14,100
12%	$9,876 to $40,125	$19,751 to $80,250	$9,876 to $40,125	$14,101 to $53,700
22%	$40,126 to $85,525	$80,251 to $171,050	$40,126 to $85,525	$53,701 to $85,500
24%	$85,526 to $163,300	$171,051 to $326,600	$85,526 to $163,300	$85,501 to $163,300
32%	$163,301 to $207,350	$326,601 to $414,700	$163,301 to $207,350	$163,301 to $207,350
35%	$207,351 to $518,400	$414,701 to $622,050	$207,351 to $311,025	$207,351 to $518,400
37%	$518,401 or more	$622,051 or more	$311,026 or more	$518,401 or more

Courtside Condos is located at 948 N. Maple Street in Dallas, Texas. The condos are just one block from campus near the tennis courts and indoor track facilities. The rent rate for unit #102 is $1,350 per month, and the tenant pays for utilities. Historical rents in the area have been growing at a rate of approximately 4% per year. Over the past three years, the condo has been vacant for about one month per year.

The asking price for the condo is $159,900, but Sally believes she can purchase it for $155,000. Annual operating expenses for the condo include $700 for property taxes, $500 for interior maintenance, $210 for a landlord condo insurance policy, and $1,080 for condo association fees. The condo association fees cover water, trash pickup, insurance, and maintenance. The association fees, local property taxes, interior maintenance, and insurance expenses have been growing at a rate of approximately 3% annually.

After investigating the local market, Sally believes that the property's future operating performance will be very similar to its historical performance. She also estimates that the property will appreciate at approximately 4% per year, providing a forecasted sales price at the end of five years of $189,000. Sally expects total selling expenses at the end of her holding period to be 8% of the sales price.

The Hidden Vale Management Company currently manages the property. They charge 7% of effective gross income and provide many services to condo owners, including filling vacancies by advertising and posting openings and overseeing regular cleaning checks and needed maintenance.

Even though the management company provides many services, it still encourages owners to make many of the significant decisions for their property. These decisions include setting rental terms, approving expenses and capital improvements, and giving final approval on tenants. By maintaining this level of involvement, the owners are considered active participants in the rental activities for tax purposes[30].

Sally has a long-standing relationship with The Mortgage Company and has decided to get a mortgage loan from them. Sally wants a thirty-year, fixed-rate loan, and she wants to use her $25,000 in savings to cover the down payment and all closing costs. The current mortgage rate offered to people with Sally's credit history and annual income is 6%.

Sally expects that her total closing costs, including mortgage fees, title, and escrow, will be approximately $3,400 (see Exhibit 12.2), leaving $21,600 for a down payment. Her loan amount would be $133,400. Because her down payment would be less than 20% of the

Exhibit 12.2: Estimated Closing Costs

1% Origination Fee	$1,334
0% Discount Points	$0
Application Fee	$200
Appraisal Fee	$550
Tax Services/Flood Certification	$90
2 Months' Property Taxes	$150
Title Company Fee	$200
Document Preparation Fee	$195
Title Insurance	$605
Recording Fees	$50
Association Fee	$26
Total	**$3,400**

30. See instructions for Form 8582 at https://www.irs.gov/forms-pubs/about-form-8582

purchase price, The Mortgage Company would require Sally to pay $80 per month for private mortgage insurance (PMI).

After researching the immediate market, Sally has compiled the following comparable data (see Exhibit 12.3).

Exhibit 12.3: Comparable Properties

	Courtside #102	Courtside #104	Courtside #203	Chatsworth #7
	Subject	Comp 1	Comp 2	Comp 3
Sale Price	$155,000 ??	$158,000	$154,000	$159,000
Sale Date	??	2 Months	5 Months	2 Months
Living Area (sq. ft.)	950	950	900	1,000
Rent (monthly)	$1,350	$1,400	$1,350	$1,350
Vacancy %/Yr.	8.33%	5%	8.33%	0%
Operating Exp. Ratio	24%	25%	24%	26%
Bedrooms	2	2	2	2
Bathrooms	2	2	2	2
Washer/Dryer?	Yes	Yes	Yes	Yes
Includes Utilities?	No	No	No	No
Covered Parking?	Yes	Yes	Yes	Yes
A/C?	Yes	Yes	Yes	Yes
Pool/Lounge?	No	No	No	No
Dishwasher?	Yes	Yes	Yes	Yes

DERIVING THE REAL ESTATE FINANCIAL STATEMENTS

Now that we've reviewed the case information, we need to construct pro forma real estate financial statements (operating and reversion). We do this one line at a time. First, let's look at a completely unpopulated annual operating statement (see Exhibit 12.4 on the following page).

Up to this point, net operating income (NOI) has been the primary emphasis of the operating statement because our focus has been on valuation. Now that we are focusing on investment analysis, many more line items on the operating statement apply to our case study. Eventually, we want to estimate after-tax cash flow for each year that Sally anticipates holding the property, but before we get there, let's review each line of the operating statement in the context of the Courtside Condos case study.

Exhibit 12.4: Blank Annual Operating Statement

Operating Statement						
	Year 0	Year 1	Year 2	Year 3	Year 4	Year 5
Potential Gross Income	--					
Less Vacancy & CL	--					
Plus Other Income	--					
Effective Gross Income	--					
Operating Expenses	--					
Property Taxes	--					
Condo Insurance	--					
Property Mgt. Fee	--					
Association Fees	--					
Interior Maintenance	--					
Total Operating Expenses	--					
Net Operating Income	--					
Less Annual Private Mortgage Ins.	--					
Less Annual Debt Service	--					
Before Tax Cash Flow	--					
Less Annual Depreciation	--					
Plus Annual Principal Paid	--					
Taxable Income/ (Loss)	--					
Less Taxes Due	--					
Tax Savings from PAL	--					
After Tax Cash Flow from Operations	--					
Initial Equity Investment						
After Tax Cash on Sale (Reversion)						
Total After Tax Cash Flow						

Potential Gross Income

Our analysis begins with the potential gross income (PGI). PGI is found by estimating the condo's potential rental income (annualized), assuming market rents at 100% occupancy. In the case study, Sally found that Courtside Condos unit #102 is expected to rent for $1,350 per month. Therefore, its PGI is $16,200 ($1,350 x 12).

Vacancy & Collection Loss

Following PGI, expected annual vacancy and collection loss (VAC) is the next line item on the operating statement. This forecast can either be a specific dollar amount or a percentage of PGI.

Forecasted VAC varies from market to market and can usually be obtained by analyzing the vacancy and collection loss of similar properties in the market area. For Courtside Condos, vacancy is expected to be one month out of the year, so annual VAC is $1,350.

Other Income

Other income (OI) consists of any nonrental income, such as revenue generated from a coin-operated laundry, vending machines, or parking fees. Deducting vacancy and collection loss from and adding other income to potential gross income results in effective gross income (EGI). The condo Sally is considering generates no nonrental income, so its EGI is $14,850.

Operating Expenses

From EGI, we subtract operating expenses (OE). Common examples of operating costs include property taxes, property insurance, HOA fees, management fees, utilities paid by the landlord, marketing and advertising, repairs and maintenance, supplies, and legal fees. Operating expenses tend to vary by property type and geographic market. In the Courtside Condos case, Sally found that property taxes were $700, condo insurance was $210, property management was 7% of EGI, association fees were $1,080 per year, and interior maintenance was $500 per year.

Net Operating Income

Net operating income (NOI) is calculated by deducting operating expenses (OE) from effective gross income (EGI). NOI is considered to be property specific and should be the same irrespective of who owns the property (assuming that owners are rational, profit-maximizing entities). This is why NOI is essential for valuation. However, in our case study, we want to examine the property from Sally's perspective, so we will venture further down the operating statement. Even so, for Courtside Condos unit #102, Sally can estimate NOI at $11,320.

After calculating NOI, we next calculate annual costs associated with mortgage debt. This includes annualized monthly mortgage principal and interest payments—called debt service (DS) payments—as well as mortgage insurance, if required by the lender, which is called private mortgage insurance (PMI). The contemporary convention is to separate these items on the operating statement. Deducting debt service (DS) and private mortgage insurance (PMI) from NOI results in before-tax cash flow (BTCF). In the Courtside Condos case study, Sally estimated PMI at $960 ($80 x 12). To calculate the annual debt service, she would need to generate an amortization statement as follows (see Exhibit 12.5):

EXHIBIT 12.5: AMORTIZATION TABLE

Period	Payment	Interest	Principal	Balance
0	-	-	-	133,400.00
1	799.80	667.00	132.80	133,267.20
2	799.80	666.34	133.46	133,133.74
3	799.80	665.67	134.13	132,999.60
4	799.80	665.00	134.80	132,864.80
5	799.80	664.32	135.48	132,729.32
6	799.80	663.65	136.15	132,593.17
7	799.80	662.97	136.83	132,456.34
8	799.80	662.28	137.52	132,318.82
9	799.80	661.59	138.21	132,180.61
10	799.80	660.90	138.90	132,041.71
11	799.80	660.21	139.59	131,902.12
12	799.80	659.51	140.29	131,761.83
Total			1,638.17	
13	799.80	658.81	140.99	131,620.84
14	799.80	658.10	141.70	131,479.14
15	799.80	657.40	142.40	131,336.74
16	799.80	656.68	143.12	131,193.62
17	799.80	655.97	143.83	131,049.79
18	799.80	655.25	144.55	130,905.24
19	799.80	654.53	145.27	130,759.97
20	799.80	653.80	146.00	130,613.97
21	799.80	653.07	146.73	130,467.23
22	799.80	652.34	147.46	130,319.77
23	799.80	651.60	148.20	130,171.57
24	799.80	650.86	148.94	130,022.63
Total			1,739.21	
25	799.80	650.11	149.69	129,872.94
26	799.80	649.36	150.44	129,722.50
27	799.80	648.61	151.19	129,571.32
28	799.80	647.86	151.94	129,419.37
29	799.80	647.10	152.70	129,266.67
30	799.80	646.33	153.47	129,113.20
31	799.80	645.57	154.23	128,958.97
32	799.80	644.79	155.01	128,803.96
33	799.80	644.02	155.78	128,648.18
34	799.80	643.24	156.56	128,491.62
35	799.80	642.46	157.34	128,334.28
36	799.80	641.67	158.13	128,176.15
Total			1,846.48	

Period	Payment	Interest	Principal	Balance
37	799.80	640.88	158.92	128,017.23
38	799.80	640.09	159.71	127,857.52
39	799.80	639.29	160.51	127,697.00
40	799.80	638.49	161.32	127,535.69
41	799.80	637.68	162.12	127,373.57
42	799.80	636.87	162.93	127,210.63
43	799.80	636.05	163.75	127,046.89
44	799.80	635.23	164.57	126,882.32
45	799.80	634.41	165.39	126,716.93
46	799.80	633.58	166.22	126,550.72
47	799.80	632.75	167.05	126,383.67
48	799.80	631.92	167.88	126,215.79
Total			1,960.36	
49	799.80	631.08	168.72	126,047.06
50	799.80	630.24	169.57	125,877.50
51	799.80	629.39	170.41	125,707.09
52	799.80	628.54	171.26	125,535.82
53	799.80	627.68	172.12	125,363.70
54	799.80	626.82	172.98	125,190.72
55	799.80	625.95	173.85	125,016.87
56	799.80	625.00	174.72	124,842.16
57	799.80	624.21	175.59	124,666.57
58	799.80	623.33	176.47	124,490.10
59	799.80	622.45	177.35	124,312.75
60	799.80	621.56	178.24	124,134.51
Total			2,081.27	

The monthly payment is $799.80, so Sally's annual debt service (DS) would be $9,598. After she deducted annual PMI and DS from NOI, Sally's before-tax cash flow (BTCF) for Courtside Condos #102 would be $762.

INCOME TAX ANALYSIS AND BENEFITS

Before calculating taxes owed on an investment property, we first need to understand two important deductions allowed by the IRS: (1) property depreciation and (2) mortgage interest.

Property Depreciation

Depreciation applies only to investment properties, not primary residences. Irs.gov says that "[any] residential rental property placed in service after 1986 is depreciated using the Modified Accelerated Cost Recovery System (MACRS), an accounting technique that spreads costs (and depreciation deductions) over 27.5 years (residential real estate) or 39 years (commercial real estate)." These irregular time frames are the periods that the IRS considers to be the "useful life" of rental properties.[31]

While investors should almost always work with a qualified tax accountant to calculate depreciation, the basic steps are (1) determining the basis of the property, (2) separating the cost of the land and buildings, (3) determining the adjusted basis if necessary, and (4) depreciating the property.

1. **Determining the basis of the property.** The basis[32] of a property is generally its cost: the amount the investor paid (in cash, with a mortgage, or in some other manner) to acquire the property. Some settlement fees and closing costs, including

---

31. Source: irs.gov
32. Examples of increases to basis include the cost of any additions or improvements (that have a useful life of at least one year) made before you place the property in service, such as money you spent to restore damaged property, the cost of bringing utility services to the property, and certain legal fees. Examples of decreases to basis include: insurance payments you receive as the result of damage or theft, casualty loss not covered by your insurance for which you took a deduction, and money you receive for granting an easement

legal fees, recording fees, surveys, transfer taxes, title insurance, and any amount the seller owes that the buyer agreed to pay (such as back taxes), are also included in the basis.

2. **Separating the cost of the land and buildings.** Investors can only depreciate building costs, not land costs, so they must determine the value of each in order to depreciate the correct amount. Investors can separate out the building and the land costs in two ways. They can either (1) use the fair market value (FMV) of each at the time they purchased the property or (2) base their estimates on assessed real estate tax values. For example, an investor bought a house for $110,000. The most recent real estate tax assessment valued the property at $90,000, of which $81,000 was for the house and $9,000 was for the land. In this situation, the investor could allocate 90% ($81,000/$90,000) of the purchase price to the house and 10% ($9,000/$90,000) of the purchase price to the land.
3. **Determining the adjusted basis (if necessary).** Investors sometimes have to increase or decrease their basis for certain events that happen between the time they buy the property and the time they have it ready for rental.
4. **Depreciating the property.** Depreciation is based on property type and the applicable depreciation rate.

A key thing to remember when calculating depreciation is to be sure to depreciate only improvements and property additions (e.g., buildings and capital expenses that extend property life) and not the land. The land is never depreciated.

For the Courtside Condos case study, let's assume that the land is worth 10% of the property value, which results in an improvement value of $139,500 ($155,000 x 0.90). Because Courtside Condos #102 is a residential property, Sally would depreciate it over 27.5 years. Therefore, the property's annual depreciation would be $5,072 ($139,500/27.5).

Mortgage Interest Deduction

When Congress made all interest tax-deductible when it created the first modern federal income tax in 1894 and when it revised the tax in 1913, it was probably thinking of business interest and not homeowner interest. At the time, most people purchased their homes with cash without borrowing money. Since interest was considered a business expense, it was naturally deducted from income before taxes, and businesses were taxed on after-tax income, just as they are today.

In real estate financial statements, mortgage interest and principal payments are both deducted to calculate before-tax cash flow. Then, principal paid is added back in further down the operating statement to calculate taxable income. Therefore, real estate operating statements do remove interest expense from taxable income as a "business expense," albeit in a roundabout way.

It is important to remember that an amortization table is beneficial for calculating interest paid annually. Also, the CUMIPMT Excel function can accomplish the same objective. However, investors should be sure to fully understand the formula (perhaps double-checking a few times) before using it in their analysis.

Taxable Income

Taxable income is calculated by deducting depreciation from and adding principal paid to before-tax cash flow. For Courtside Condos #102, depreciation was estimated to be $5,072 per year, and mortgage principal was estimated to be $1,638 for the first year (see amortization table in Exhibit 12.5). Therefore, Sally's taxable income for the first year would be –$2,672 (BTCF $762 – Depreciation $5,072 + Mortgage Principal $1,638).

Taxes Due

Because Courtside Condos #102 would experience a paper loss according to the IRS in its first year, Sally would not have any taxes due to her rental income. Instead, it should probably reduce her overall tax liability by using the losses from her investment property to offset her other income. Before considering this option, let's review two important tax concepts: passive income and active income.

Passive Activity Loss (PAL) Rules

All rental activities and income are considered passive. The IRS allows taxpayers to offset passive income with passive losses. However, exceptions exist for real estate professionals and "active participants" in real estate investments. Investors who do not meet the requirements to be considered a real estate professional usually benefit the most from the special allowance for "active participants."

To be considered a real estate professional, investors need to be involved in real property development, redevelopment, construction, reconstruction, acquisition, conversion, rental, operation, management, leasing, or brokerage. For investors who qualify as professionals, real estate investment income is considered active income, which is fully deductible from ordinary income.

Active participation is a different concept and refers to landlords who actively approve tenants, set rental rates and terms, and approve capital and repair expenditures. If investors qualify as active participants, they receive a special allowance to offset up to $25,000 of ordinary income with passive losses. However, it is important to note that this is the case only if the investor's MAGI (taxable income) is less than $100,000. If the investor's MAGI is greater than $100,000 but less than $150,000, his or her special allowance is reduced by 50% of the amount of his or her income that is greater than $100,000. Finally, if these criteria are correctly met, investors' passive activity loss (PAL) is calculated by multiplying their taxable losses by their marginal tax rate.

Sally, our investor, would qualify as an active participant and has MAGI of less than $100,000. Therefore, she could take the loss of $2,672 on Courtside Condos #102 and use it to offset her other income. This would result in savings from Passive Activity Loss Rules of $588 ($2,672 x 0.22 tax bracket).

After-Tax Cash Flow

Now that we know that Sally would not owe taxes and that she would get a benefit of $588 from PAL, we can calculate her first-year after-tax cash flow as follows:

Before-tax cash flow	$762
less taxes	0
plus PAL	$588
After-tax cash flow	$1,350

Now that we have completed the operating statement for the first year, let's complete the operating statement over the remaining four years of the five-year holding period. According to the case study, rents are forecast to grow at 4% per year, and operating expenses are forecast to grow at 3% per year. Applying these rates to the first-year estimates produces the following completed operating statement (see Exhibit 12.6):

Exhibit 12.6: Completed Operating Statement

Operating Statement						
	Year 0	Year 1	Year 2	Year 3	Year 4	Year 5
Potential Gross Income	--	$16,200	$16,848	$17,522	$18,223	$18,952
Less Vacancy & CL	--	-$1,350	-$1,404	-$1,460	-$1,519	-$1,579
Plus Other Income	--	$0	$0	$0	$0	$0
Effective Gross Income	--	$14,850	$15,444	$16,062	$16,704	$17,372
Operating Expenses	--					
Property Taxes	--	-$700	-$721	-$743	-$765	-$788
Condo Insurance	--	-$210	-$216	-$223	-$229	-$236
Property Mgt. Fee	--	-$1,040	-$1,081	-$1,124	-$1,169	-$1,216
Association Fees	--	-$1,080	-$1,112	-$1,146	-$1,180	-$1,216
Interior Maintenance	--	-$500	-$515	-$530	-$546	-$563
Total Oper. Expenses	--	-$3,530	-$3,646	-$3,766	-$3,890	-$4,019
Net Operating Income	--	$11,321	$11,798	$12,296	$12,814	$13,354
Less Annual Private Mortgage Ins.	--	-$960	-$960	-$960	-$960	-$960
Less Annual Debt Service	--	-$9,598	-$9,598	-$9,598	-$9,598	-$9,598
Before Tax Cash Flow	--	$763	$1,240	$1,738	$2,256	$2,796
Less Annual Depreciation	--	-$5,072	-$5,072	-$5,072	-$5,072	-$5,072
Plus Annual Principal Paid	--	$1,638	$1,739	$1,846	$1,960	$2,081
Taxable Income/ (Loss)	--	-$2,672	-$2,093	-$1,488	-$856	-$195
Less Taxes Due	--	$0	$0	$0	$0	$0
Tax Savings from PAL	--	$588	$460	$327	$188	$43
After Tax Cash Flow from Operations	--	$1,350	$1,701	$2,065	$2,444	$2,839
Initial Equity Investment						
After Tax Cash on Sale (Reversion)						
Total After Tax Cash Flow						

Termination (Reversion) Statement

After constructing the operating statement, you're probably excited to see the word *termination*. The Termination, or Reversion, Statement calculates the cash that "reverts" to the owner upon sale of the property and considers two important tax calculations: (1) capital gains and (2) depreciation recapture.

Capital Gains Tax

The IRS discusses the proper treatment of capital gains (losses) in Topic 409:

> Almost everything you own and use for personal or investment purposes is a capital asset. Examples include a home, personal-use items like household furnishings, and stocks or bonds held as investments. When you sell a capital asset, the difference between the adjusted basis in the asset and the amount you realized from the sale is a capital gain or a capital loss. Generally, an asset's basis is its cost to the owner. (irs.gov)

Capital Gain = Net Sales Proceeds — (Original Purchase Price + Improvements)

To calculate capital gains taxes upon the sale of an investment property, investors must first determine whether the property was held for less than (short-term) or more than (long-term) one year. Short-term capital gains and losses are taxed as ordinary income at the investor's marginal tax rate. However, long-term capital gains and losses are taxed at either 0%, 15%, or 20% (see Exhibit 12.7), so holding an asset for longer than a year can be extremely beneficial.

EXHIBIT 12.7: 2020 CAPITAL GAINS TAX TABLE

Filing Status	0% Rate Applies	15% Rate Applies	20% Rate Applies
Single	Up to $40,000	$40,000 to $441,450	Above $441,450
Married Filing Jointly	Up to $80,000	$80,000 to $496,600	Above $496,600
Head of Household	Up to $53,600	$53,600 to $469,050	Above $469,050
Married Filing Separately	Up to $40,000	$40,000 to $248,300	Above $248,30

Unless investors are excited by the thought of paying more taxes, they quickly realize that long-term capital gains tax rates are much lower than their marginal tax rate.

Depreciation Recapture Tax

While investors hold an investment property, the IRS allows them to deduct depreciation attributed to the property's building improvements according to a straight-line schedule (27.5 years for residential properties and 39 years for nonresidential properties). As shown previously, this consistently lowers taxes during the holding period. However, this changes when investors sell their property. If the property has not depreciated at the rate calculated, then investors must pay a "recapture" tax on that depreciation at either their marginal tax rate or 25%, whichever is lower.

Now that we understand the basic concepts of long-term capital gains and recapture taxes, let's calculate the after-tax cash flow at reversion for Courtside Condos #102. We can use the following template for this calculation (see Exhibit 12.8):

Exhibit 12.8: Blank Reversion Statement

Termination (Reversion) Statement	
Gross Future Sales Price	
Less Selling Expenses	
Net Sales Proceeds	
Less Mortgage Balance	
Before-Tax Cash on Sale	
Net Sales Proceeds	
Less Cost Basis	
Capital Gain (Economic Gain)	
x Capital Gains Rate	
Capital Gains Taxes	
Accumulated Depreciation	
x Recapture Tax Rate	
Recapture Taxes	
Before-Tax Cash on Sale	
Less Capital Gains Taxes	
Less Recapture Taxes	
After-Tax Cash on Sale	

Let's start with the first line-item, Gross Future Sales Price. This is the price that Sally expects to get from the condo when she sells it in the future. Since Sally plans to hold the property for five years and expects an appreciation rate of 4% per year, the forecast future sales price is $189,000. From the Gross Future Sales Price, we deduct selling expenses of 8%, or $15,120, providing Net Sales Proceeds of $173,880. After we have deducted selling expenses, we deduct the balance owed to the mortgage lender (refer to the amortization table in Exhibit 12.5), which amounts to $124,135. This results in a Before-Tax Cash on Sale of $49,745.

After paying the selling expenses and paying off the lender, Sally needs to settle up with Uncle Sam by deducting capital gains taxes and recapture taxes, if she owes any. To calculate capital gains taxes, we first deduct the Cost Basis from the Net Sales Proceeds. The cost basis is equal to the original purchase price plus any capital improvements. In the Courtside Condos case information, there is no mention of capital improvements, so the capital gain is simply $18,880 (Net Sales Proceeds of $173,880 – Cost Basis of $155,000).

We now need to estimate the future capital gains tax rate. Because they do not know what the capital gains rate will be in the future (five years in this case), many real estate investment analysts simply use the highest capital gains rate currently in the tax code. In this case, we would use 20%. By applying this rate to the capital gain of $18,880, the capital gains tax amounts to $3,776 ($18,800 x 0.20).

Next, we need to calculate the recapture taxes. We do this by first summing the annual depreciation we have taken over the entire holding period. Since Sally plans to deduct $5,072 in depreciation per year, her total accumulated depreciation would be $25,360 ($5,072 x 5 years). Because Sally is in the 22% marginal tax bracket, her recapture tax rate is 22%, so recapture taxes would amount to $5,579 ($25,360 x 0.22). If her marginal tax rate were higher than 25%, the recapture tax rate would cap out at 25%.

After deducting capital gains and recapture taxes, the after-tax cash flow at reversion is estimated at $40,390, as shown in Exhibit 12.9.

Exhibit 12.9: Completed Reversion Statement

Termination (Reversion) Statement	
Gross Future Sales Price	$189,000
Less Selling Expenses	$15,120
Net Sales Proceeds	$173,880
Less Mortgage Balance	$124,135
Before-Tax Cash on Sale	$49,745
Net Sales Proceeds	$173,880
Less Cost Basis	$155,000
Capital Gain (Economic Gain)	$18,880
x Capital Gains Rate	$0.22
Capital Gains Taxes	$3,776
Accumulated Depreciation	$25,360
x Recapture Tax Rate	$0.22
Recapture Taxes	$5,579
Before-Tax Cash on Sale	$49,745
Less Capital Gains Taxes	$3,776
Less Recapture Taxes	$5,579
After-Tax Cash on Sale	$40,390

Now that we have estimated the after-tax cash on sale, we can take that number, move back to the operating statement, and complete the remaining rows of the table. First, we include our initial equity investment of –$25,000 in year 0, and then we add the reversion value of $40,390 in year 5. After that, we bring all of the numbers to the bottom row. It is important to remember that in the fifth year, we need to add the after-tax cash flow from operations to the after-tax cash flow from reversion to obtain the total after-tax cash flow. The completed operating statement is shown in Exhibit 12.10.

Exhibit 12.10: Completed Operating Statement (with Reversion)

Operating Statement						
	Year 0	Year 1	Year 2	Year 3	Year 4	Year 5
Potential Gross Income	--	$16,200	$16,848	$17,522	$18,223	$18,952
Less Vacancy & CL	--	-$1,350	-$1,404	-$1,460	-$1,519	-$1,579
Plus Other Income	--	$0	$0	$0	$0	$0
Effective Gross Income	--	$14,850	$15,444	$16,062	$16,704	$17,372
Operating Expenses	--					
Property Taxes	--	-$700	-$721	-$743	-$765	-$788
Condo Insurance	--	-$210	-$216	-$223	-$229	-$236
Property Mgt. Fee	--	-$1,039.50	-$1,081	-$1,124	-$1,169	-$1,216
Association Fees	--	-$1,080	-$1,112	-$1,146	-$1,180	-$1,216
Interior Maintenance	--	-$500	-$515	-$530	-$546	-$563
Total Oper. Expenses	--	-$3,530	-$3,646	-$3,766	-$3,890	-$4,019
Net Operating Income	--	$11,321	$11,798	$12,296	$12,814	$13,354
Less Annual Private Mortgage Ins.	--	-$960	-$960	-$960	-$960	-$960
Less Annual Debt Service	--	-$9,598	-$9,598	-$9,598	-$9,598	-$9,598
Before Tax Cash Flow	--	$763	$1,240	$1,738	$2,256	$2,796
Less Annual Depreciation	--	-$5,072	-$5,072	-$5,072	-$5,072	-$5,072
Plus Annual Principal Paid	--	$1,639	$1,739	$1,846	$1,960	$2,081
Taxable Income/ (Loss)	--	-$2,671	-$2,093	-$1,488	-$856	-$195
Less Taxes Due	--	$0	$0	$0	$0	$0
Tax Savings from PAL	--	$588	$460	$327	$188	$43
After Tax Cash Flow from Operations	--	$1,350	$1,701	$2,065	$2,444	$2,839
Initial Equity Investment	-$25,000					
After Tax Cash on Sale (Reversion)						$40,390
Total After Tax Cash Flow	-$25,000	$1,350	$1,701	$2,065	$2,444	$43,229

Investment Measures and Analysis

Now that we have completed the operating statement, we can begin to analyze the anticipated performance of the property to see if it meets Sally's investment criteria. Investors should recognize the subjectivity inherent in investment analysis, since each investor has different investment criteria based on his or her objectives. Many investors tend to focus on first-year performance because they are uncertain about the future forecasts in their pro forma financial statements. In other words, most investors are quite confident about their estimated operating data during the first year of operations but are much less confident about subsequent years. Thus, many investors like to drill down on the first-year numbers to make sure they meet their criteria, and only examine holding period measures like NPV and IRR if the first-year numbers are acceptable.

Exhibit 12.11 lists some of the first-year investment measures most commonly used by investors.

Exhibit 12.11: First-Year Measures

Measure	Formula	Explanation
Payback period	Equity investment/ATCF	Years until initial equity is recovered
Profit margin	ATCF/EGI	After-tax profit as a percent of EGI
Default ("BE") ratio	(Operating exp. + debt service)/EGI	Obligations as a percent of EGI
Operating expense ratio	Operating exp./EGI	Operating expenses as a percent of EGI
Debt coverage ratio	NOI/Debt service	NOI as a percent of annual debt service
Loan-to-value ratio	Loan amount/Property value	Loan amount as a percent of total property value
EGI multiplier	Purchase price/EGI	Valuation multiplier
Capitalization rate	NOI/Purchase price	Overall capitalization rate for valuation
Before-tax return	BTCF/Equity investment	Return on cash equity invested before taxes
After-tax return	ATCF/Equity investment	Return on cash equity invested after taxes

For the Courtside Condos case study, each of these first-year investment measures is calculated as follows:

Investment Measures

Payback Period	=	Equity Investment	=	$25,000	=	18.50 years
		After-Tax Cash Flow		$1,350		
Profit Margin	=	After-Tax Cash Flow	=	$1,350	=	9.09%
		Effective Gross Income		$14,850		
Default Ratio	=	Operating Exp. + Debt Service	=	$13,128	=	88%
		Effective Gross Income		$14,850		
Operating Expense Ratio	=	Operating Expenses	=	$3,530	=	23.77%
		Effective Gross Income		$14,850		
Debt Coverage Ratio	=	Net Operating Income	=	$11,320	=	1.18
		Debt Service		$9,598		
Loan-to-Value Ratio	=	Loan Amount	=	$133,400	=	86%
		Purchase Price		$155,000		
Effective Gross Inc. Multiplier	=	Purchase Price	=	$155,000	=	10.44
		Effective Gross Income		$14,850		

Capitalization Rate	=	Net Income	=	$11,320	=	7.3%
		Purchase Price		$155,000		
Before-Tax Return	=	Before-Tax Cash Flow	=	$762	=	3.0%
		Equity Investment		$25,000		
After-Tax Return	=	After-Tax Cash Flow	=	$1,350	=	5.4%
		Equity Investment		$25,000		

First-year investment measures are informative by themselves, but when investors compare them to the first-year measures for other investment properties, they provide even greater insights. After calculating and comparing first-year measures, the natural next step is to calculate the holding period measures of NPV and IRR, which are described in Exhibit 12.12.

Exhibit 12.12: Holding Period Measures

Measure	Interpretation
Net Present Value (NPV)	Positive NPV = Accept the investment
Internal Rate of Return (IRR)	Rate at which NPV = 0

For the Courtside Condos case study, the holding period measures of NPV and IRR are $9,091 and 16.69%, respectively. A positive NPV coupled with a high IRR usually indicates that an investment should be pursued. However, Courtside Condos #102's first-year measures suggest that its overall forecast performance is highly correlated with its expected appreciation in value. This finding indicates that the overall performance of this investment is highly contingent upon one item—its price appreciation. If this property does not appreciate in line with Sally's forecast, its returns will be much lower, and the overall investment may be a disappointment.

At this point in the analysis, the investor (Sally) must consider all of the data and make a final decision. Some investors would look at the first-year numbers, which are not great, and decide that they are good enough to justify betting that the condo will appreciate in value and that its overall performance will be great. Other investors would shy away from the gamble on appreciation and choose not to pursue the investment. In the end, no amount of numerical analysis saves investors from the decision of whether or not to purchase a property.

RELATED RESOURCES

How Rental Property Depreciation Works
http://www.investopedia.com/articles/investing/060815/how-rental-property-depreciation-works.asp#ixzz4BUp6Yj3o

The History of the Mortgage Interest Deduction
http://taxfoundation.org/blog/history-mortgage-interest-deduction

Common Real Estate Return Metrics
https://medium.com/@EquityMultiple/learning-series-common-real-estate-return-metrics-7a2f241f8524

CHAPTER 13

Real Estate Risk Analysis

INTRODUCTION

Understanding financial risk is vitally important to successful real estate investment. Therefore, the purpose of this chapter is to explore modern techniques for quantifying and measuring risk that lead to better investment decisions.

QUANTITATIVE METHODS

This chapter outlines four methods for quantitatively assessing real estate investment risk: (1) single-point models, (2) scenario analysis, (3) what-if analysis, and (4) Monte Carlo simulation. This provides an overview of the strengths, weaknesses, and potential uses of each method.

SINGLE-POINT MODELS

Single-point models project investment outcomes using a single set of assumptions. Analysts often employ single-point models when they construct pro forma financial statements based on forecasts of rental revenue, vacancy, operating expenses, capitalization rates, and tax rates. Analysts can then use these single-point, pro forma financials to calculate decision metrics, such as net present value, internal rate of return, payback period, and after-tax cash-on-cash return. Single-point models are employed ubiquitously by business school students and industry professionals alike because they are intuitive to construct and use. However, they create a false sense of precision that can blind analysts to the risks of potential investments. Therefore, single-point models are best used as a starting point for more sophisticated risk-analysis techniques and not as the sole basis for decision-making.

Single-Point Models	
PROS	CONS
• Easy to build • Intuitive to use • Useful as a starting point for advanced techniques	• Create a false sense of precision • Give no intuition about the potential range or likelihood of outcomes

Partitioning the IRR is one technique that analysts can use to gain greater insight into the metrics generated by a single-point model. Partitioning the IRR consists of separately discounting the after-tax operating cash flows and the after-tax reversion cash flow of an investment at the internal rate of return to determine the percentage of the total return that comes from each component. The following example illustrates how to partition the IRR:

Exhibit 13.1: Partitioning the IRR

Assume the following initial equity investment, after-tax operating cash flows, and after-tax reversion cash flow for a five-year real estate investment:

Year	0	1	2	3	4	5
Initial Equity Investment	<75,000>					
After-tax Operating Cash Flows		2,800	3,000	3,100	3,450	3,500
After-tax Cash Flow from Reversion						150,000
Total ATCF	<75,000>	2,800	3,000	3,100	3,450	153,500

These assumptions result in an 18.1% internal rate of return for this investment.

Step 1: Discount the After-Tax Operating Cash Flows at the IRR:

$$\frac{2{,}800}{(1+.181)} + \frac{3{,}000}{(1+.181)^2} + \frac{3{,}100}{(1+.181)^3} + \frac{3{,}450}{(1+.181)^4} + \frac{3{,}500}{(1+.181)^5} = \$9,701$$

Step 2: Discount the Reversion Cash Flow at the IRR:

$$\frac{150{,}000}{(1+.181)^5} = \$65,299$$

(Notice that the sum of these two discounted cash flow values is $75,000, the value of the initial equity investment. This is NOT a coincidence, since the IRR is the discount rate that makes the present value of all future cash flows equal to the initial outlay.)

Step 3: Divide the discounted cash flows by the Initial Investment:

$$\textit{Operating Cash Flows}: \frac{9{,}701}{75{,}000} = 13\%$$

$$\textit{Reversion Cash Flow}: \frac{65{,}299}{75{,}000} = 87\%$$

These calculations show that only 13% of the return on this investment is attributable to operating cash flows, while a full 87% comes from the final sale of the property. This presents a potential risk to investors since a decline in property value could destroy the attractiveness of this investment.

SCENARIO ANALYSIS

Scenario analysis is another popular risk-analysis technique that addresses some of the short-comings of single-point models. An analyst conducting scenario analysis constructs multiple single-point models for an investment under varying sets of assumptions. Typically, these would include a best, worst, and most-likely set of assumptions (see Exhibit 13.3).

Exhibit 13.2: Sample Scenarios

	Worst Case	Most Likely Case	Best Case
Rent Growth	–1%	3%	6%
Vacancy	5%	2%	0%
Operating Expenses	30%	25%	20%
Property Appreciation	0%	4%	8%

Scenario analysis is useful because it helps the analyst get some sense of the spread or range of outcomes possible for a single investment. However, it provides little to no insight into the relative likelihood of the different outcomes.

Scenario Analysis	
PROS	CONS
• Easy and intuitive to conduct • Gives some sense of spread for possible outcomes	• Gives little information about the likelihood of each scenario

WHAT-IF ANALYSIS

What-if analysis is another expansion of single-point models. However, unlike scenario analysis, what-if analysis consists of working with individual variables rather than sets of assumptions. To perform what-if analysis, an analyst changes one assumption in a single-point model while holding all other assumptions constant, and records new values for each output variable. This approach allows the analyst to gain a sense of the output variables' sensitivity to changes to a given assumption. Like scenario analysis, however, what-if analysis provides no information about the likelihood of various outcomes. Additionally, what-if analysis is extraordinarily time-consuming and can produce an overwhelming amount of data. Because it is so inefficient, analysts should not utilize what-if analysis as a regular risk-assessment tool.

What-If Analysis	
PROS	CONS
• Relatively easy to conduct • Provides some insight into a model's sensitivity to assumptions	• Extremely time-consuming • Generates an overwhelming amount of data • Gives no insight about the probabilities of different outcomes

MONTE CARLO SIMULATION ANALYSIS

Monte Carlo simulation is a modern risk-assessment technique that relies on probability distributions and sampling to overcome the limitations of the static models previously discussed. Monte Carlo simulation is superior to every other risk-analysis method presented in this chapter because it gives insight into both the range of possible values for each output metric and the likelihood of observing each value. Furthermore, Monte Carlo simulations are relatively easy to run using commercially available software packages.

Numerous software packages are available that add Monte Carlo simulation capabilities to Microsoft Excel, including @Risk, Crystal Ball, and ModelRisk. These add-ins allow users to define a probability distribution around each input variable in a single-point model. Then, the add-ins randomly select values for each input variable based on their probability distributions. By aggregating the output values calculated over a specified number of trials, the add-ins are able to estimate a probability distribution for each output variable (see Exhibit 13.3).

EXHIBIT 13.3: SAMPLE OUTPUT PROBABILITY DISTRIBUTION

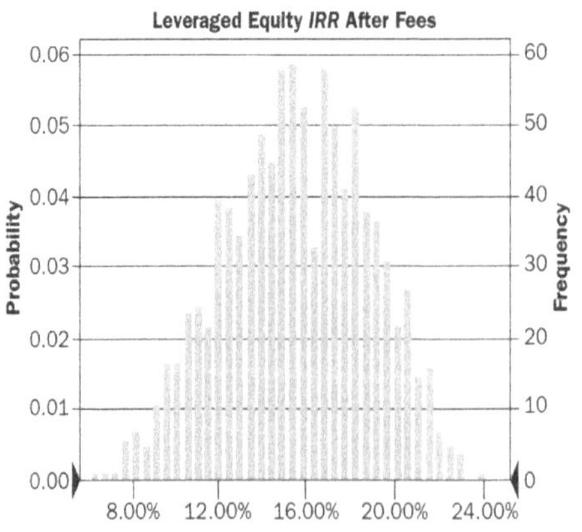

Statistics	Forecast Values	Percentiles	Forecast Values
Trials	1,000	0%	4.66%
Mean	15.52%	10%	10.97%
Median	15.54%	20%	12.55%
Mode	-	30%	13.77%
Standard Deviation	3.37%	40%	14.71%
Variance	0.11%	50%	15.54%
Skewness*	-0.16075	60%	16.60%
Kutosis†	2.62	70%	17.46%
Coefficient of Viability‡	0.21712	80%	18.55%
Minimum	4.66%	90%	19.88%
Maximum	24.68%	100%	24.68%
Range Width	20.02%		
Mean Standard Error	0.11%		

Selecting the Correct Distribution

When an analyst runs a Monte Carlo simulation, he or she must select the proper distribution for each input variable. In this text, we will discuss two of the most commonly used distributions, triangular and normal, though most software packages allow users to select many other types of distributions (see Exhibit 13.4).

Exhibit 13.4: Commonly Used Distributions

Triangular Distribution

A triangular distribution is created using three inputs: a minimum value, and a most-likely value. For example, if an analyst thought market rents would likely grow at 3%, with a best and worst case of 6% and 1%, respectively, he or she would define the following triangular distribution:

Based on this distribution, the analyst's Monte Carol simulation package would randomly select market grown rates between 1% and 6%, with most values clustered around 3%.

Normal Distribution

Normal distributions take on a familiar bell-curve shape and are defined by two variables, mean and standard deviation. The mean provides a measure of central tendency, while the standard deviation provides a measure of the spread of the distribution. The following graph depicts a normal distribution for mortgage interest rates with a mean of 5.75% and a standard deviation of 0.50%.

For any normal distribution, observations will fall within one standard deviation of the mean 68% of the time, so under these assumptions, a Monte Carlo simulation add-in would select a mortgage interest rate between 5.25% and 6.25% on roughly two-thirds of its trials. The remaining one-third of the trials would use a mortgage interest rate further from the mean, and 99.7% of all selections would be within three standard deviations of the mean, or between 4.25% and 7.25%.

Interpreting Simulation Output

In addition to displaying an appropriate distribution for each output variable, Monte Carlo simulation add-ins calculate numerous statistics to help analysts evaluate simulation results. For example, the statistical output to the right of Exhibit 13.3 reveals that the IRR distribution depicted has a mean of 15.52% and a standard deviation of 3.37%. The percentiles listed next to the statistics provide insight into the likelihood of various outcomes. The percentile output in Exhibit 13.3 shows that the project has only a 30% chance of earning less than 13.77% and a 40% chance of earning more than 16.60%. Many simulation add-ins also allow users to calculate the probability of observing an output value over a given range. Exhibit 13.5 shows the probability of earning an internal rate of return greater than 14%.

Exhibit 13.5: Probability of IIR > 14%

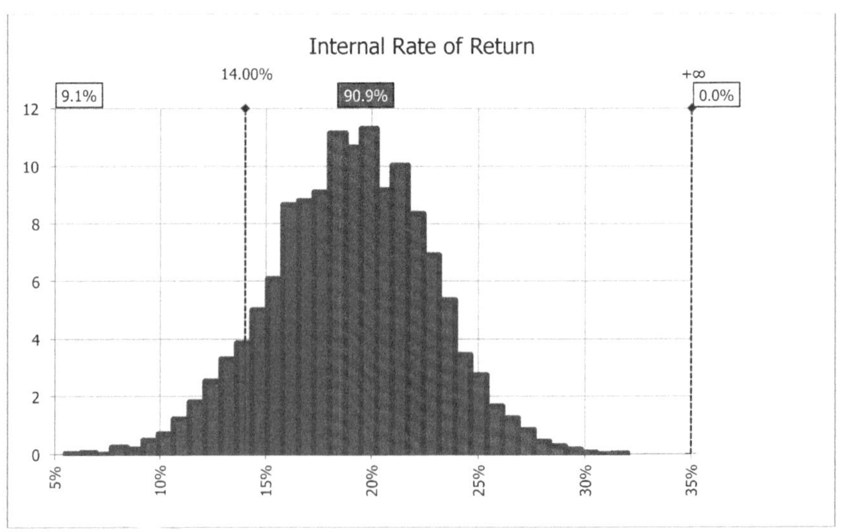

Most Monte Carlo simulation add-ins also produce sensitivity, or "tornado," charts that display the sensitivity of a given output variable to each input variable. The longer the bar next to an input variable, the more sensitive the output variable is to changes in that input. Furthermore, bars extending to the right indicate inputs that are positively correlated with the output, while bars extending to the left represent negatively correlated inputs. Exhibit 13.6 contains an example sensitivity chart for IRR.

EXHIBIT 13.6: SAMPLE SENSITIVITY CHART: IIR

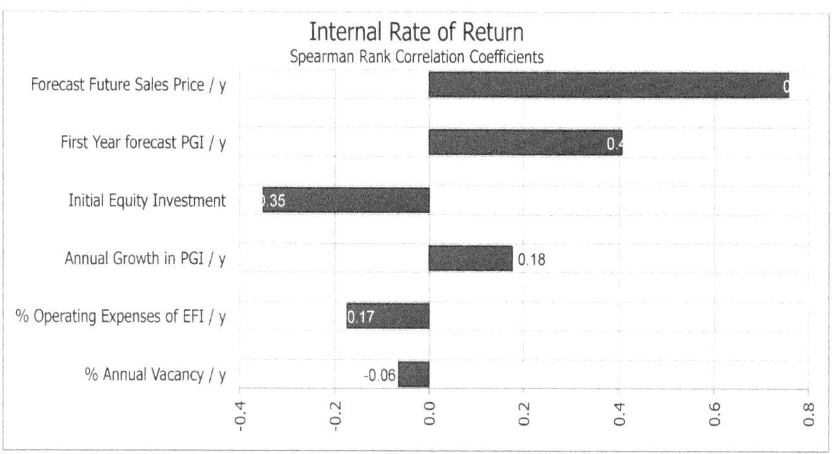

Monte Carlo Simulation	
PROS	CONS
• Is relatively easy to conduct • Produces probability distributions and statistics for each output variable • Provides detailed information about input sensitivity	• Requires additional software, which can be expensive • Requires the analyst to define a probability distribution for each input

CONCLUSION

In this chapter, we reviewed four techniques for evaluating real estate investment risk: (1) single-point models, (2) scenario analysis, (3) what-if analysis, and (4) Monte Carlo simulation. Though each of these techniques possesses various strengths and weaknesses, Monte Carlo simulation is by far the most robust, providing the greatest insight into the financial risk inherent in an investment.

RELATED RESOURCES

Related Article

Barrett Slade, "Property Risk Assessment: A Simulation Approach," The Appraisal Journal 74, no. 4 (2006): 347–57.

Property Risk Assessment: A Simulation Approach

https://professional.sauder.ubc.ca/re_creditprogram/course_resources/courses/content/344/344_additionalcases2.pdf

History of Monte Carlo Simulation

https://www.elderresearch.com/blog/monte-carlo-simulation

Selecting the Appropriate Distributions for Your Model

https://www.vosesoftware.com/riskwiki/Selectingtheappropriatedistributionsforyourmodel.php

CHAPTER 14

Commercial Property Negotiations, Contracts, Title, & Closing

INTRODUCTION

When investors are getting ready to negotiate and enter into a contract to purchase an investment property, many of the principles outlined in chapters 5 and 6 are directly applicable. However, one item is unique to the purchase of investment properties—the letter of intent.

LETTER OF INTENT

The acquisition of an investment property is more complicated than the acquisition of an owner-occupied home because investors have to be concerned with not only the physical asset itself but also with the investment aspects of the property. For instance, when people enter into a contract to buy a home, they generally want to ensure that the property is physically sound (i.e., does not have any undisclosed material defects), that the property appraises for at least the agreed-upon sales price, and that they can obtain mortgage financing. For investment properties, people want these same assurances. However, obtaining each assurance is generally more costly and time-consuming than with a home. Additionally, investors usually want a thorough audit and investigation of the operating performance of the property, including a detailed review of its rental revenue and operating expenses.

Obtaining these assurances is known on the street as a buyer's due diligence, and the period over which they are completed is known as the due diligence period. Both buyer and seller are engaged in this process, and neither wants to expend the necessary time and resources unless he or she has some assurance that the other party is serious about the transaction. This is where a letter of intent comes into play. A letter of intent is a loose agreement between a buyer and seller that signals that both parties are serious about negotiating in good faith and that the buyer will be given a period of time (the due diligence period) to complete due diligence and will afterward enter into a formal, binding contract. A letter of intent also assures the buyers that the seller will not sell the property to another party while the buyer is completing his or her due diligence.

In short, a letter of intent is a written document that conveys a buyer's interest to purchase and a seller's interest to sell a property and lays out a road map for how the negotiation and deal will proceed. Letters of intent generally contain a soft offer price, the dates during which the buyer will complete his or her due diligence, and duties that must be performed by both parties as they work toward a formal purchase contract.

Once the due diligence period is over, the parties either enter into a formal purchase contract or walk away without further obligation. If the parties execute a legal contract, then the terms of the contract take on many of the same characteristics discussed in chapter 6, including earnest money, escrow, and weasel clauses.

Completing the purchase of, or closing on, a small investment property requires investors to think about how they would like to hold the title to the property. Investors who obtain mortgage funds with personal guarantees may initially have to take title in their own name. After taking title, many investors choose to form a Limited Liability Company (LLC) and transfer ownership of the property to the LLC, which they own. This ownership structure provides for liability protection and cleaner accounting. Almost all investors should retain qualified legal counsel and tax advice to determine their optimal ownership structure.

RELATED RESOURCES

Using a Letter of Intent for Making Offers on Commercial Real Estate (including Template)
https://www.commercialpropertyadvisors.com/using-a-letter-of-intent-when-making-offers-on-commercial-real-estate/

How to Form a Real Estate LLC
https://www.fortunebuilders.com/forming-a-real-estate-llc/

A Comprehensive Approach to Real Estate Deal Due Diligence
https://groundbreaker.co/real-estate-due-diligence-guide/

CHAPTER 15

Property Management

INTRODUCTION

Investment real estate requires property management, which is monitoring and overseeing the operations of the real estate. Owners may elect to manage a property themselves or hire a property manager who operates the real estate on their behalf for a fee. This chapter answers several questions relating to property management, including why it may be beneficial to hire a property manager, how to find a property manager, what the duties of a property manager are, and how much it costs to hire a property manager.

WHY HIRE A PROPERTY MANAGER?

Property managers provide expertise in managing real estate in their local market. Different asset classes in real estate—such as residential, office, and industrial—are nuanced in how they operate. For example, apartment complexes usually have short leases that range from one to two years. Shorter leases lead to higher turnover rates, requiring more work to find tenants and maintain occupancy. Many investors do not have the time to dedicate themselves to finding new tenants because of other responsibilities.

HOW DO YOU FIND A PROPERTY MANAGER?

Proper property management requires skill and hard work. When looking for a property manager, investors should research candidates' track records and read reviews from previous customers. Since property managers deal with both owners and tenants, investors should verify that a property manager has a good reputation with both parties.

Should You Hire a Local or National Property Manager?

Local property managers tend to be closer to the property and more available to handle emergencies that inevitably surface. Local property managers often have a better understanding of the local real estate market, which may help them operate the property more efficiently than a national manager. Local property managers are also more likely to manage small properties. National property managers typically limit their services to large commercial properties. Local property managers may not have the capacity to handle large properties.

Should You Hire a Licensed and Certified Property Manager?

Many states require that property managers who charge a fee for their services undergo training and receive licensure from the state. Many property managers also pursue and obtain professional certifications that provide evidence of their training and knowledge on property management. These certifications provide owners some assurance of what they can expect from the property manager. Property management certifications come from a variety of associations.

What Associations Certify Property Managers?

A number of different associations certify property managers. Following is a list of several prominent associations:

BOMA—Building Owners and Managers Association
- Founded in 1907, BOMA is for commercial property owners and managers.
- Website: boma.org

ICSC—International Council of Shopping Centers
- Founded in 1957, ICSC is for retail real estate.
- Website: icsc.com

IREM—Institute of Real Estate Management

- Founded in 1933, IREM is for residential and commercial properties.
- Website: irem.org

NAA—National Apartment Association

- Founded in 1939, NAA is for apartment properties.
- Website: naahq.org

NARPM—National Association of Residential Property Managers

- Founded in 1987, NARPM is for smaller residential properties.
- Website: narpm.org

What Services Do Property Managers Provide?

Not all property managers offer the same services. Understanding an investment property and the services needed to maintain and efficiently run the property helps investors determine what duties their property manager should perform. The following exhibit shows the most common services provided by property managers:

EXHIBIT 15.1: MOST COMMON PROPERTY MANAGEMENT SERVICES

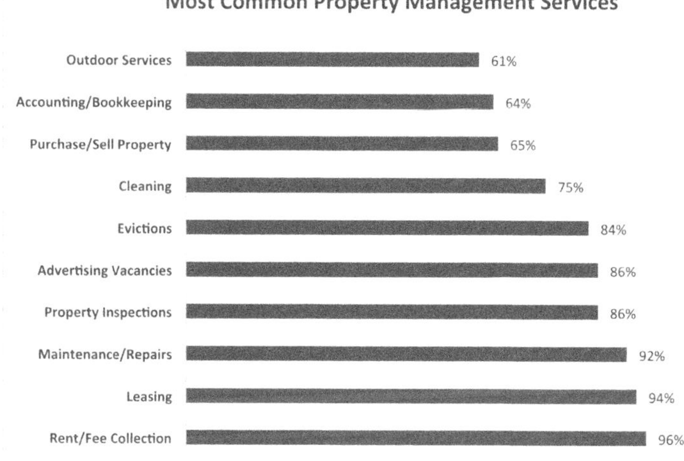

Source: *iPropertyManagement: Property Management Industry Statistics*[5]

Each of these services is discussed in the following list. This list is not exhaustive but can help prospective investors understand the types of services provided by property managers.

- **Rent Collection:** Rent is typically paid on a monthly basis. Property managers are responsible for ensuring that rent is paid on time, usually through an electronic payment system.
- **Leasing:** Large commercial properties are often leased with the help of commercial leasing agents, who advertise and show properties and assist in negotiating lease terms between tenants and owners. With small investment properties, property managers are typically responsible for performing these duties and keeping their properties occupied.
- **Maintenance/Repairs:** Property managers are responsible for ensuring that properties are adequately maintained and that needed repairs are taken care of in a timely manner. They accomplish these duties by hiring maintenance personnel, such as handymen and plumbers, to take care of small repairs and by contracting with outside providers for larger issues.
- **Property Inspections:** Property managers perform periodic inspections to ensure that tenants are caring for the properties in a manner consistent with the terms of their lease. If a property inspection reveals that a tenant is not caring for the property adequately, then property managers take action to rectify the problem.
- **Advertising Vacancies:** Often, property managers are responsible for finding new tenants when a property is vacant. This may require advertising and showing the property to prospective tenants.
- **Evictions:** When tenants violate their lease terms, property managers are responsible for implementing the eviction process, which may require the services of an attorney or other legal professionals.
- **Cleaning:** Property managers are responsible for ensuring that their properties are clean and compliant with local health codes.

- **Purchasing/Selling Property:** Managers know local properties and their local market very well, so they can often add value when they assist with the purchase or sale of a property.
- **Accounting/Bookkeeping:** Properties have income and expenses that require proper accounting. Accurate bookkeeping is essential for tax purposes and efficient property operation. Property managers either perform these duties themselves or retain professionals to do so.
- **Outdoor Services:** Some properties have landscaping that must be maintained. Some property managers take care of their properties' landscaping.

HOW MUCH DOES IT COST TO HIRE A PROPERTY MANAGER?

The cost of property management varies based on several variables, including the number of properties or units under supervision, the type of property, and the local real estate market.

- **Number of Properties or Units:** Economies of scale affect the fee paid. Generally, property management fees, on a percentage basis, decline with the number of properties or units under management. Single properties often have high property management fees on a percentage basis.
- **Type of Property:** Some property types, such as apartments, are more operationally intensive, resulting in a higher property management fee.
- **Local Market:** Local market conditions and competition for property management services affect the property management fee structure in a given market.

Property management fees are usually structured in two ways: flat or percentage.

- **Flat Fee:** A flat fee is a fixed fee that remains constant regardless of how the property performs. Flat fees are more common with single-family residential properties. Commercial properties seldom have flat management fees.

- **Percentage Fee:** Property managers usually charge 8%–12% of monthly rental income (effective gross income) for smaller properties and 4%–7% for larger properties.

RELATED RESOURCES

10 Things to Ask before Choosing a Property Manager
https://www.bizjournals.com/bizjournals/how-to/growth-strategies/2016/12/10-things-to-ask-choosing-a-property-manager.html

The 300 Most Popular Property Management Companies in America (by State)
https://www.allpropertymanagement.com/blog/post/300-most-popular-property-management-companies-in-america/

When Should a Landlord Hire a Property Management Company?
https://www.nolo.com/legal-encyclopedia/landlord-hire-property-management-company-29885.html

PART IV

REAL ESTATE INVESTMENT ALTERNATIVES

CHAPTER 16

Real Estate Investment Trusts (REITS)

INTRODUCTION

Some investors are not comfortable with the potential risk and leverage required to own income-generating real estate, so REITs offer an alternative form of real estate investing. Real Estate Investment Trusts (REITs) were established in the 1960s as a way for individuals to invest in income-generating real estate without personally owning real estate.

A REIT is a corporation, public or private, that owns, operates, and finances income-generating real estate properties and sells equity to individual and institutional investors. Many corporations have real estate on their balance sheets (office buildings, warehouses, etc.), but REITs are unique because they earn nearly all of their income from real estate.

As of January 2020, REITs owned approximately $3 trillion in gross real estate assets across 520,000 properties, with more than $2 trillion of that total from public listed and nonlisted REITs and the remainder from privately held REITs.[33] The IRS shows that about 1,100 REITs in the United States have filed tax returns, with about 225 REITs traded as public companies, and 184 traded on the New York Stock Exchange. They have a combined equity market cap of

---

33. "REITs by the Numbers," Nareit, www.reit.com/data-research/data/reits-numbers.

more than $1 trillion.[34] Of the publicly traded REITs, thirty are members of the S&P 500.[35]

HOW TO QUALIFY AS A REIT

To qualify as a REIT, a company must have the bulk of its assets and income connected to real estate investment and distribute at least 90% of its taxable income to shareholders annually in the form of dividends. A company that qualifies as a REIT may deduct dividends that it pays out to its shareholders from its corporate taxable income. Because of this particular tax treatment, most REITs pay out at least 90% of their taxable income to their shareholders and, therefore, owe no corporate tax. In addition to paying out at least 90% of its taxable income annually in the form of shareholder dividends, a REIT must meet the following criteria:

- Be an entity that would be taxable as a corporation but for its REIT status
- Be managed by a board of directors or trustees
- Have shares that are fully transferable
- Have a minimum of 100 shareholders after its first year as a REIT
- Have no more than 50% of its shares held by five or fewer individuals during the last half of the taxable year
- Invest at least 75% of its total assets in real estate assets and cash
- Derive at least 75% of its gross income from real estate–related sources, including rents from real property and interest on mortgages financing real property
- Derive at least 95% of its gross income from such real estate sources and dividends or interest from any source
- Have no more than 25% of its assets consist of nonqualifying securities or stock in taxable REIT subsidiaries

---

34. "Frequently Asked Questions about REITs," Nareit, https://www.reit.com/what-reit/frequently-asked-questions-about-reits.
35. Will Ashworth, "5 Types of REITs and How to Invest in Them," Investopedia, January 29, 2020, www.investopedia.com/articles/mortgages-real-estate/10/real-estate-investment-trust-reit.asp.

TYPES OF REITS

According to the SEC, there are three main types of REITs: equity, mortgage, and hybrid.[36] Equity REITs own and operate residential and commercial buildings and receive income from rental income from tenants. Mortgage REITs (mREITs) invest in underlying commercial and residential mortgages and mortgage-backed securities (MBS). mREITs provide important liquidity to the housing market by helping to finance the purchasing and sales of real estate and tend to be more leveraged than equity REITs. Hybrid REITs are a mix of the two and invest in both properties and mortgages.[37] These types of REITs can be broken down further, as some REITs specialize in different kinds of real estate investing. These include retail, residential, healthcare, office, and mortgage.

1. **Retail REITs:** Approximately 24% of REIT investments are in shopping malls and freestanding retail. Retail REITs make money by collecting rent from their tenants, who are businesses. Finding new tenants in retail spaces is typically more challenging than finding new tenants in residential real estate. However, much of the investments in retail REITs are in long-term leases, which reduces the cost of turnover. The long-term outlook for retail REITs is less promising, as consumers are starting to shift their spending to online shopping rather than brick and mortar. The surge of e-commerce has resulted in diminished demand for retail properties. However, some types of retail businesses do well in times of recession or innovation (e.g., drug stores, discount stores, and automotive repair shops).
2. **Residential REITs:** Residential REITs are rental properties in which people reside. The majority of holdings by residential REITs come in the form of apartment complexes and manufactured housing, with a small percentage of REITs

36. "Investor Bulletin: Real Estate Investment Trusts (REITs)," Office of Investor Education and Advocacy, https://www.sec.gov/files/reits.pdf.
37. "What Is a Hybrid REIT?" Millionacres, https://www.fool.com/millionacres/real-estate-investing/reits/what-hybrid-reit/.

specializing in single-family rentals. The biggest residential REITs tend to focus on high-cost areas where the rental rates are higher and home affordability is low (New York City, San Francisco, Chicago, etc.). REITs with the most available capital tend to be the most successful. Single-Family Rental (SFR) REITs make up only 2% of the REIT ETFs.[38] Combined, the three largest SFRs own about 150,000 homes in the United States. SFRs are a capital-intensive, low-yield investment vehicle.

3. **Healthcare REITs:** Healthcare REITs invest in properties such as hospitals, medical centers, nursing facilities, and retirement homes. The success of healthcare REITs is directly tied to the healthcare system. The operators of these facilities are dependent on occupancy fees, Medicare and Medicaid reimbursements, and private pay. The COVID-19 pandemic threatened healthcare REITs, as senior housing was devastated by the virus all over the country. However, with Baby Boomers looking to retire, the demand for senior living should remain stable.
4. **Office REITs:** Office REITs invest in office buildings and usually collect rental income from tenants who sign long-term leases. The success of office REITs is tied to the state of the economy, especially at a local level. Unstable economic environments and volatile employment rates will affect the vacancy rates in the office spaces. The onset of COVID-19 in the United States could prove to be a devastating blow to office REITs, as many companies transitioned to allow employees to work at home.
5. **Mortgage REITs:** Mortgage REITs invest in mortgages as opposed to real assets. The performance of mortgage REITs rises and falls with interest rates. High interest rates result in a decrease in the book value of mortgage REITs, driving stock prices lower.

---

38. "Single-Family Rentals: REITs Flex Their Muscle," Seeking Alpha, May 9, 2019, https://seekingalpha.com/article/4261864-single-family-rentals-reits-flex-muscle.

INVESTING IN REITS

There are two main ways to invest in REITs. Some REITs are registered with the SEC and traded publicly on an exchange, and some REITs are not. There are nuances with investing in both publicly traded and nontraded REITs.

First, investing in publicly traded REITs is just like investing in a standard, dividend-paying security. Their shares are available for purchase with most standard brokerages, and the fees associated with buying or selling shares are the same as any other company. These publicly traded firms are required to make regular disclosures to the SEC, and they are subject to specific stock exchange rules on corporate governance. You can also choose to buy REIT ETFs to diversify your investments further. As previously stated, REITs usually specialize in a specific type of real estate investing, and REIT ETFs allow you to have exposure to all aspects of real estate.

Additionally, you may simplify your portfolio by consolidating many different income streams into one source.[39] One of the cons of owning REIT ETFs instead of shares of individual firms is that returns will be lower than owning a specific REIT due to the extra fees the ETF imposes. Most of the large financial firms offer REIT ETFs, such as Vanguard, Charles Schwab, BlackRock, and Fidelity. Some ETFs specialize in high yield, short, and international investments.[40]

Second, some REITs are not publicly traded but register with the SEC to take advantage of the tax benefits of being an REIT. The operations of the nontraded firm are very similar to the publicly traded REITs, but they are different in some important ways.[41] First, they are illiquid investments. They are more closely related to VC/PE investments in the way that investors receive returns on their investments. The timing of the liquidity events is entirely up to the management of the

---

39. Dan Caplinger, "Your Complete Guide to REIT ETFs," *Millionacres*, September 4, 2019, www.fool.com/millionacres/real-estate-investing/reits/your-complete-reit-etf-guide/.
40. Eric Rosenberg, "The 8 Best REIT ETFs of 2020," *The Balance*, November 20, 2019, https://www.thebalance.com/best-reit-etfs-4174043.
41. "Investor Bulletin: Real Estate Investment Trusts (REITs)," Office of Investor Education and Advocacy, https://www.sec.gov/files/reits.pdf.

REIT and could be years after the investment. Second, the value of the company is not transparent. As with most private companies, it can be difficult to know the value of the shares of the company because they are not traded on a public exchange. Nontraded REITs do not provide estimates of the value per share for months after raising capital, which means you do not know the value of your investment. Third, there are significant fees associated with investing in nontraded REITs. These shares are typically sold by financial advisors and include sales commissions and other fees that may be as high as 9%–10%.

Investing in REITs differs from investing in regular dividend-paying stocks. Investors in REITs are responsible for paying taxes on the dividends received and on capital gains from the investment.

RELATED RESOURCES

National Association of Real Estate Investment Trusts (NAREIT)
https://www.reit.com

Definitive List of Real Estate ETFs
https://etfdb.com/etfdb-category/real-estate/

Benefits of REITs
https://news.morningstar.com/classroom2/course.asp?docId=145579&page=2&CN=

Drawbacks of REITs
https://news.morningstar.com/classroom2/course.asp?docId=145579&page=3&CN=

CHAPTER 17

Publicly Traded Real Estate Firms

INTRODUCTION

There are many ways to invest in real estate beyond owning actual property. One of the more common forms of alternative real estate investing is Real Estate Investment Trusts (REITs), which were covered in the previous chapter. This chapter discusses other types of publicly traded real estate companies, including those that are associated with real estate in unconventional or indirect ways.

PUBLIC REAL ESTATE FIRMS

One type of public real estate firm is asset management companies. These companies have a variety of assets and business plans, from office buildings to infrastructure to pensions. Brookfield Asset Management Inc. is the largest asset management company, with significant investments in real estate.

Real estate development firms include another alternative to direct real estate investment. Developers operate a broad range of activities, from renovating existing buildings to building new structures on vacant land. Development companies often finance, organize, and oversee significant projects from start to finish. They take on considerable risk in anticipation of a substantial return on investment. These companies might lease the property at the end of the project or sell the property for a profit. Real estate development companies are involved in a variety of different property types, including single-family residential, office, retail, and industrial properties.

Many companies act as an essential complement to the real estate market with their services, data, and analytics, such as Zillow (Z); CoStar Group, Inc. (CSGP); and Reis, Inc. (REIS). These companies provide relevant platforms, analytics, and data for real estate participants. There are also prominent real estate software companies like Black Knight, Inc. (BKI); Ellie Mae, Inc. (ELLI); and AppFolio, Inc. (APPF) that assist in mortgage and property management needs.

Although they might not be involved in typical real estate operations, residential and commercial real estate construction companies are dependent on a healthy real estate market. These companies include D. R. Horton, Inc. (DHI); PulteGroup, Inc. (PHM); and Toll Brothers, Inc. (TOL). Related to these construction companies are construction equipment manufacturers like Caterpillar, Inc. (CAT) and Deere & Company (DE) and engineering firms like Fluor Corporation (FLR) and Jacobs Engineering Group, Inc. (JEC). There are also publicly traded companies that do business in the materials needed to build residential and commercial real estate. Like the construction companies, their success is dependent on new properties being built. This encompasses companies in HVAC, refrigeration, plumbing, cabinets, concrete, flooring, lighting, paint, windows and doors, and other wood products.

RELATED RESOURCES

Publicly Traded Real Estate Companies
https://fintel.io/industry/list/real-estate

Real Estate Technology: Trends and Overview
https://builtin.com/consumer-tech/real-estate-technology

Modernizing Real Estate: The Property Tech Opportunity
https://www.forbes.com/sites/valleyvoices/2019/02/22/the-proptech-opportunity/#5b701ffc5826

CHAPTER 18

Real Estate Tax Liens

INTRODUCTION

Tax liens present a unique opportunity to invest in real estate. Tax lien certificates offer investors high rates of return with relatively low risk. While there are several important nuances involved, if done right, tax liens can be a lucrative part of any portfolio. Not all states offer tax lien certificates to private investors. However, the option to buy liens online is available to everyone.

REVIEW OF LIENS

A lien is a financial interest in a property that must be repaid before property ownership can be transferred. Several types of liens can be attached to a property: mechanic's liens, mortgage liens, and home equity liens are among the most common. An important aspect of liens is that the first lien on a property has priority over the other liens in the event of default. If a mortgage lien were attached to a home before a home equity lien, for example, the holder of the mortgage lien would have the right to foreclose on the property, and the home equity lien would be effectively wiped out.

The government always holds the first lien on a property, and it is almost always a lien for property taxes, so this means that the government is the first to recover amounts owed if the property owner defaults on the payment of property taxes. Before a lender, contractor, and so on can recoup losses on a property, the holder of the tax lien must be paid. The certificate for that tax lien is held with the county treasurer's office. The property owner must pay the full amount of delinquent taxes with a stated amount of interest. If the delinquent taxes are not paid before the end of a specified redemption period, the county has the right to foreclose on the property to recoup its losses. Alternatively, a private investor can decide to pay the delinquent taxes for the property and claim ownership of the tax lien certificate through a public auction. The property owner then pays the delinquent taxes and interest to the investor.

According to the National Tax Lien Association, the market for tax lien certificates is as high as $14 billion a year, and less than a third of those liens get picked up by private investors.[42] The interest rate paid on delinquent taxes differs by state, but it is often greater than 15%. This is the case in states such as Arizona, Florida, Iowa, and Wyoming. That rate is government-mandated, meaning it is essentially a risk-free rate. With the right due diligence, high rates of return are consistently achievable with little risk.

CHARACTERISTICS OF TAX LIENS

Some tax lien investors are interested only in collecting high rates of interest on their principal paid. Others hope to foreclose and gain ownership of properties through their tax liens for pennies on the dollar. Before buying a tax lien, potential investors need to establish their objective. Several lien characteristics are worth considering, including the interest rate, penalties/fees, the redemption period, the foreclosure process, and the number of liens on the property. These tax lien characteristics differ greatly by state.

Interest Rate: The interest rate is a stated percentage. It doesn't change due to market conditions. Naturally, tax liens with higher interest rates have higher demand than those with lower interest rates.

---

42. Kayleigh Kulp, "Here's Why You Could Have Property Tax Liens in Your Portfolio," CNBC, January 30, 2017, https://www.cnbc.com/2017/01/27/heres-why-you-could-have-property-tax-liens-in-your-portfolio.html.

Penalties/Fees: Some states tack on various fees to tax lien certificates. These fees, paid by the homeowner to the holder of the certificate, can dramatically increase the yield received by the investor.

Redemption Period: Each state allows different lengths of time for homeowners to pay their delinquent taxes before the holder of the first lien on the property can pursue foreclosure. Redemption periods almost always range from sixty days to four years.[43] Investors hoping to foreclose on properties might be more interested in shorter redemption periods, while investors that are solely concerned with preserving their principal and earning the interest of the tax lien might purchase tax liens with longer redemption periods.

Foreclosure Process: If the property owner doesn't pay his or her property taxes by the end of the redemption period, the holder of the tax lien may begin the process of foreclosure on the property. States grant different types of deeds to holders of tax liens that pursue foreclosure, and some states are easier to foreclose in than others. Before purchasing a tax lien in a given state, it is important to understand the process of foreclosure in that state. Some states, such as Kentucky, don't allow holders of tax lien certificates to foreclose on properties at all.

Number of Outstanding Liens: The number of liens on a property is available to the public and can be very helpful in performing due diligence. If an investor is the first person to purchase a tax lien on a property, for example, then he or she may not be able to foreclose on the property. If there are several years of delinquent taxes on a property, but a private investor has never purchased a lien during that time, the property might be worthless. If there is a mortgage on the property, an investor's chances of receiving the initial investment and interest are very high because the bank responsible for the mortgage would be required to pay the holder of the tax lien before it foreclosed on the property.

These are just a few of the characteristics that must be researched before a tax lien is purchased. All of this information is available to the public, usually on the treasurer office's page of a county website.

---

43. Alan Northcott, *Investing in Real Estate Tax Liens & Deeds*, 2nd edition Atlantic Publishing Group, 25.

THE AUCTION

Tax liens are sold at the county level at an annual auction. Much of the time, counties in the same state do auctions on the same day of the year so as to prevent the same investors from attending several different auctions. Because many auctions are now online, more and more outsider investors are gaining access to tax liens.

Pre-Auction

Usually at least two weeks before the annual auction, the county will publish a list of the tax liens that will be offered for sale. Thousands of properties could be available, so it's probably not realistic to research every property in depth. At the very least, it's important for an investor to understand the basic characteristics of the liens he or she is interested in. The investor must have a good idea of his or her budget and use that to narrow the pool of possible liens. The investor should look up properties using the county's parcel search feature or by viewing parcel maps. He or she should also check recent tax charges and payments, make sure the property value that secures the tax lien justifies the cost of the lien, and have a list of properties in mind before the auction begins.

The investor must register for the auction with the county treasurer's office before the date of the auction. Some counties only allow high-net-worth investors, and many require sizable deposits before the auction begins.

Auction

Different states have different methods of auctioning off tax lien certificates. Some states, like Florida, do interest rate bidding. In Florida, the stated interest rate on tax lien certificates begins at 18%. If more than one investor bids on a certificate, the investors proceed to bid down the interest rate until the investor willing to receive the lowest rate wins the certificate. Another method of auctioning tax liens is premium-bidding. In states such as South Dakota, the opening bid at tax lien auctions is the dollar amount of the delinquent property taxes. The interest rate remains the same for every tax lien, and the investor willing to pay the highest premium in a bidding war wins the tax lien.

In other states, including Iowa, where interest rates on tax liens are 24%, random bidding is used to auction off tax liens. An investor's registration number is selected from a hat, and the investor is given the right to purchase a particular tax lien. If the selected investor is not interested in purchasing the tax lien certificate, another investor is randomly chosen. Random-selection auctions are unfavorable for investors hoping to purchase a particular tax lien, but they level the playing field somewhat and give all investors the same opportunity to purchase high-quality certificates. With the other two types of auctions, interest rates are frequently bid down well below the stated interest rate, or premiums are bid up well above the amount of delinquent taxes.

Post-Auction

After the auction, investors must pay for purchased tax liens within a specified time frame. Failure to do so results in forfeiture of tax liens, and such liens then remain in possession of the county. After a lien is won at auction and paid for, there is not much else to do besides collect interest payments from the corresponding property owner.

OVER-THE-COUNTER SALES

Because of the attractive returns presented by tax lien investing, large banks and high-net-worth investors often send representatives to auctions and make it very difficult for individual investors to purchase high-quality liens at auction. However, depending on the county, there's a good chance that less than half of the available liens will be purchased at auction. Unsold property-tax liens remain in possession of the county. The county, then, may offer the liens to the general public in the form of an over-the-counter market. Not all states that sell tax lien certificates have over-the-counter markets. Some states, such as Montana, require their counties to sell all tax liens if possible. Other states, like Nebraska, for example, have the option to sell tax liens after an auction or to retain ownership of unsold liens.[44]

---

44. Alan Northcott, *Investing in Real Estate Tax Liens & Deeds*, 2nd edition, Atlantic Publishing Group, 112.

Pros: The most significant advantage of buying tax liens over the counter is that there is no bidding. An investor can purchase a lien at the exact dollar amount of the corresponding delinquent taxes, at the interest rate mandated by the state. One does not have to bid up the premium, bid down the interest, or hope to be randomly selected to purchase a particular lien. Also, because these liens are not purchased at an auction, an investor can spend more time researching the list of available liens.

Cons: Many of the best liens are scooped up by banks and wealthy investors during the auction. Investors hoping to purchase a high-quality lien through an over-the-counter market may have to sift through pages of worthless tax liens before they find one that they are interested in.

Just because a tax lien is being offered over the counter does not necessarily mean that it is worthless (although it certainly could be). Sometimes, there are more tax liens available for sale at an auction than there are investors able to buy them. Sometimes smaller tax liens fall through the cracks because banks and accredited investors aren't interested in them. And sometimes, bidders get caught up in the excitement of an auction and agree to pay more than they are able for a tax lien certificate. When this happens, the lien remains with the county and may be listed in the over-the-counter market.

RISKS

Liquidity is one of the risks of investing in tax liens. Investors pay the delinquent taxes upfront, but they can't be totally sure when they will recoup their initial investments. Redemption periods vary, foreclosure processes differ, and other state or federal liens may prevent investors from ever recouping their investment. At the very least, investors may have to wait several years during the redemption period to be repaid. The biggest risk of tax lien investing, however, is the risk of purchasing a lien on a worthless property.

Investors should be wary of purchasing liens on landlocked land, liens on properties that could have environmental hazards associated with them, liens on oddly shaped properties, or liens on properties that simply shouldn't have tax liens attached to them (condo common areas, roundabouts, roads, and so on).

CONCLUSION

Tax liens, while not very sexy investments, somewhat defy the risk-return tradeoff. There is certainly risk involved in purchasing tax liens, but there is no volatility. Returns are government mandated, and they are generally much higher than other investment securities with similar risk profiles. Investing in tax liens provides an interesting opportunity for investors without deep pockets to diversify into real estate. Before purchasing their first tax lien certificate, investors should do sufficient research. A little due diligence goes a long way with tax lien investing.

RELATED RESOURCES

Upcoming Online Auction Information

http://www.realauction.com/

National Tax Lien Association

https://www.ntla.org/

County Search

https://www.naco.org/

Book: *Investing in Real Estate Tax Liens and Deeds,* Revised 2nd Edition, Alan Northcott

Difficulties of Tax Lien Investing Due Diligence

https://www.biggerpockets.com/member-blogs/1419/13003-difficulties-of-tax-lien-investing-due-diligence

PART V

REFERENCE CHAPTERS

CHAPTER 19

Property Rights

INTRODUCTION

Real estate property rights give utility or value to land and buildings (the realty). Navigating the complexities of a real estate transaction and the subsequent ownership of the property requires a basic understanding of fundamental property rights. This chapter discusses (1) personalty versus realty, (2) the various property rights associated with absolute ownership, (3) common public and private limitations to absolute ownership, and (4) some of the different types of property ownership.

PERSONALTY VERSUS REALTY

Property is commonly classified as either personalty or realty. Whenever a property is purchased, the owner receives the right to the land and anything permanently affixed to it (e.g., homes, garages, landscaping, etc.). This type of property is typically referred to as realty. The law distinguishes one other type of property: personalty, or personal property. Personalty is considered to be anything that is movable or not permanently attached to the land. Typically, realty and personalty are clearly identifiable. However, disputes can often occur over fixtures. Fixtures are items that were once personalty but have become realty because they have been attached to the property.

Hardly anyone would believe that they have the right to take the kitchen sink with them after they sell their property, but they might consider taking the wall-mounted flat-screen TV. The TV was once personal property, but how it has been attached to the wall may determine whether it is considered a fixture and, therefore, realty. Fixtures can remain the property of the seller if they are specifically excluded in the sales contract. Similarly, the buyer can negotiate the purchase of the seller's personal property if it is specifically delineated in the sales contract. In the event of a dispute about ownership after the real estate is sold, the matter is typically resolved in a court of law.

COMMERCIAL LEASE EXCEPTIONS

While fixtures are typically considered to be owned by the holder of the real estate, there are some exceptions for commercial properties. Commercial tenants often make significant improvements to the real property to operate their business. These improvements are typically referred to as trade fixtures and include such things as display counters, cubicles, shelving, booths, and storage cabinets. These fixtures typically remain the property of the tenant after the lease term ends.

BUNDLE OF RIGHTS

The value of real estate comes from the right to use the property in both general and specific ways. Consider the value of owning a property that you were forbidden to access in any way. Such a property would not be worth owning and therefore would have little or no value to you. In the US, most properties are sold "fee simple," meaning that they are purchased with complete or absolute ownership barring some exceptions or limitations that will be discussed later. Fee simple ownership is the most complete bundle of rights that anyone can acquire in the US.

Physical Rights of Fee Simple Ownership

When a buyer purchases a property, he or she is also buying a bundle of rights from which properties derive their value. Three of these physical rights are (1) surface rights, (2) subsurface rights, and (3) air rights.

Surface Rights

Surface rights are the legal rights to ownership of both the land and any permanently attached improvements. This includes buildings, landscaping, streets, gutters, and other improvements on or to the land. Therefore, anything permanently attached to the land is owned by the holder of the surface rights.

Subsurface or Mineral Rights

Subsurface or mineral rights extend physical ownership below the surface of the earth. The holder of these rights is considered the owner of any natural resources beneath the property, including oil, gas, and minerals. In theory, these rights extend to the earth's core. If an entity owns mineral rights but not the surface rights to a property, it typically still has the right to set up operations on the surface of the property to extract resources.

Air Rights

Air rights convey ownership of the space above the surface of the property. These rights are typically limited to five hundred feet. Space above this level is generally considered public air space. This allows airlines to operate without violating private ownership rights. More recently, the use of drones has resulted in the change of some air rights.[45]

FUNDAMENTAL RIGHTS OF FEE SIMPLE OWNERSHIP

As mentioned previously, fee simple ownership includes absolute ownership of the physical property. In addition to physical rights, the

---

45. See http://fortune.com/2016/09/25/drone-shotgun-airspace-rights/.

property owner is also entitled to three other fundamental rights: (1) the right of exclusive possession and control, (2) the right of quiet enjoyment, and (3) the right of disposition.

Right of Exclusive Possession and Control

The right or exclusive possession and control allows the owner to prevent trespass by private and even public entities (unless a search warrant is granted). In the case of trespass, the owner retains the right to collect damages from the trespasser. This right also allows the owner to use the property as collateral when seeking loans.

Right of Quiet Enjoyment

Contrary to the name, the right of quiet enjoyment has nothing to do with noise. Instead, this right allows the property holder to collect rent from the property and to collect money from the sale of the property. This right also grants the holder the right to use the property without unfounded disturbances from hostile claimants to the title. This means that, in conveyance of the title, the owner has assurance that no one else holds superior claims of ownership.

Right of Disposition

The right of disposition permits the owner of real property to transfer ownership to another party in any way he or she chooses. Methods of conveying property include sale, gift, or will. Some state or federal laws may still restrict who the property can be sold to (e.g., no foreign ownership).

LIMITATIONS TO ABSOLUTE OWNERSHIP

While fee simple ownership of a property is often referred to as absolute ownership, in reality, ownership is not absolute. Both public and private entities may place restrictions on property rights and uses. The value of a property will likely be impacted by these limitations because the uses and rights associated with the property have been restricted.

PUBLIC LIMITATION TO ABSOLUTE OWNERSHIP

The government's ability to limit property rights and uses comes from the US and state constitutions. These powers were granted to the government to protect the public interest. Fee simple ownership is subject to four principal public limitations: (1) eminent domain, (2) escheat, (3) police power, and (4) taxation.

Eminent Domain

Eminent domain is the government's right to take property from a private owner for a public purpose. This limitation finds its roots in the Takings Clause of the Fifth Amendment, which says that "private property [shall not] be taken for public use, without just compensation." The legal process the government uses to take property is called condemnation. Property may be taken by the government for any number of public uses, including the construction of highways, railroads, schools, or public utilities. Under the law, the owners of the condemned property must be "justly" compensated for their loss. "Just compensation" is typically interpreted to mean "fair market value," which will be determined in a court of law if the government and private owners cannot come to an agreement on the property's value.

Escheat

If the sole owner of a property dies without a will or any known heirs, the state takes ownership as the owner of last resort. Ownership will transfer to the state only after attempts have been made to locate any living heirs or other legal claimants. Typically, the property will return to private ownership through a subsequent sale of the property. This limitation ensures that property is always owned by either a public or private entity.

Police Power

Police power gives the government the right to restrict property uses to protect the health, safety, moral character, and general welfare of the population. This limitation is designed to limit the negative externalities that would result from everyone using their property as they pleased. For instance, many cities use the rights given to them through police power to restrict the discharge of firearms. If property owners were free to discharge firearms on their property within the city limits, they would be jeopardizing the safety of others.

Included within police power is the government's ability to set zoning laws. Zoning ordinances dictate the structural and architectural design of buildings as well as the allowable uses of the property. Zoning laws are often used to separate alternative types of uses, including commercial, industrial, and residential properties in a city. These laws typically also specify building height restrictions and setback requirements, which determine how far buildings must be from neighboring properties and/or streets. Zoning can have a significant impact on the value of a property (consider the value of land zoned as rural versus high-density commercial). However, governments are generally not required to compensate property owners for any adverse effects of zoning changes.

Taxation

Property taxation is the government's right to raise revenues from property owners. The function of government is to preserve and protect the public interest, but the government is unable to accomplish its purpose without funding. Taxes are typically collected as a percentage of a property's assessed value. The assessed value is a government (county) appraisal of the market value of the property, though it is typically less than the true market value of the property. Annual property taxes are calculated based on the assessed value.

PRIVATE LIMITATION TO ABSOLUTE OWNERSHIP

In addition to the four public limitations to fee simple ownership, it is possible for private parties to place limitations on a property's uses. These private restrictions are typically conveyed through (1) deed restrictions, (2) property liens, or (3) easements.

Deed Restrictions and Restrictive Covenants

Deed restrictions and restrictive covenants are private agreements that limit property use. They are often outlined in the language of the property deed. Usually, the seller of a property creates the restriction and includes it as a condition of the sale of the property.

Property Liens

Property liens are documents filed with the county against a specific property and are claims against the owners representing a debt to a creditor. Liens must be removed from a property for it to be sold since liens "cloud" the property title. In this way, liens ultimately restrict an owner's ability to sell the property and collect money from the sale. If, and when the property is sold, the creditors are paid off from the proceeds of the sale to remove their claim on the property. Creditors are paid based on the seniority of the lien. The government is always considered to be in the first position (most senior) in the event that a property owner owes outstanding taxes on the property. Most often the primary mortgage lender is in the second position, followed by any other creditors who have filed liens against the property (e.g., secondary mortgages, contractors, automobile or boat creditors, etc.). Common lien types include a mortgage, mechanics (contractors), judgment, and tax.

Easements

An easement is used to grant property uses to others while maintaining ownership of the property. There are two main types of easements: (1) easements appurtenant and (2) easements in gross.

An easement appurtenant is a type of easement between two adjacent properties. The property that receives the right to use the other property is called the dominant estate, while the property giving the right is called the servient estate (see Exhibit 19.1). The owner of the dominant estate typically pays the owner of the servient estate for the right to cross his or her property.

Exhibit 19.1: Easement Appurtenant

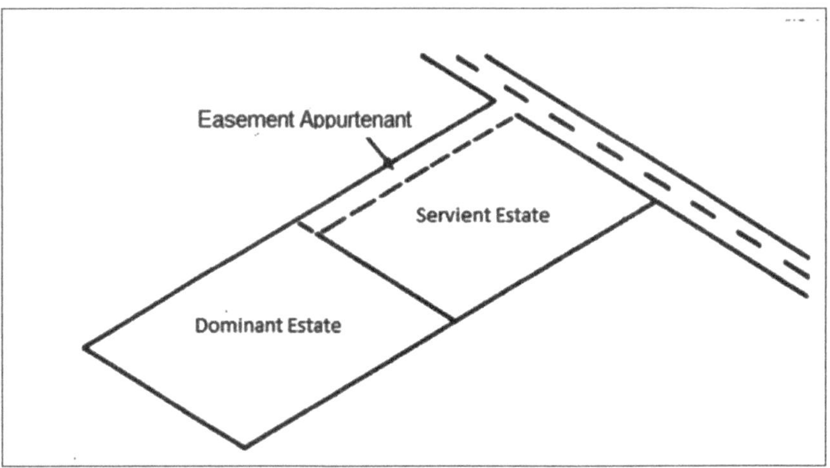

Although the owner of the dominant estate has been granted the right to use the servient estate, the servient estate is generally still responsible for the taxes and other liabilities of the property. Because the property itself retains the right, easements appurtenant are almost always transferred with the property ownership.

Like easements appurtenant, easements in gross grant specific property uses, but to individual entities rather than to a property. A common example of an easement in gross is granting utility companies the right to run pipes under your land or electric lines above your land. Easements in gross are often transferrable to third parties but remain exclusive: only the holder of the easement has the right to use the property in the specified manner.

Encroachments

Sometimes a third party will use another property without the owner's consent or approval (i.e., without an easement). This could be as simple as building a fence slightly beyond one's property line or having a tree overhang onto another's property. If property owners do not enforce their property rights when another encroaches on their property, they could eventually lose rights to the encroaching party through adverse possession. Adverse possession occurs if the nonpermitted use of a property is sustained over a long enough period (which varies by state), at which time the encroaching party could gain title to the property. For example, if a neighbor builds a fence on your side of the property line and you do not enforce its removal, then, given enough time, your neighbor may become the owner of your property on his or her side of the fence.

OTHER TYPES OF OWNERSHIP

In addition to fee simple property ownership, there are many other types of ownership that grant a subset of the absolute ownership rights that come with a fee simple estate. Although not an exhaustive list, some different types of ownership are described here:

Determinable Fee Estates

In a determinable fee estate, fee simple ownership is granted until a specified event occurs, at which point ownership reverts to the original owner or grantor of the determinable fee estate. For example, an owner might donate land to be used for a school with the condition that the land will revert to the original owner if it is used for any other purpose. Ownership reversion is automatic by force of law.

Fee Simple Subject to Condition Subsequent

Fee simple subject to condition subsequent is very similar to a determinable fee estate. In both cases, ownership is transferred upon a condition that the property will revert to the grantor of the estate upon certain events. The difference is that under fee simple subject to condition subsequent, reversion is not automatic but at the option of the grantor. If a reversion event occurs, (e.g., the property is not being used for a school), the grantor has the right to repossess the property but may choose not to do so.

Ordinary Life Estate

Ordinary life estate grants fee simple use of a property until the holder's death, at which point the property reverts to the original owner or to another specified party.

Leasehold Estate

Leasehold estates grant the holder the right to occupy a property for a length of time. Rent is typically paid to the lessor in exchange for occupation rights. At this time, all granted property rights revert to the lessor (owner) at the end of the lease.

Estate for Years

An estate for years is a type of leasehold estate with a defined beginning and ending date of the tenancy. The tenant is expected to vacate the property at the end of the lease term. The lease terms are almost always given in writing to document the specific period of the tenancy.

Periodic Tenancy

Periodic tenancy is another type of leasehold estate but without a definite beginning or ending period. These are often informal conveyances of leasehold rights that may not even be in writing. Since no formal ending date is provided, states typically have laws governing the termination process of a periodic tenancy.

RELATED RESOURCES

History of the Federal Use of Eminent Domain
https://www.justice.gov/enrd/history-federal-use-eminent-domain

Utah County Assessor's Office
http://www.utahcounty.gov/Dept/assess/index.asp

What Are House Fixtures?
https://www.thebalance.com/what-are-house-fixtures-1798755

Tenants' Rights Basics
https://realestate.findlaw.com/landlord-tenant-law/tenants-rights-basics.html

CHAPTER 20

Land (Legal) Descriptions

INTRODUCTION

A land or legal description describes land parcels in relation to a public land survey system. Because real estate is fixed in location, there must be a system that uniquely and precisely identifies a property's boundaries. Within the US there are three common and accepted methods for legally describing real estate: (1) metes and bounds, (2) government or rectangular survey, and (3) recorded plat (lot and block). These methods, when correctly used, provide the means of identifying the boundaries for a parcel of land and are an essential item on any real estate contract, deed, or mortgage document.

METES AND BOUNDS

The metes and bounds survey system is the oldest known method of identifying a parcel of land. Used by the Founding Fathers when they came to America, the metes and bounds system is the primary method used in twenty states, including the thirteen states that made up the original thirteen colonies and those states that had land allocated prior to 1785 (which includes states adjacent to the original thirteen colony states). This system is also the primary method used by Texas, as it was an independent republic prior to becoming a state.

Historically, the metes and bounds system used prominent landmarks to mark the Point of Beginning (POB), which constitutes a corner of the subject property. For the Founding Fathers, the POB may have been the a large oak tree. Today, USGS benchmarks are used as a reference point to mark the POB. After the POB has been located, the legal description follows the property boundaries by giving cardinal directions and the distances of a property's boundaries.

Exhibit 20.1 is an example of a metes and bounds legal description: "From reference mark located at the USGS benchmark, proceed north 400 feet to POB, thence east 350 feet, thence north 500 feet, thence south 45 degrees west 305.164 feet, thence west 175 feet, thence south 250 feet to POB." The following sketch shows the boundaries of this metes and bounds legal description.

Exhibit 20.1

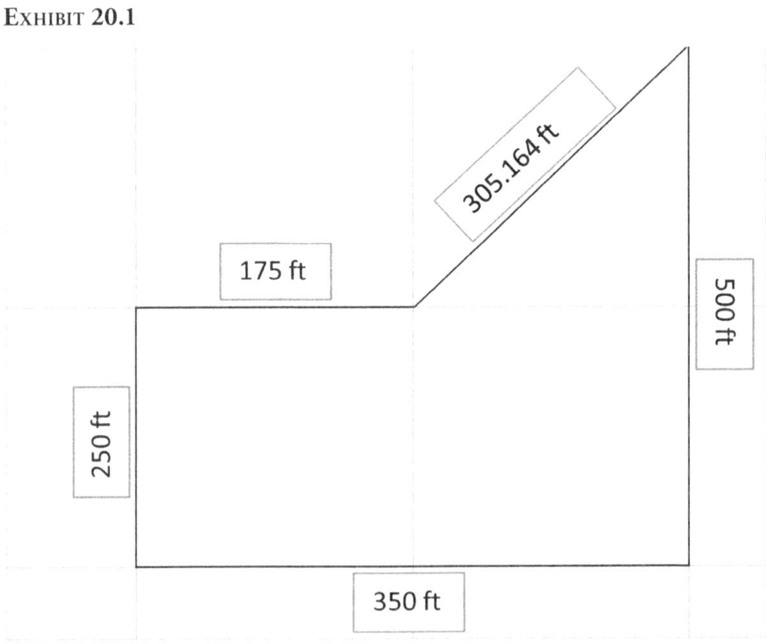

Answer: 109,375 square feet, 2.511 acres

GOVERNMENT OR RECTANGULAR SURVEY

As you can imagine, the metes and bounds survey system is tedious to use when surveyors need to describe large tracts of land and many properties. For that reason, the rectangular survey system was created.

The majority of states in the US use this system to legally describe property boundaries. This system is based on Principal Meridians, which run north to south, and Base Lines, which run east to west. Principal Meridians typically have a unique name, such as the Gila and Salt River. Principal Meridians (PM) and Base Lines (BL) may span over more than one state.

To provide further division, there are Range Lines, which travel north to south six miles apart, and Township Lines, which run east to west, also six miles apart. These lines make up six-mile by six-mile squares, called townships, as shown in Exhibit 20.2.

Exhibit 20.2

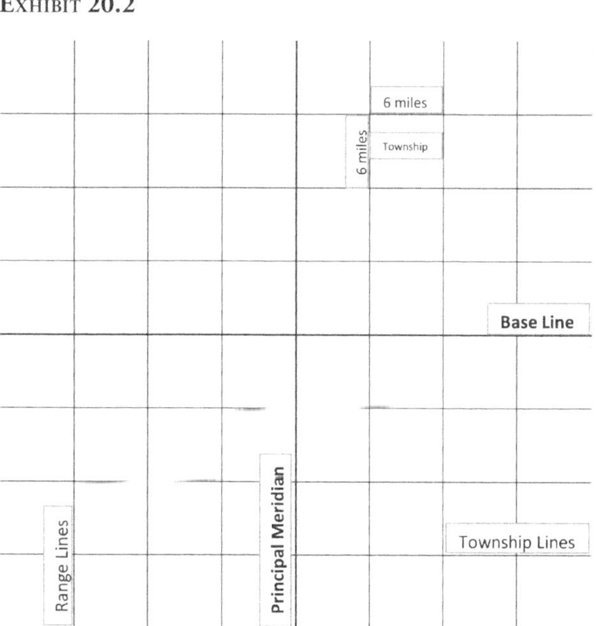

Next, each township is divided into thirty-six one-mile increment squares called sections, as shown in Exhibit 20.3. Each section contains 640 acres. The sections are labeled from 1 to 36 starting in the upper-right corner and continuing left until the end of the row. At the end of the row, the numbering continues down a row and then right until the end of the row. The 36th section is in the right-bottom corner, as shown in the following example. Finally, the rectangular survey system splits each section up using halves and quarters to locate the specific parcel of the property it is trying to define.

Exhibit 20.3

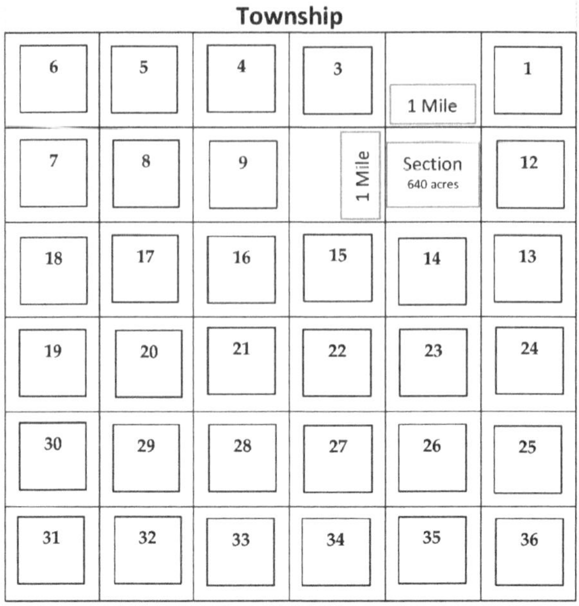

Township

6	5	4	3	1 Mile	1
7	8	9	1 Mile	Section 640 acres	12
18	17	16	15	14	13
19	20	21	22	23	24
30	29	28	27	26	25
31	32	33	34	35	36

Exhibit 20.4 shows how to identify a parcel with the following legal description: "The S1/2, NE1/4, NW1/4, of Section 8, T3N, R2W, Salt Lake Principal Meridian and Baseline."

Exhibit 20.4

Salt Lake City
T3N
R2W
Base Line
Range Lines
Principal Meridian
Township Lines
Township 3 North, Range 2 West
Section
8
Section 8
NE4
S2
NW4

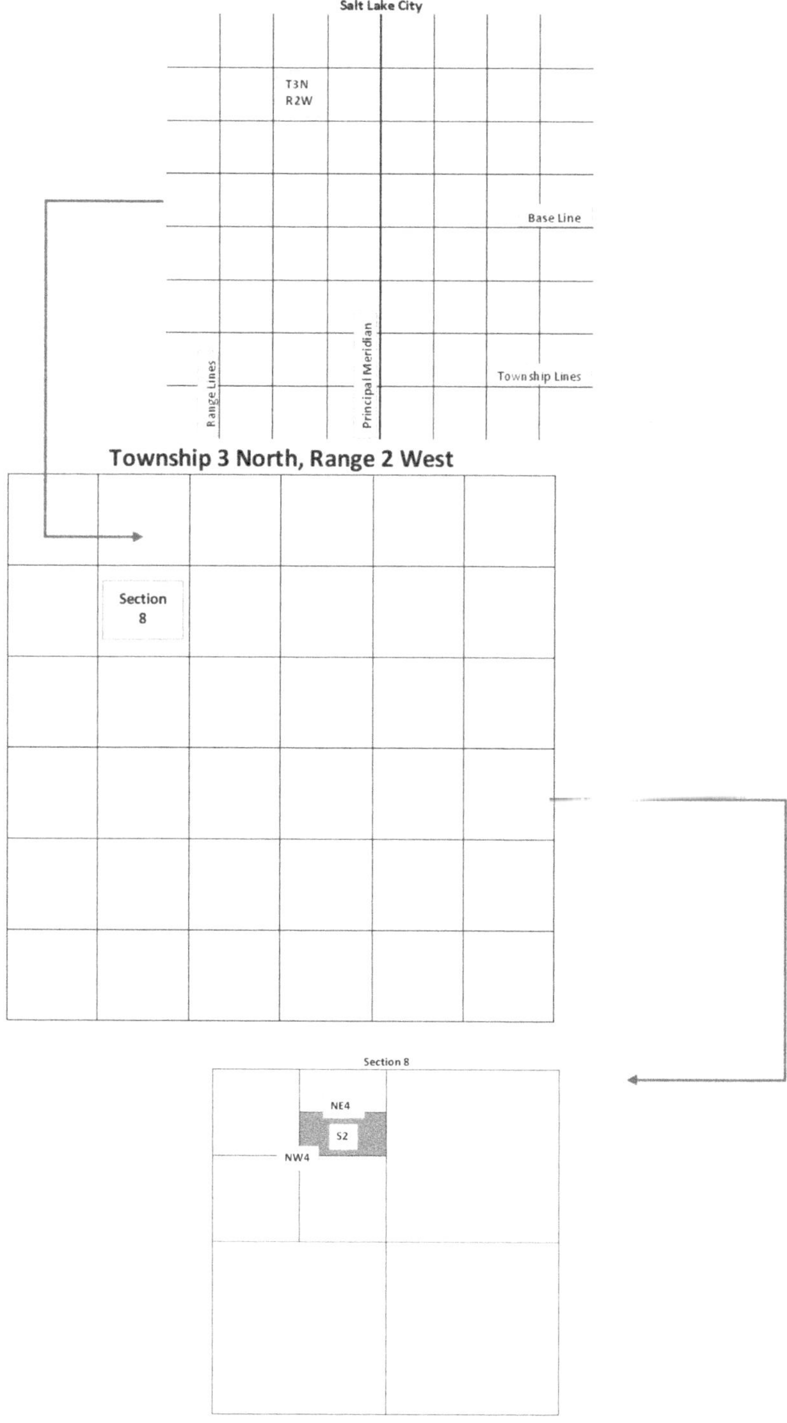

RECORDED PLAT (LOT AND BLOCK)

A lot and block legal description is mainly used for the ease of describing subdivisions. A subdivision is a plot of land bought and owned by one person or company. That owner then divides up the land into lots/homes, parks, streets, and so forth and sells the lots/homes to individual buyers. These buyers fully own their little piece of land inside of the subdivision, which is why it is important that we can effectively describe what land they own.

The entire subdivision plat will be recorded with the county recorder's office, using metes and bounds, the rectangular survey system, or a combination of both. Each lot on the plat is given a number that is tied to the subdivision name.

As an example, Exhibit 20.5 locates Lot 5 of the Sunny Pines Community subdivision.

Exhibit 20.5

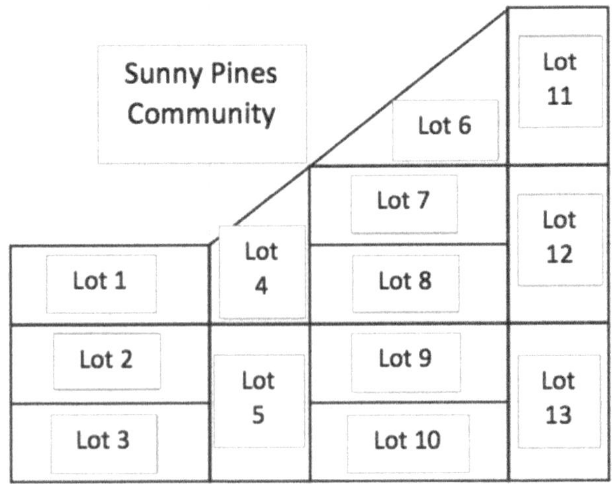

CONCLUSION

As a final note on legal descriptions, it is important to know that in some cases the different methods are used together to provide a legal description for a property. In one legal description of a property, both the rectangular survey system and the metes and bounds system may be used to specify the boundaries of the property.

RELATED RESOURCES

Metes and Bounds System
https://legaldictionary.net/metes-and-bounds/

Video: Rectangular Survey System
https://www.youtube.com/watch?v=KqsLpghno1U

Lot and Block System
http://study.com/academy/lesson/using-the-lot-block-survey-system.html

CHAPTER 21

Zoning and Entitlements

INTRODUCTION

Zoning, in one form or another, has been around since almost the very beginning of the United States of America and can have a dramatic effect on property value and the land use rights of the property owner. Understanding zoning and land use controls by local municipalities is essential for a prospective homeowner and real estate investor.

HISTORY AND DEFINITION

Zoning can be traced back as far as Jamestown, Virginia, where the settlement was planned and set up for the well-being of the people.[46] Wikipedia provides a nice definition and overview of zoning with the following:

> Zoning is the process of dividing land in a municipality into zones (e.g., residential, industrial) in which certain land uses are permitted or prohibited. In addition, the sizes, bulk, and placement of buildings may be regulated. Zoning is the most common regulatory divider local governments use to help carry out urban plans. The type of zone determines whether

---

46. Edward T. McMahon, "Zoning at 85," Urban Land, Urban Land Institute, November 21 2011, https://urbanland.uli.org/industry-sectors/zoning-at-85/.

> planning permission for a given development is granted. Zoning may specify a variety of outright and conditional uses of land. It may also indicate the size and dimensions of the land area as well as the form and scale of buildings. These guidelines are set in order to guide urban growth and development.[47]

The ability or authority of a community to restrict property use through zoning was granted to states by the Tenth Amendment to the Constitution. This right or authority is known as police power, which is one of the four limitations to the fee simple estate.[48] Police power is essentially the right of each community to ensure its health, safety, welfare, and moral character.

To provide these protections, zoning ordinances regulate how the land may be used. They legislate "intensity or density of development, height, bulk and placement of structures, amount and design of parking, and a number of other aspects of land-use and development activity."[49]

In other words, the ordinances can dictate that certain areas are for single-family housing instead of multifamily housing, how tall buildings can be, how much of the land a building may cover, and so on. Exhibit 21.1 provides examples of a few of these restrictions.

---

47. "Zoning," Wikipedia, https://en.wikipedia.org/wiki/Zoning.
48. "Police Power," West's Encyclopedia of American Law, 2nd ed. (Gale Group, 2008; 7 Apr. 2018, https://legal-dictionary.thefreedictionary.com/Police+Power.
49. Edward T. McMahon, "Zoning at 85." Urban Land, Urban Land Institute, November 21, 2011, https://urbanland.uli.org/industry-sectors/zoning-at-85/.

EXHIBIT 21.1

Height Restrictions
104 ft
41 ft
28 ft
Bulk Restrictions
56.25% Area
75 ft
100 ft
75 ft
100 ft
56.25% Area
100 ft
56.25 ft
100 ft
28.13 ft
56.25% Area
28.13 ft
100 ft
100 ft
Setback Restrictions
25 ft
15 ft
Building
15 ft
40 ft

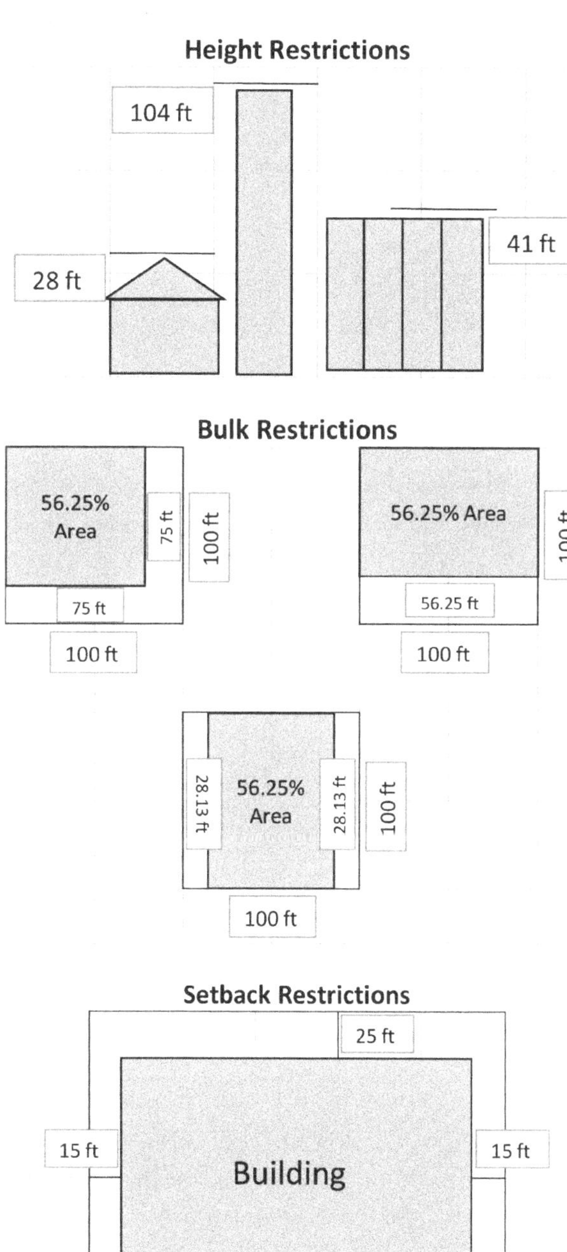

REZONING PROPERTIES

At times, the existing zoning of a parcel is suboptimal and does not provide for the highest and best use of the site. In this case, it can be advantageous to petition the local municipality to rezone the property to an alternative use or zone. Some investors see financial opportunity in purchasing a property and then rezoning it to higher and better use. This action may increase the value of the property, allowing the investor to resell it for a profit.

Rezoning can be a difficult process because an investor must convince the local government authorities that the change in use results in the highest and best use of the site by enhancing the value of nearby properties and benefiting the community at large.

Rezoning is also very political and requires an understanding of the rezoning process. Generally, the rezoning process is accomplished in the following six steps.

Step 1: The property owner completes an application for a zoning change that includes a description of the property, its current zoning classification, its prospective zoning classification, its intended future use, and an application fee.

Step 2: The city zoning and planning representatives place a sign on the site notifying the public of a hearing before the Planning and Zoning Commission that will consider a zoning change on the property. The city also provides other public notices and typically notifies nearby property owners of the public hearing.

Step 3: The employees at the city Zoning and Planning Department review the zoning application and consider its merits in the context of the current zoning regulations and general plan of the city. After reviewing the application, these planners formulate a recommendation to the Planning and Zoning Commission.

Step 4: The Planning and Zoning Commission holds a public hearing to consider the application. During the meeting, the commissioners seek input from the applicant, the employees at the city Zoning and Planning Department, and the public.

Step 5: The commissioners vote to either accept, reject, or table the application for zone change. If the vote were to approve the zoning change, the application goes to the city council for their consideration. If the votes were to reject, it still goes to the city council. However, approval by at least a three-fourths majority is required to override the commission's recommendation.

Step 6: In some jurisdictions, the mayor is also allowed to weigh in and either ratify or deny the zoning request.

RELATED RESOURCES

Police Power
http://legal-dictionary.thefreedictionary.com/Police+Power

Zoning
http://en.wikipedia.org/wiki/Zoning

Zoning at 85
http://urbanland.uli.org/industry-sectors/zoning-at-85/

Preparing for a Zoning Change
http://www.ccim.com/cire-magazine/articles/abcs-zoning

CHAPTER 22

Time Value of Money

INTRODUCTION

Conducting even the most basic real estate analysis requires a working knowledge of the time value of money. The basic idea is that a dollar today is worth more than a dollar in the future.

A simple illustration shows the validity of this concept. Suppose you are given the option by a new employer of receiving your latest paycheck now or in one year. Which option would you prefer? Unless you are exceptionally poor at managing your finances, you would prefer to have the money now. The money should be worth more to you now than in one year for at least three reasons: (1) purchasing power, (2) opportunity cost, and (3) default risk.

PURCHASING POWER

A dollar received in one year will likely purchase fewer goods and services than a dollar now because of inflation. For example, a dollar in the 1960s could buy you approximately three gallons of gas or a full meal at a local diner. Finding those types of deals in today's economy would be a real boon.

OPPORTUNITY COST

Receiving a dollar in one year would not allow you to make full use of that dollar over the next year. A dollar received today could be invested to make more dollars or spent on goods or services during the year.

DEFAULT RISK

A dollar promised to you by your employer in one year is less likely to be collected than one promised to you the same day. Several factors, such as employer financial difficulty, confusion regarding the obligation, and so on, could prevent you from collecting that dollar in one year.

Though you would not accept an equal dollar payment for your paycheck from your employer in one year, what if the employer offered to pay 5% more dollars? What if the employer offered 20% or 50% more? At some point, the additional amount received in one year would compensate you enough to justify accepting a later payment. The formulas presented in this chapter can help you compare cash flows and their value at distinct periods in time.

FUTURE VALUE (FV)

A common question involving the time value of money is how much an investment will be worth at some date in the future. If you can obtain the interest rate at which the investment will grow, and the number of periods that will pass until the investment is withdrawn, you can determine the value of the cash flow at a future date. The relationship among these variables is shown in the following formula:

$$FV = PV(1 + i)^n$$

FV = future value	i = interest rate
PV = present value	n = number of periods

For example, suppose you have \$1,000 you would like to invest in a retirement account. You expect to earn 8% annual interest, and you plan to withdraw the investment in thirty years. The future value of the investment can be derived as follows:

$$FV = \$1{,}000\ (1 + 0.08)^{30} = \$10{,}062.66$$

How is it that a modest interest rate (8%) can multiply an investment by more than ten times in thirty years? This increase is because of compounding interest. Compounding interest, or interest on interest, can significantly increase the future value of a lump sum. In year 1, interest is calculated on the original investment of \$1,000, totaling \$80. But in year 2, interest is calculated on the new outstanding balance of \$1,080, totaling \$86.40. This upward trend in interest continues throughout the investment period, and by year 30, the annual interest earned is about \$745.38.

While understanding the underlying algebra of time value of money (TVM) calculations is a good idea, these calculations are now rarely calculated by long-hand. The use of financial calculators and spreadsheet programs such as Microsoft Excel can make quick work of TVM calculations, even as they become more complex. Following is the format for entering a future value calculation into Microsoft Excel:

= *FV (rate, nper, pmt, [pv], [type])*

FV = future value	pmt = annuity payment (discussed later)
rate = interest rate	[pv] = present value
nper = number of periods	[type] = timing of payments (discussed later)

Note: Square brackets [] indicate an optional argument.

For the problem discussed earlier, the future value would be calculated as follows:

=FV(0.08,30,0,–1000) = \$10,062.66

Notice a few important things about the previous formula:

- The pmt argument was set at zero (discussed later).
- The pv argument was set at a negative $1,000. This convention goes back to earlier financial calculators designed to help keep cash inflows and cash outflows separate. In this instance, we are investing, or experiencing a cash outflow, so we enter the present value as a negative number. If we were receiving the money today and paying it back later, we would use a positive number in this argument.
- This [type] argument was simply left blank. This is permissible for optional arguments [denoted in brackets], and the [type] argument is usually omitted except in the case of an annuity due (discussed later).
- If you forget the order of the arguments, don't fret. Each time you enter a formula into Excel, a "screen tip" will appear to remind you of the arguments in that formula.

PRESENT VALUE (PV)

Rather than calculating the future value of a lump sum, the investor may want to determine what "present value" would be required today to grow to a specified amount or value in the future. Or, to put it another way, how much would you be willing to give up today in order to receive a stipulated amount in the future? Simply by rearranging the future value formula to solve for present value PV, you can use the following algebraic formula to calculate the present value of a lump sum:

$$PV = \frac{FV}{(1+i)^n}$$

And the formula in Excel is likewise similar to the future value formula:

= *PV (rate, nper, pmt, [fv], [type])*

Now suppose you anticipate being able to sell an investment property for $200,000 in five years. How much would you be willing to pay today if you wanted to earn 5% annually on the investment?

To solve this problem, enter the appropriate values into Excel's PV formula:

=PV(0.05,5,0,200000) = –$156,705.23

This result suggests that you should be willing to pay $156,705.23 for this property to receive $200,000 in five years. This investment would earn you a 5% annual rate of return.

RATE (i)

A third question relating to time value of money is the rate of return that is expected in an investment. The derivation of the future value formula solving for rate algebraically is as follows:

$$i = \left(\frac{FV}{PV}\right)^{\frac{1}{n}} - 1$$

These formulas continue to grow in complexity, so the ease of Excel's entry simplifies calculation substantially:

– *RATE (nper, pmt, pv, [fv], [type], [guess])*

Suppose you had the opportunity to purchase an investment property for $195,000 today, and you expect to sell the property in five years for $245,000. What is the implied annual rate of return from this investment?

Again, we turn to Excel to assist in solving this problem:

= RATE(5,0,–195000,245000) = 4.67%

The investment offers an annual rate of return of 4.67%. This calculation provides you with the information to make an investment decision.

NUMBER OF PERIODS (NPER)

A final question relating to the value of a lump sum payment is the time needed to realize a certain return. The derivation of the future value formula solving for the number of periods algebraically is as follows:

$$n = \frac{ln\left(\frac{FV}{PV}\right)}{ln(1-i)}$$

The corresponding Excel formula is provided here:

=NPER (rate, pmt, pv, [fv], [type])

As an example of this calculation, suppose you want to know how long it will be until a $100,000 property is worth $200,000, assuming it will appreciate at 3% annually.

To solve this equation, note the following Excel inputs:

=NPER(0.03,0,–100000,200000) = 23.45 years

If inflation is constant at 3%, it will take 23.45 years for the value of the property to double.

ANNUITY CALCULATIONS

An annuity is a series of equal amounts received, one each period, for a specified number of periods. There are two types of annuities you need to know to properly calculate annuities:

Regular Annuity: An annuity in which the payments are received at the end of each period.

Annuity Due: An annuity in which the payments are received at the beginning of each period.

FUTURE VALUE OF AN ANNUITY

Some investments may generate the same cash flow each period for the term of the investment. If the investor wanted to calculate the future value of the equal cash flows over the term of the investment, he or she could calculate the individual future value of each cash flow and sum them up. This process, however, could be very tedious if there are many cash flows. Luckily, mathematicians have derived a closed-form equation that will calculate the future value of a series of equal cash flows as follows:

$$FVA = PMT\left[\frac{(1+i)^n - 1}{i}\right]$$

The corresponding Excel formula is provided here:

= FV (rate, nper, pmt, [pv], [type])

As an example of this calculation, suppose that an investment will provide $10,000 per year in cash flow for ten years, earning a 5% annual rate of return.

To solve this problem in Excel, note the following inputs:

= FV(0.05,10,–10000,0,0) = $125,778.93

Therefore, $10,000 per year, growing at 5% per year for ten years, will result in $125,778.93 at the end of ten years.

SINKING FUND

As investors, we sometimes want to know how much we need to sink away (save) each period over a specified number of periods to accumulate a specific amount. Using the previous equation and solving for PMT results in the following formula:

$$PMT = FVA\left[\frac{i}{(1+i)^n - 1}\right]$$

The portion of the equation in the brackets is known as the sinking fund factor because once we multiply the factor by the forecast future value, it tells us how much we must sink away (save) each period to accumulate a specific amount. The corresponding Excel formula is provided here:

= *PMT (rate, nper, pv [fv], [type])*

Let's assume that an investor wants to accumulate $1,000,000 in thirty years, and he or she can earn a 5% annual rate of return.

To solve this problem in Excel, note the following inputs:

= PMT(0.05,30,0,1000000,0) = $15,051.44

Therefore, he or she would need to save $15,051.44 each year at a 5% annual rate of return for thirty years to accumulate $1,000,000.

PRESENT VALUE OF AN ANNUITY

Rather than calculate the future value of an annuity, an investor may want to calculate the present value of an annuity. Suppose an investment promises to pay $10,000 per year for five years. Also, suppose that the investor wants to earn an 8% annual rate of return. To calculate the present value of this annuity, he or she could calculate the present value of each individual cash flow and then sum them up. Or, a more efficient approach would be to use the present value annuity equation that has been derived by mathematicians as follows:

$$PVA = PMT\left[\frac{1-\frac{1}{(1+i)^n}}{i}\right]$$

The corresponding Excel formula is provided here:

= PV (rate, nper, pmt, [fv], [type])

Inserting the previous inputs into the Excel function results in the following:

= PV(0.08,5,10000,0,0) = $39,927.10

Therefore, the investor would be willing to pay $39,929.10 today in exchange for $10,000 each year for the next five years. This investment would provide an annual rate of return of 8% on the investment.

A CONSTANT PAYMENT

Purchasing real estate often requires that the buyer obtain a mortgage loan to complete the acquisition. In the context of the time value of money, the mortgage loan is the PVA of the previous equation. Given a specified term and interest rate, it is possible to calculate the PMT by using the present value annuity equation and solving for PMT as follows:

$$PMT = PVA\left[\frac{i}{1-\frac{1}{(1+i)^n}}\right]$$

The portion of the equation within the brackets is known as the mortgage constant and provides the periodic payment when multiplied by the mortgage amount (PVA). The equivalent Excel function is as follows:

= *PMT (rate, nper, pv, [fv], [type])*

As an example, suppose you are considering obtaining a $200,000 mortgage that will charge 5% annual interest over thirty years. What is the annual payment you would be required to pay?

To solve this in Excel, note the following inputs:

= PMT(0.05,30,200000,0,0) = –$13,010.29

You would have to pay $13,010.29 annually for a mortgage with those terms.

MONTHLY COMPOUNDING

Interest rates are usually quoted on an annual basis, but payments are often made more regularly than once each year. In real estate, payments are typically made monthly. Therefore, the compounding is monthly. When the compounding is more frequent than yearly, the previous equations can easily be manipulated to provide the correct result. This is done by dividing the interest rate by the number of periods in the year and multiplying the term by the number of periods in the year.

For example, take the terms of the mortgage payment calculation derived earlier. The interest rate was 5%, and the term was over thirty years. If payments were made monthly instead of annually, how much would the monthly payments be?

Using the Excel function shown previously, we divide the 5% interest by 12 and multiply the thirty years by 12 as follows:

= PMT(0.05/12,30 * 12,200000,0,0) = –$1,073.64

The new monthly payment would equal $1,073.64 instead of an annual payment of $13,010.29.

Note that the monthly payment of $1,073.64 is not equal to the annual payment of $13,010.29 divided by 12, which would equal $1,084.19. Take care not to make this common mistake. Because payments are made more quickly on the loan, less interest accrues on the mortgage, and less money is needed over the life of the mortgage.

Note that the same process could be followed to match any compounding interval but that monthly intervals are the most common for real estate transactions.

ANNUITY DUE

Most time value of money calculations are made with the assumption that the cash flows occur at the end of the period. However, sometimes it is necessary to specify that cash flows occur at the beginning of the period. Adjusting TVM calculations in Excel for an annuity due (the technical term for payments due at the beginning of the period) is as simple as adding a 1 to the optional [type] argument.

For example, if the monthly mortgage payment just contemplated was to be paid by the first of each month, the calculation would look like the following.

= PMT(0.05/12,30 * 12,200000,0,1) = –$1,069.19

Note that the monthly payment for the annuity due mortgage is about $5 less than the payment with the standard calculation because payments are being made earlier, allowing less time for compounding interest to accrue.

AMORTIZATION SCHEDULE

The mortgage payment is fixed or constant over the term of the loan and is comprised of both principal and interest. However, these two inputs vary each period. Also, the amount of the principal that is paid each period reduces the outstanding balance as well. Given the dynamic nature of interest, principal, and outstanding balance over the life of the loan, it is sometimes helpful to create an amortization table depicting these changes.

As an example, assume the bank will loan you $50,000 over five years at 10% annual interest. Also assume the payments will be made annually. First, using the preceding methodology, we calculate the annual payment:

= PMT(0.10,5,50000,0,0) = $13,189.87

Next, we calculate the amount of interest being paid by multiplying the interest rate by the outstanding balance:

0.10(50,000) = $5,000

Then, we calculate the amount of principal being paid by subtracting the interest payment from the total payment:

$$13{,}189.87 - 5{,}000 = \$8{,}189.87$$

Finally, we calculate the new outstanding balance by subtracting the principal being paid from the old outstanding balance:

$$50{,}000 - 8{,}189.87 = \$41{,}810.13$$

We repeat these steps for each period to complete the amortization schedule of the loan as follows:

Period	Payment/ Debt Service	Interest	Principal	Amount Outstanding
0	-	-	-	50,000.00
1	13,189.87	5,000.00	8,189.87	41,810.13
2	13,189.87	4,181.01	9,008.86	32,801.27
3	13,189.87	3,280.13	9,909.74	22,891.53
4	13,189.87	2,289.15	10,900.72	11,990.81
5	13,189.87	1,199.08	11,990.79	0.00

Notice how the interest paid declines each period, and the principal paid increases each period. At the end of the term, the amount outstanding is zero (the preceding table has a bit of a rounding error). While making these calculations, be sure to use the correct compounding interval.

CALCULATING THE OUTSTANDING BALANCE

Often, when conducting financial analysis for an investment, it is helpful to calculate the amount outstanding on a mortgage loan. As previously shown, one way to do this is to construct an amortization table. However, a more efficient way is to discount the payments over the remaining term to obtain the present value of the remaining payments.

As an example, assume that five years ago, you purchased a home and obtained a loan for $100,000. The terms of the loan were 10% annual interest compounded monthly for thirty years. You can calculate your current outstanding balance as follows. First, calculate the monthly payment:

= PMT(0.10/12,30 * 12,100000,0,0) = $877.57

Second, discount the payments over the remaining term (30 – 5 = 25 years) to calculate the present value of the mortgage:

= PV(0.10/12,25 * 12,877.57,0,0) = $96,574.15

Therefore, the outstanding balance is $96,574.15.

Another way to approach this problem is to use the future value of an annuity (FVA) function and calculate the future value of the monthly payments over the term that has passed (five years) as follows:

= FV(0.10/12,5 * 12,877.57,–100000,0) = $96,574.15

We arrive at the same outstanding balance of $96,574.15.

NET PRESENT VALUE (NPV)

The net present value (NPV) calculates the difference between what an investment costs and what it is worth to the investor. That bears repeating: the net present value is the difference between what an investment costs and what it is worth. A positive net present value usually suggests investing, while a negative one would not. This method gives an investor a way to compare real estate assets to stocks, bonds, and a host of other potential investment opportunities.

The NPV of an investment can be found via the following formula:

$$NPV(i, N) = \sum_{t=0}^{N} \frac{CF_t}{(1+i)^t}$$

N = total number of periods

CFt = cash flow in a period

i = discount rate

Put in simpler terms, if you were to take every cash flow, including the initial outlay, from an investment and discount it back to the present time and then add all of those present value calculations together, you would derive the NPV of the investment. In Excel, this calculation is made fairly simple with the following formula:

= NPV (rate, value1, [value2], ...)

Suppose you were to make an investment that cost $100, paid out $30 after one year, $65 after two years, and $20 after three. If your discount rate is 10%, what is the investment worth to you?

Using Excel, the sensible way to input this would be as follows:

= NPV(0.10,–100,30,65,20) = –$3.62

Unfortunately, this is not how Excel's NPV function works. Instead, Excel's NPV formula calculates the discounted present value of all cash flows, whereas the traditional capital budgeting NPV analysis analyzes the return of the project starting at the first cash flow. This means the initial outlay (IO) of the project should be subtracted out separately from the NPV function, as follows:

= NPV(30,65,20) – 100 = –$3.98

The difference here is small, and the investment would be rejected either way, but if the numbers were instead in millions or billions, that change would make a big difference. Using the correct second formula , an investor would reject this hypothetical investment because it would cost him or her $3.98 more than it is worth.

INTERNAL RATE OF RETURN (IRR)

While the net present value calculation is the most heralded by financial purists, the most quoted multiyear financial metric in real estate circles is the internal rate of return. The internal rate of return (IRR) is the discount rate at which an investment will have a net present value of zero. The formula for IRR in Excel follows and is usually as simple as typing in the formula and then selecting the cells that have the appropriate cash flows. Entering an estimate in the [guess] field may increase calculation speed:

= IRR (values[guess])

IRR has many benefits, the biggest of which is its easy comparison across asset classes. Most portfolio returns are quoted on a percentage basis, so if your investment portfolio earns about 10% and the asset had an expected return of 20%, you would know immediately that the expected return of that asset would exceed your current portfolio return.

Despite its wide adoption, there are three important weaknesses to remember regarding the IRR. First, the IRR assumes reinvestment at the rate it calculates. This often makes assets with large, quick returns on the investment look more valuable than they really are since the funds are assumed to be reinvested at the rate that prevails throughout the investment window when in reality there may not be an opportunity to invest at that same rate at a later time. Second, there may be multiple solutions if there is more than one sign change in the cash flows. In this case, do not use the IRR for decision-making purposes. Third, the size of cash flows is not evaluated, just the percentage return. Given two mutually exclusive investment opportunities, one with a 400% IRR and an investment of $1 is surely going to be rejected against a 40% IRR investment of $1,000,000, but the higher IRR suggests the first is better. These weaknesses aside, the IRR is a valuable metric and will likely continue as the most important multi-year investment measure in real estate.

UNDERSTANDING THE DISCOUNT RATE

Calculating an appropriate discount rate is essential for calculating the net present value of an investment, and understanding the appropriate discount rate for the investment is vital to understanding whether the projected IRR is sufficient to justify investment in the project.

To calculate an appropriate discount rate, we will start by breaking up the discount rate into several components that can later be summed to calculate the total discount rate. Possible inclusions into the discount rate for real estate investment include the following considerations.

RISK-FREE RATE

The risk-free rate is included in nearly every discount rate calculation and is usually the quoted US Treasury interest rate on a note or bond equal (or close to) the projected investment horizon. For example, an investment with an expected ten-year hold would use the risk-free rate on the most recent ten-year Treasury bond.

DEFAULT (OF EQUITY) RISK PREMIUM

Investors (including lenders) are often paid out according to different priority levels. Those who are paid first incur less risk than those who are paid last, so the required rate of return to those who are paid last is higher, and this difference represents the default (or equity) risk premium.

LIQUIDITY PREMIUM

If you had ten minutes to sell your stock or bond portfolio, you could probably go online and get nearly full value in return. Selling a house (or other real estate asset) in such a time frame would be unreasonable. Even a deadline of a month or more may create significant price pressure and reduce the amount for which the asset can sell. Investors require a premium if their assets are difficult to sell for market value—a liquidity premium.

INDUSTRY PREMIUM

Real estate is a highly cyclical industry. When the outlook is positive on real estate, there may be no industry premium or a negative industry premium, but when the real estate market is perceived as overheated, there may be a significant industry premium added to the discount rate.

ASSET RISK PREMIUM

Some pieces of real estate have had similar cash flows for many years and are subject to very low risk. Others have highly volatile cash flows and should be discounted at a higher rate. Size, location, condition, and asset type are among the variable types that should be considered when setting the asset risk premium.

NONDIVERSIFIABLE RISK PREMIUM

A commonly known investment strategy is to diversify investments, but at times this can be difficult or impossible. For example, if you want to purchase and rent out a condominium unit, you may not have capital left to invest in other assets. An investor that is not in a fully diversified portfolio should increase the discount rate.

CONTROL RISK PREMIUM

When you give over your money to others and have little control over how that money is utilized, you run some risk that funds will not be optimally invested for your benefit. That risk premium is often called the control risk premium.

INTERNATIONAL RISK PREMIUM

Exchange rate and governmental risk can significantly increase the required return for an investor.

In theory, each investor would calculate a value for each of these fields, sum them together, and calculate the appropriate discount rate for a real estate investment. While you may wish to take this approach, in practice, most investors consider some of these factors and then estimate a rate they will require on their investment. When calculating a discount rate for an investment, the discount rate should approximate the opportunity cost of investing the funds in a similarly risky investment. This cost, and thus the appropriate discount rate, will depend on who the investor(s) is. Examples of opportunity cost discount rates used in the industry include the following.

COST OF EQUITY

The most common discount rate used for evaluating real estate projects is the cost of obtaining equity financing. Because most real estate investment properties have a mortgage for that specific property, estimating the debt service required is straightforward. If you use this method, you should calculate leveraged cash flows (i.e., include debt service payments) to the investor and discount them at the rate that your investors require to continue to invest.

WEIGHTED AVERAGE COST OF CAPITAL (WACC)

If instead of leveraging specific real estate assets a company selectively leverages some assets or gets portfolio loans and thus leverages its company more similarly to most Fortune 500 companies, the weighted average cost of capital (WACC) should be used. The WACC is calculated using the equation that follows. When using the WACC as a discount rate, you should base the returns on the unleveraged cash flows (i.e., net operating income minus any capital expenditures or returns).

(% Debt x AfterTax Cost of Debt) + (% Equity x Cost of Equity)

When a company has limited access to capital at less than prohibitive cost, it should base its discount rate on the other investments it could make or a more arbitrary management target and then select the projects that will maximize the NPV for the portfolio.

RELATED RESOURCES

The Limitations of IRR
https://fundrise.com/education/blog-posts/the-limitations-of-internal-rate-of-return-irr-for-predicting-investment-su

Limitations of the Net Present Value Method
http://www.projectnpv.com/9.html

Video: Time Value of Money
https://www.khanacademy.org/economics-finance-domain/core-finance/interest-tutorial/present-value/v/time-value-of-money

CHAPTER 23

Brokerage

INTRODUCTION

In 2019 HomeLight estimated that there were more than two million active real estate agents in the US.[50] Of these, more than 1.3 million were Realtors®, or members of the National Association of Realtor®, one of the largest trade organizations in the country. So why is this industry so large? It comes down to two primary reasons—the size of the transaction and the lack of experience by the participants.

Purchasing a home is typically the most significant financial decision made by a household, and it is made infrequently (the typical family moves about every seven years on average). Hence, most families have minimal experience with this transaction, and they don't want to mess it up. Given that, most households seek help from licensed agents and brokers who have both the training and experience to assist them through the complexities of the housing transaction. Because many homebuyers retain the services of real estate agents and brokers, it is essential to understand their business and how to use their services. This chapter is not meant to provide training for someone who desires to become a real estate agent or broker but only to acquaint a prospective property buyer with the general aspects of the brokerage business and how to interact with an agent or broker.

---

50. Catrina, Sun-Tan, "Here's How Many Real Estate Agents There Are in the U.S. (And Why It's Hard to Find a Great One)," HomeLight, January 23, 2019, https://www.homelight.com/blog/how-many-realtors-in-the-us/.

AGENTS AND BROKERS

To become a licensed real estate agent, one must generally complete a specified number of hours of coursework and pass a state exam. The specifics of these qualifications depend on the state where the license is sought. Real estate agents must "hang their license" with a real estate broker who oversees their work, and they typically join the board(s) of Realtors® in their service area. This represents a significant investment for many individuals but is done by almost all real estate agents to gain access to the network (i.e., the MLS) and information necessary to assist in real estate transactions.

Real estate agents often bring value to a home purchasing team because of their understanding of the real estate acquisition process, from the search to closing. While there is usually another professional that may do better at specific aspects of the purchasing process (e.g., an appraiser may determine value better, an attorney may negotiate and/or understand contracts better, and an inspector may understand home damage and necessary repair costs better), competent real estate agents are well-versed enough in all aspects of the purchasing process to provide material assistance.

Agents have what is known as a fiduciary responsibility to those they represent. Covenants implied in any agency agreement include care, confidentiality, loyalty, obedience, accounting, and disclosure. A competent real estate agent does everything in his or her power to help a client but ultimately allows clients to make their own decisions.

Compensation for real estate agents depends entirely on the contracted agreement between the principal and the agent. As a general rule, real estate agents are paid by commission at closing, so their compensation is less certain than many of the professionals discussed in this chapter. But real estate agents are often rewarded for this uncertainty with higher fees when transactions do close—usually calculated as a percentage (e.g., 1% to 10%) of the purchase price. Contract terms for real estate agents are often negotiable and can be vastly different from area to area and agent to agent. Because of these different terms, using due diligence in selecting a real estate agent is absolutely essential.

There are two general types of residential real estate agents: (1) seller or listing agents, who are contracted to sell a property, and (2) buyer agents, who assist a buyer in purchasing a property. Both are common, but listing agents are more common. Listing agents are generally charged with marketing and selling a property. Their experience in this process, access to the MLS, and ability to maintain a more objective viewpoint on a property are often attractive to sellers. Properties listed as "For Sale by Owner" that are otherwise identical should theoretically net a higher sales price to the owner. However, frequently, these sellers are poor negotiators, and the net effect is negligible.

Buyer agents can be one of two types. First, a buyer agent may be a licensed agent who happens to be showing you properties and is willing to assist with an offer contract but receives compensation as a commission split from the listing agent. In this case, there is no explicit contract with the agent who is assisting you. Second, a buyer agent may be someone who has an explicit contract with you to find a property and negotiate the best price. In this case, the agent's compensation may be fixed, and the agent may be entitled to compensation even if he or she doesn't ultimately find a home that you end up buying. For instance, if you find a home that is offered as "For Sale by Owner," you may still be required to compensate the buyer agent. Given the complexities of the buyer/agent relationship, it is essential that you ask a lot of questions and understand any legal documents that the agent may ask you to sign.

Attorneys are well employed in the real estate field, and with good reason—there is significant complexity and a lot of money at stake. Trying to purchase or sell real estate without consulting an attorney with real estate expertise is usually a recipe for disaster. However, if there were a circumstance in which a real estate attorney's services would not be necessary, it would be in the purchase of a single-family residence. To prevent predatory selling and lending, states generally require the use of a standardized purchase contract with addendums if a real estate agent is involved. These contracts are usually well-litigated and leave little to ambiguity to protect less-sophisticated buyers and sellers.

Real estate attorneys are usually compensated on an hourly rate that is likely higher than the hourly rate charged by any of the other specialists discussed in this chapter. But as a homebuyer, if you have any questions about the contract you plan to sign, spending an hour or two with an attorney to make sure everything is in order could be some of the best money you ever spend. And if you ever engage in a nonstandard home purchase, legal assistance is a necessity.

THE REAL ESTATE TRANSACTION

To understand the role that agents and brokers play in a real estate deal, let's work through a typical transaction. First, we begin with a seller, Mary, who has a desire to sell her property. She can market the property herself, or she can retain the services of a licensed real estate agent. Let's assume that Mary wants to sell her home, so she contacts Bill, a licensed agent who lives in her neighborhood. Bill agrees to come to her house to discuss a listing contract. Prior to arriving at her home, Bill logs into the Multiple Listing Service (MLS) and researches the listing and transaction prices of similar homes in the area. When he meets with Mary, he shows her the comparables and provides his opinion of market value. He then offers to list the property at or above the market value estimate.

After reviewing the data, Mary agrees with Bill's opinion of value and enters into a listing agreement for him to help her sell the property. A listing agreement is a formal contract that stipulates the terms of the listing contract, including the listing price, the term of the listing agreement, the commission rate, and the duties of both parties. For the most part, the agent agrees to exercise diligence in marketing and help the seller sell the property, and the seller agrees to facilitate the marketing of the property and to pay the commission if the agent brings a ready, willing, and able buyer to the table.

After Mary and Bill sign the listing agreement, Bill is required to have his designated broker review and sign the agreement. Only after the agreement is signed by the listing broker is it a binding listing contract. Shortly after the listing broker signs the contract, Bill enters the specific details of the property and the terms of the listing agreement into the MLS and broadcasts the availability of the property to all other brokers and agents that are members of the MLS. Bill also advertises the property with online marketing platforms, such as

Zillow and Trulia, and posts a marketing sign in the front yard. When Bill publishes the data on the MLS, he also notifies the other agents and brokers that if they bring a ready, willing, and able buyer to the table, he will split the commission with them.

Sarah, an agent with another brokerage, finds a buyer who is interested in the property. After some discussion and analysis, the buyer decides to make an offer on the property. Sarah helps the buyer complete a Real Estate Purchase Contract (REPC) and then, after review by her designated broker, conveys the document to Bill, the listing agent. After Bill and his designated broker review the offer, Bill presents the offer to Mary, the seller. If Mary decides to accept the offer, she signs the REPC, and the property is under contract. If Mary chooses not to accept the offer, she may decline it outright, or she may counter with revised terms of her own. If she counters, the revised REPC goes back to the buyer's agent, and the process starts over. Often, the process will go back and forth several times until both parties are satisfied with the terms of the contract and a deal is solidified. When that occurs, the signed contract goes to an escrow officer at a title company that assists both parties (buyer and seller) to complete the requirements of the contract and close the deal. At the close of escrow, the selling commissions are then paid to the respective agents/brokers.

RELATED RESOURCES

Utah Real Estate Sales Agent Licensing
https://realestate.utah.gov/realestate/salesagent.html

Utah Real Estate Broker Registration
https://realestate.utah.gov/realestate/broker.html

Real Estate Agent versus Broker: What's the Difference?
https://www.zillow.com/agent-resources/blog/real-estate-broker-vs-agent/

CHAPTER 24

Rent versus Buy Decision

INTRODUCTION

This chapter addresses the advantages and disadvantages of renting or buying a home. First, a discussion of the advantages and disadvantages of renting are presented, followed by the advantages and disadvantages of buying.

RENTING

Over the past two decades, renting a home has grown in popularity. The financial crisis around 2008 furthered this trend, leading some to call renting The New American Dream. Following are some of the chief advantages and disadvantages of renting.

Advantages of Renting

High Mobility: Residential lease contracts are typically for one year or less, so they are ideal for people who seek mobility.

Lower Initial Costs: Real estate purchases generally involve large sums of money and considerable uncertainty about the future, so buying real estate requires a larger upfront financial commitment. Even when financed with a mortgage loan, a real estate purchase requires a significant down payment.

Maintenance Costs: Most residential rental contracts require that repairs and maintenance be performed by the landlord, saving the tenant time and money.

Easier to Budget: Because the landlord typically covers maintenance costs, the tenant is responsible only for the lease payment and utilities, making budgeting more straightforward. If desired, tenants may even find a landlord willing to include utilities in the lease payment, making budgeting even easier.

Communal Living: While there are exceptions (e.g., condominiums, renting a single-family house), renting is usually associated with communal living. Many people like the social opportunities and shared amenities (e.g., a swimming pool, tennis courts, laundry facilities) that communal living often allows.

Disadvantages of Renting

Rate Hikes: One downside of renting is that rents may increase suddenly and unexpectedly. Rental tenants often grow attached to their residence and neighborhood but are later forced to leave due to a new rate hike they are unwilling or unable to pay.

Status: Though the stigma has arguably decreased over the past couple of decades, renting is generally viewed as a lower-class means of living. Rentals are usually lower in quality compared to residences for sale. Many people who may be better off financially by renting decide to buy to avoid the stigma of renting.

Dealing with a Landlord: Some landlords do not respond with respect and care in a timely manner to concerns expressed by tenants, leading to frustration and anger. A residence that fits your needs perfectly may still present a headache if the landlord proves disagreeable.

Limited Financial Benefits: In a traditional real estate market, a well-maintained residence appreciates in value over time. However, benefit accrues only to the owner, not the tenant. The tenant also forfeits any tax benefits that accrue to the owner.

Communal Living: Just as it can be an advantage, communal living can be a disadvantage. Renters are usually severely limited in the changes they can make to a property and may be restricted in their use of the residence (e.g., no pets, kids, etc.). Noisy and obnoxious neighbors can also make life unpleasant.

BUYING

Buying has significant advantages, but there are also significant drawbacks. Following are some of the advantages and disadvantages of buying.

Advantages of Buying

Permanence and Pride of Ownership: Though renting is referred to by some as the New American Dream, the traditional American Dream involves owning a suburban house with a white picket fence. Owners generally put more care into their residences, and owning a home is often cited as a prerequisite to upper tiers of social status.

Fixed Monthly Payment: While your landlord may raise rent at a moment's notice, most homeowners finance their homes with a level payment mortgage (LPM). The LPM originator (often a bank) cannot raise your rate during the term of the mortgage, often thirty years. This level monthly payment allows for more long-term certainty compared to renting.

Leverage: Though leverage is a two-edged sword, in a traditional market, real estate values increase over time. An owner gets the full benefit of appreciating property value and can use this additional equity for several financial objectives.

Economic Incentives: The US federal government has a long history of subsidizing homeownership. The government allows homeowners to deduct mortgage interest and property taxes from their income for tax purposes. Also, the government allows for a nice capital gains exemption for a primary residence. Specifically, if the homeowner has lived in the residence in at least two of the last five years, he or she may exempt $250,000 in capital gain if he or she is single filing an individual return, and $500,000 if he or she is married filing a joint return.

Forced Savings: Though cited less often by younger generations, one benefit of holding a mortgage is that it requires putting money away in the form of principal payments that reduce the mortgage balance. People who find themselves in difficult financial circumstances can often use these forced savings to avoid financial ruin by getting a home equity loan or obtaining a reverse mortgage.

Disadvantages of Buying

Significant Upfront Costs: Buying a home is often a painful process that involves substantial upfront costs and coordination. Buyers often underestimate both the cost of acquiring real estate and the time needed to search, inspect, and coordinate the financing and purchase of a home.

Higher Living Expenses: Many homeowners forget to budget or do not budget nearly enough for the upkeep of the property. Average maintenance costs per year are often around 1% of property value per year. To compound the problem of forgetting to budget, the timing of these expenses is difficult to predict, and needing to replace a furnace in the middle of winter can be a shock to the family budget. The time required to deal with these problems and to keep the residence in good shape (e.g., maintain the lawn and garden) is often significant.

Increased Risk: Buying a home entails a substantial financial commitment. Real estate markets are unpredictable, and equity in a home may be lost. During the financial crisis of 2008 and the Great Recession that followed, many homeowners witnessed this phenomenon.

Poor Diversification: Related to the increased risk, homeowners often have poorly diversified investment portfolios. Having such a large chunk of a person's net worth tied to one property is likely suboptimal, and the homeowner may look at ways to pull equity out of a home and place it in other investments.

Disposition: While many buyers find buying a home to be a painful process, selling a home is often even more difficult. Preparing and showing the home, paying commissions, timing closings and moves, and accepting far less money than the owner thinks the home is worth are common complaints made by owners who participate in the selling process.

GENERAL GUIDELINES

Even after understanding the advantages and drawbacks of renting and buying, making the decision can be difficult. Here are a few things to keep in mind.

Length of Occupancy

Deciding whether to rent or buy is often as simple as calculating how long you expect to stay in a particular location. The upfront costs of buying make renting more favorable in the short term, while the level payment and property appreciation usually make buying more favorable in the long term. Research has shown that the average length of stay needed to justify buying over renting is between two and three years, so that should give you a ballpark figure. But make sure to calculate your net benefit of renting/buying if you may be anywhere near this range.

Comparison Shop

You might think that current rental prices will correlate almost entirely with buying prices, but often this is not the case. Rental rates usually increase slightly from year to year, but home values may fluctuate more broadly, so carefully researching both markets is essential to making an informed decision.

Know Your Numbers

Many people have no idea that mortgage interest is tax-deductible or forget to factor that into their decision. Know your numbers (how much you can afford) and take the time to budget the decision properly.

Don't Rely on Free Advice

Sales agents earn a commission when they help with the sale of a home but not when someone rents. Therefore, they have an incentive to encourage buying over renting, even though there may be compelling reasons for someone to rent rather than buy.

SUMMARY

The rent versus buy decision is a critical first step in determining a course of action for utilizing real estate. There are benefits and drawbacks to each alternative. Generally, renting makes the most sense for shorter-term users, while buying makes sense for longer-term users. However, this is not always the case, so each situation should be analyzed separately.

RELATED RESOURCES

The New Math of Renting versus Buying:
http://online.wsj.com/news/articles/SB100014240527023039481 04579534230618539424

End of White Picket Fences: Has America Awoken from Its Home Ownership Dream?
https://www.nickminer.com/wp-content/uploads/WL7-21.pdf

Gazing at the Horizon: Why the Buy/Rent Equation Is Changing
http://www.zillow.com/research/q4-2014-buy-rent-breakeven-9380/

CHAPTER 25

Careers in Real Estate

INTRODUCTION

Real estate is a diverse industry with countless opportunities in various asset classes and sub-disciplines. Many people would love to have a career in real estate but have difficulty determining where to start. This chapter is intended to provide a broad introductory education to real estate careers. Following a discussion of primary asset classes, applicable information on various careers is presented.

ASSET CLASSES

Real estate is traditionally divided into two broad categories: residential and commercial. Commercial real estate generally refers to all types of real estate that facilitate business commerce. The most basic types of commercial real estate include office, retail, industrial, and hotels. Many companies (depending on the subdiscipline) deal in multiple asset classes, but others focus on one specifically. Residential real estate is generally referred to as properties in which families/individuals reside. Apartments are generally included in the residential category. However, because of the income-producing characteristic of apartments, some practitioners would refer to these properties as commercial.

OFFICE

Office real estate is what it sounds like—office space for businesses. Although the building can take many forms (downtown high rise, suburban mixed-use, etc.), the concept is always the same. Office real estate is desirable because of longer leases. One challenge that often arises is the specific needs of individual tenants. Tenants often need improvements made to the property that may be paid by the owner. Interestingly, the demand for types of office space is shifting with shifting demographics. Office real estate also tends to be rather cyclical.

RETAIL

Retail properties include restaurants, grocery stores, shopping malls, convenience stores, and other types of stores. Retail real estate's value and riskiness are heavily dependent on the perceived strength of the tenants in the building. Many retail leases are triple-net, which is preferred by landlords. With a triple net lease, the tenant pays his or her portion of all operating expenses. Retail real estate is also typically divided into either single-tenant or multi-tenant properties. Single-tenant properties are usually easier to manage because there is only one tenant. They are also riskier because you will have no cash flow if the one space is not filled. Retail real estate has experienced significant changes with the rise of e-commerce.

INDUSTRIAL

Industrial properties include warehouses, production facilities, and other real estate related to the logistics of running businesses. Industrial real estate has recently seen a substantial increase in demand, primarily due to the increase in online shopping. Because of this, industrial real estate has done very well lately, and investors are very optimistic about the future for industrial real estate.

APARTMENTS

Apartments are an asset class that has been viewed as a safer investment in real estate. The logic behind the safe reputation is that people will always need a place to live and sometimes can't afford a home. Changing demographics have increased the demand for multifamily housing and reaffirmed this safe view. Because of this, the primary concern with apartments is usually oversupplying in a market. Multifamily real estate is also more management intensive, and most owners employ a property management company to manage properties.

SINGLE-FAMILY RESIDENTIAL

Single-family residential real estate is another way of referring to homes. While most homes are owner-occupied and are not investments, there is a large market for single-family residential rentals. Some companies have started investing in single-family residential real estate on a large scale, but the industry (on an institutional level) is still in its infancy.

HOSPITALITY

Hotels are typically viewed as the riskiest asset class with short (often one-night) leases and high operating leverage. Hotels also see more volatility due to the high number of hotel stays paid with discretionary income. This higher risk is often rewarded with higher returns on average. The big hotel companies typically operate as franchisees who take fees from the owner of the actual real estate, which can bring challenges (like meeting specific quality standards) and advantages (like tapping into advertising platforms). Another problem for hospitality real estate is the emergence of new competitors, like Airbnb, that have provided a substitute for hotel rooms.

REAL ESTATE CAREERS

There are many career opportunities in real estate but some of the more prominent include appraising, brokerage, consulting, corporate real estate, development, escrow and title, investment, mortgage lending, and property management. Each of these career opportunities is discussed in more detail below.

APPRAISING

Real estate appraisers estimate property value. Generally, appraisers specialize in either residential (homes) or commercial (income properties) real estate. Estimating property value requires that the appraiser identify the scope and purpose of the appraisal with the client, physically inspect the property, perform market research, perform analysis of data to arrive at a value estimate, and prepare a report for the client. Appraisers are also sometimes called on to testify in court for real estate cases.

Many appraisers are self-employed. Self-employment allows appraisers to choose their hours. Compensation is fee-based. When working as a company employee, appraisers have a nice work-life balance and a stable job.

While some companies will hire and train an appraiser, most appraisers obtain required licenses and certifications on their own. There are several licensing options for appraisers, and many institutions require one or more of these licensing options.

Related Websites:

https://www.appraisalinstitute.org/appraisal-profession/

BROKERAGE

Real estate brokers (or agents) are like other brokers in the sense that they help facilitate a transaction between buyers and sellers. Most of an agent/broker's time is spent marketing his or her services and showing properties to potential clients. Some of the services agents and brokers provide include listing a property for sale on the local MLS, showing properties, and assisting with the negotiations and sales contract.

The lifestyle of a successful broker is quite desirable. Because brokers are independent contractors, they set their schedules. The compensation structure is typically 100% commission, so there is no cap to what a broker can make. But there is also no floor. In general, the brokerage business is hard to break into but can be very lucrative and flexible if done well.

Because of high turnover and commission-based compensation, brokerages are generally looking for talented individuals to add to their team. Some larger companies also provide internships that include rotational programs with other disciplines (market research, capital markets, property management, etc.) as well as brokerage.

Related Websites:

www.realtor.com/careers
www.thebalancesmb.com/are-you-right-for-a-real-estate-agent-career-2866775
www.nreionline.com/brokerage/2018-top-brokers
www.cbre.com/research-and-reports
www.marcusmillichap.com/research/researchreports
https://www2.colliers.com/en/Countries/United-States/Commercial-Real-Estate-Research
www.us.jll.com/en/trends-and-insights
www.realestateexpress.com

CONSULTING (ADVISORY)

Real estate advisory professionals provide consulting services on transactions, valuation, portfolio strategy, risk, and other real estate–specific functions.

The lifestyle of a real estate advisory professional is similar to those in other consulting fields and typically includes significant travel. Some of the largest companies with real estate advisory services include the big accounting and brokerage firms. The recruiting timeline for real estate advisory positions is similar to those in accounting.

Related Websites:

www.adventuresincre.com/real-estate-consulting-jobs/
www.glassdoor.com/Jobs/KPMG-real-estate-advisory-Jobs-EI_IE2867.0,4_KO5,25.htm

CORPORATE REAL ESTATE

Corporate real estate professionals work within a company. Some of their duties include determining optimal sites, negotiating leases and/or purchases, and assisting in any other business decisions that involve real estate. Lifestyle and compensation typically follow the pattern of corporate finance jobs. Many large companies, such as Walmart, Costco, Marriott, and others, have a significant need for internal real estate professionals.

Related Websites:
realestate.washington.edu/5165-2/

DEVELOPMENT

Real estate development firms develop or redevelop real estate projects. Developers have many duties. Some of these include selecting and acquiring sites, working with city officials for rezoning approvals, working with architects on design, working with mortgage bankers for financing, working with contractors during construction, and working with marketing firms for promotion.

Because of the cyclical nature of development, the lifestyle of analysts at a development firm can vary. In bull markets, analysts tend to be very busy underwriting deals and/or overseeing construction. In bear markets, however, many development companies tend to be hit pretty hard.

Development companies generally hire based on the need at the time, so it is difficult to put a timeline on exactly when these companies recruit. In general, development companies are known for recruiting close to the time of hiring.

Related Websites:
info.simoncre.com/the-commercial-real-estate-development-process

ESCROW AND TITLE

Title and escrow are an essential part of a real estate transaction. Title officers ensure that a title is clean by searching the public record to ensure that there is no encumbrance or cloud on the title. If there are encumbrances on the title, they alert the parties to the transaction and assist in removing these obstacles. Title officers also provide title insurance to buyers. Escrow officers assist both the buyer and seller in completing the terms of the contract. Many title companies are small and tend to hire as a need arises. Therefore, most do not offer an internship or apprentice analyst program.

Related Websites:

https://work.chron.com/types-job-positions-offered-title-companies-17049.html

INVESTMENT ANALYST

Some firms specialize in the acquisition and development of investment properties. These firms seek to provide competitive returns to their investors of financial capital. Some of these firms include pension funds, endowments, and private equity companies. Some of the larger companies include Blackstone (New York), Brookfield Asset Management (Toronto), Starwood Capital Group (Miami), Lone Star Funds (Dallas), The Carlyle Group (Washington, DC) Morgan Stanley Real Estate Investment Group (New York and San Francisco), Bridge Investment Group (Salt Lake City), BlackRock (New York), and USAA Real Estate (San Antonio). Many of these global firms recruit very early for summer internships and jobs.

Related Websites:

www.perenews.com/database/#/PERE-50
www.irei.com
www.nreionline.com/

MORTGAGE LENDING

Very few real estate deals are completed without some type of loan. Because of this, mortgage lenders are crucial players in the real estate industry. Analysts in the mortgage lending industry typically underwrite deals to determine if the bank/institution should lend money to the borrower. Underwriting could include performing market research and property due diligence, communicating with clients, and preparing loan documents.

The lifestyle for mortgage lenders differs widely by company. In general, the lending industry has a reputation for being traditional in terms of work-life balance. The large banks typically start their recruiting process in the fall and often offer internship programs as well as full-time opportunities. Other smaller lending institutions recruit later, depending on their need.

Related Websites:

www.monster.com/career-advice/article/Mortgage-Loan-Officer-Careers

PROPERTY MANAGEMENT

Property management groups oversee the day-to-day operations of real estate, which could include overseeing leasing, maintenance, and miscellaneous operations. Some real estate firms have a property management group within a larger real estate company, and some companies focus only on property management. Either way, having a good property manager can be key to successful real estate investments. Property management is known as being very stable with a good work-life balance.

A significant portion of property management companies are local companies. However, many of the larger brokerage companies like CBRE, JLL, and Colliers have a property management arm. Like many real estate companies, property management companies usually hire on a need basis. Because of this, the recruiting timeline will vary, but companies often start the recruiting process a few months before the start date.

Related Websites:

www.cbre.com/real-estate-services/investor/property-management
www.buildium.com/resource/property-management-career-guide/
www.boma.org

Glossary

Active participation: Requires the individual own at least 10% of the rental property and make management decisions in a significant sense.

Adjustable rate mortgage (ARM): Variable rate mortgage in which the interest rate is periodically adjusted based on a financial or economic index.

Age-life method: Method of estimating percentage of depreciation attributable to property improvements by dividing the effective age by the total economic life.

Air rights: Legal rights of the space above owned land without interference by others.

Amortization schedule: Table detailing each periodic payment on an amortizing loan, indicating what portion of each payment is for interest and for principal.

Annual debt service (DS): Total principal and interest required to be paid in a calendar year.

Annual operating statement: Also called a profit and loss statement; displays revenues and then subtracts operating expenses to calculate net income.

Annuity: A series of equal amounts or payments received, one each period, for a specified number of periods.

Annuity due: Annuity in which the payment is made at the beginning of the period.

Balloon payment: When a mortgage doesn't amortize fully by the date of the final payment, the final payment is larger than previous payments to fully pay off the loan.

Basis: The original value of an asset, usually the purchase price.

Before-tax cash flow (BTCF): The net operating income minus the debt service.

Buyer agent: Real estate agent that represents only the interests of the buyer in a transaction.

Capital gains: Profit from the sale of property.

Closing: The final step in a real estate transaction when ownership is transferred to the buyer.

Conforming conventional loan: Mortgage loan that meets the GSE guidelines.

Cost approach: Valuation method that estimates the value of a property by adding land value to the depreciated cost new of the improvements.

Covenant of marketable title: Implied promise in a contract that there are no encumbrances on the land or property.

Debt-to-income ratio: Total monthly debt payments divided by gross monthly income; used in mortgage underwriting.

Deed restrictions and restrictive covenants (CC&Rs): Private rules and regulations that specify uses and other aspects of a parcel of land.

Depreciation recapture tax: Taxes levied on accumulated depreciation of property at sale.

Determinable fee estate: Ownership interest reverts to the grantor or grantor's heirs automatically when a stated event or condition occurs.

Direct capitalization: Method used to convert an estimate of a single year's income expectancy into an indication of value in one direct step by dividing the NOI by the cap rate.

Dominant estate: Parcel of real property that has an easement over another piece of property.

Earnest money: Deposit paid to confirm a contract.

Easement: Right to cross or otherwise use someone else's land for a specified purpose.

Easement appurtenant: Right to use adjoining property.

Easement in gross: Right to use another person's land (not an adjacent property owner; think utility companies running power or sewer lines).

Effective gross income (EGI): Rental income after deducting vacancy and adding other income.

Effective gross income (EGI) multiplier: Valuation measures found by dividing the property's sale price by its gross annual rental income.

Eminent domain: Right of a government to expropriate private property for public use with payment of compensation.

Encroachment: Intrusion on a person's property (think fence built over a property line).

Equity capitalization rate: Before-tax cash flow divided by the equity investment.

Escheat: Reversion of property to the state when the owner dies without any heirs.

Escrow: Bond, deed, or other document kept in the custody of a third party, taking effect only when a specified condition has been fulfilled.

Estate for years: Leasehold estate for a specific period of time, which is not automatically renewed and ownership reverts back to grantor.

External obsolescence: Factor that reduces the value of a property because of something external to the property itself (think being next to train tracks or a dump).

Fee simple: land ownership in which the owner holds all rights on the land.

Fee simple subject to condition subsequent: Similar to a fee simple estate but is subject to a specific use or triggering event, after which grantor regains ownership.

FICO score: A person's credit score as calculated by the Fair Isaac Corporation.

Floor area ratio (FAR): Ratio of the building's total floor area to the area of the land upon which it is built.

Frontage-to-depth ratio: Ratio of the lot frontage to the depth of the lot.

Functional obsolescence: Reduction in the usefulness or desirability of a building because of an outdated design feature.

Gross lease: Type of commercial lease in which the landlord pays for the building's operating expenses.

Holding period measures: Measures used to determine desirability of an investment during the holding period.

Income approach: Valuation method that considers the present value of future cash flows of a property.

Internal rate of return (IRR): Discount rate that makes the net present value of an investment equal to zero.

Investment measures: Measures used to determine the desirability of an investment by considering the property cash flows.

Leasehold estate: Ownership of a temporary right to hold land or property (think renting an apartment or home).

Lender's policy: Insurance that protects the lender's interests in the property should a problem with the title arise.

Level payment mortgage (LPM): Mortgage that requires the same dollar payment each month or payment period.

Listing agent: Real estate agent who helps homeowners sell their home.

Loan-to-value ratio (LTV): Ratio of a loan amount to the value of the asset purchased.

Maturity date: Date on which the principal amount of a mortgage becomes due and is repaid in full.

Metes and bounds: System of describing land.

Mortgage capitalization rate (mortgage constant): Ratio between the annual amount of debt service to the total loan amount.

Multiple listing service (MLS): Comprehensive listing of properties for sale used by Realtors®.

Negative leverage: Occurs when the cost of borrowing money is greater than the return a party makes on an equity investment.

Net operating income (NOI): Annual net operating income generated by an income-producing property.

Net present value (NPV): Difference between the present value of cash inflows and the present value of cash outflows.

Nonconforming conventional loan: Loan that will not be bought by Fannie Mae or Freddie Mac.

Operating expenses (OE): Costs associated with the operation and maintenance of an income-producing property.

Opportunity cost: Loss of potential gain from other alternatives when one alternative is chosen.

Ordinary life estate: Ownership of land for the duration of a person's life.

Owner's policy: Insurance that protects the buyer should a problem arise with the covered title.

Periodic tenancy: Tenancy that continues for successive periods until the tenant gives the landlord notice of intent to end the tenancy.

Personalty: Personal or movable property.

Points: Fees paid directly to the lender at closing in exchange for a reduced interest rate.

Police power: Capacity of the states to regulate behavior and enforce order for the betterment of the health, safety, moral character, and general welfare of residents in the area.

Positive leverage: Occurs when the cost of borrowing money is less than the return a party makes on an equity investment.

Potential gross income (PGI): Total rental income a property could make if it is 100% leased at market rent.

Prepayment: Settlement of a debt or installment payment before its official due date.

PITI (principal, interest, taxes, insurance): Mortgage payment that is the sum of monthly principal, interest, property taxes, and property insurance.

Private mortgage insurance (PMI): Insurance that reimburses the lender if a mortgage defaults.

Property liens: Legal claim on a tract of real estate granting the holder a specified amount of money upon the sale of the property.

Property reversion: Net sales proceeds from the future sale of a property.

Realty: Real, fixed property.

Reconciliation: The act of reconciling the three approaches to valuation, including the sales comparison approach, the income approach, and the cost approach.

Recorded plat (lot and block): Survey system to locate and identify land, usually in densely populated metropolitan areas and suburban areas.

Rectangular (government) survey: Survey system that divides land into townships and sections.

Regular annuity: Annuity in which payments are made at the end of the period.

Replacement allowance (RES): Allowance set aside to replace short-lived items in a property (think replacing the roof).

Reversionary capitalization rate: Cap rate used to derive the reversion value of the property; sometimes known as the exit cap rate.

Right of disposition: Right to sell property.

Right of exclusive possession and control: Right to prevent others from coming onto one's property.

Right of quiet enjoyment: Right to possess the property in peace, without disturbance by hostile claimants to the title.

Sales comparison approach: Valuation method that compares a property with other properties that have similar characteristics and have been recently sold.

Servient estate: Estate that grants the easement across the property.

Settlement: Process finalizing a real estate transaction.

Sinking fund: Fund formed by periodically setting aside money for a future use.

Subsurface (mineral) rights: Rights to the earth below owned land and any substances found therein.

Surface rights: Rights to the surface of the earth.

Title: Right to a bundle of rights in a property.

Title insurance: Policy that covers the loss of ownership interest in a property due to legal defects of the title.

Triple net lease: Form of lease in which the tenant is responsible for paying the operating expenses of the property.

Vacancy and collection loss (V&CL): Amount of money or percentage of operating income that is lost due to vacancy or nonpayment of rents.

Yield capitalization: Method of converting future income from an investment into present value by discounting each year's income using an appropriate discount rate.

Index

A

B

F

H

I

L

M

N

~O~

~P~

~R~

❧V❧

❧Z❧

Acknowledgments

This educational publication is designed to provide accurate information regarding the subject matter covered and to facilitate learning about the subject matter. It is provided with the understanding that the publisher is not engaged in rendering legal, accounting, or other professional services. If legal advice or additional expert assistance is required, the services of a competent professional person should be sought.

This work was supported by the James Passey Professorship and the Peery Institute of Financial Services at the Marriott School at BYU. I thank Curtis Woodbury, Chris Childers, Ian Blades, Avery Smith, Lauren Tavernier, Caleb Nickolaisen, Ben Bates, Brynn Carter, Billy Affleck, Spencer Evans, and Natasha Fenn for assistance with this publication.

About the Author

Barrett A. Slade, PhD, is the James Passey Professor of Finance at the Marriott School of Business at Brigham Young University. Dr. Slade enjoys teaching students about real estate finance and investment. He also enjoys conducting research about real estate markets and has an extensive publication record with articles appearing in numerous real estate finance and economics journals including *Real Estate Economics*, the *Journal of Real Estate Finance and Economics*, the *Journal of Real Estate Research*, the *National Tax Journal*, and the *Journal of Real Estate Portfolio Management.*

Barrett received a B.S. in economics and an M.S. in managerial economics from BYU, and a PhD in business administration with an emphasis in real estate from the University of Georgia. Prior to his academic assignment at BYU, Barrett was the owner of Slade & Associates, Inc., a real estate consulting firm, and he held the positions of vice president and chief appraiser at First Interstate Bank of Arizona.

— Notes —

— Notes —

— Notes —

— Notes —

— Notes —